CIRCLING THE EDGE

LISTENING TO THE WHISPERS OF THE WILD SOUL

WILMA G. RUBENS

◆ FriesenPress

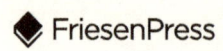

One Printers Way
Altona, MB R0G 0B0
Canada

www.friesenpress.com

Copyright © 2022 by Wilma G. Rubens
First Edition — 2022

All rights reserved.

No part of this publication may be reproduced in any form, or by any means, electronic or mechanical, including photocopying, recording, or any information browsing, storage, or retrieval system, without permission in writing from FriesenPress.

Photographs provided by the author.

Photo of Shona Rubens by Malcolm Carmichael, Banff Photographer, www.carmichaelphoto.com

Photo of Chris Rubens by Garrett Grove www.garrettgrove.com

Cover photo of Mount Allan, by John Dunn, Wilderness explorer and photographer, www.articlight.com

Author photo by Caroline Marion, Canmore Photographer.

ISBN
978-1-03-914109-4 (Hardcover)
978-1-03-914108-7 (Paperback)
978-1-03-914110-0 (eBook)

1. BIOGRAPHY & AUTOBIOGRAPHY, PERSONAL MEMOIRS

Distributed to the trade by The Ingram Book Company

For Clive, Christopher and Shona,
my grandchildren Tilly and Huxley,
and all who love our magnificent planet –
I dedicate this book to you with all my wild heart.

Glacier Valley, Sonamarg, Kashmir by the author

What people say:

"Wilma shares her journey from a repressive childhood to global travel, an expansive spirituality, and embraces human diversity. While ghosts of her mother's biblical voice follow her, the reader feels privileged to witness the emergence of Wilma's own wise voice."

Patricia Morgan, Canadian Therapeutic Counsellor and author of *Love Her As She Is: Lessons from a Daughter Stolen by Addictions*

"Wilma's search for self takes her on many adventures. Her story encourages the reader to embrace life, explore their talents and express their unique wisdom."

Margaret Edmunds, Retired Head of Social Work at Mount Royal College and author of *A Handbook of Interactive Exercises for Groups*

"Still she had reached the place in life where, if you are lucky, looking back provides the resilience to look forward."
~ Lisa Kogan

CIRCLING THE EDGE

"Never doubt that something invisible can change the world."
~ Wilma G. Rubens

TABLE OF CONTENTS

1
CHAPTER 1
Poisoned Apples

13
CHAPTER 2
Scarlet Longing

22
CHAPTER 3
Chameleon Summer

27
CHAPTER 4
Thumbs Up in the USA

38
CHAPTER 5
Overland on a Shoestring

54
CHAPTER 6
Crossroads

77
CHAPTER 7
College Interlude

81
CHAPTER 8
Mountain Madness in Kashmir

113
CHAPTER 9
"Two Mrs and no Mr?"

146
CHAPTER 10
Deepest, Darkest England

164
CHAPTER 11
Aotearoa - Land of the Long White Cloud

184
CHAPTER 12
Full Tilt

193
CHAPTER 13
Against the Wind

209
CHAPTER 14
Ragged Edges

219
CHAPTER 15
U-turn on the Edge

228
CHAPTER 16
The Crux

238
CHAPTER 17
The Holy Sport of Mothering

248
CHAPTER 18
Tussles and Defiance

255
CHAPTER 19
Lust for Adventure

264
CHAPTER 20
Sisters

270
CHAPTER 21
Wasps and Yoga

277
CHAPTER 22
Mountain Mama

284
CHAPTER 23
Kashmiri Socks - Gratitude and Grace

289
EPILOGUE

291
APPENDIX
Meet Me on the Edge - Writing Tips

297
ACKNOWLEDGEMENTS

298
ABOUT THE AUTHOR

A Rainbow of Desire
by Wilma G. Rubens

Words float like clouds
Words blow in on the west wind
Words plant like seeds
Words chewed like cud in a deer's mouth
Forge past limitation

Stories bubble up from her depth
And are regurgitated with wisdom

As she climbs upward
Stretching herself
Like a galaxy of stars
She expands her spiral of light

CHAPTER 1
Poisoned Apples

*"Calvinist negativity embedded in the elegant steeples
guarded the sinners in the cemetery
humiliations stunted our growth
pitted people against one another
shamed our Scottish accents"*
~ Wilma G. Rubens, "Entangled Enchantments"

Scotland, December 1957

I grew up certain that our week revolved around my father's Sunday sermons. One Saturday, at the white enamel gas stove, I perched on a three-legged stool, stirring the melting butter. Leaning over my shoulder, Mother poured in brown sugar and cocoa powder.

"Don't burn yourself," she said.

"I won't," I said, inhaling the chocolate. When she disappeared into the pantry, I gingerly dipped my eight-year-old finger into the mixture and popped it into my mouth. The sweet concoction trickled like velvet down my throat.

"Here's the soya flour, raisins, and coconut." Mother wrapped her warm hand over mine and stirred. "We'll make balls and roll them in coconut."

That evening, our family sat around the table: Mother, Father in his white dog collar, and my two sisters: Ruth, a willowy blonde at fifteen and seven years older than me; and nine-year-old Dorothy with bountiful curls, a stark contrast to my page-boy hair that hung poker straight. Munching on a coconut ball, careful not to talk with my mouth full, I challenged my father: "Can I go to the Brownies with my friend?"

"No!" he said, then snapped his jaw shut.

"The Brownies have a Brown Owl. They do badges on fires and first aid," I continued.

"Wilma, our Ebenezer Church has the Girls' Brigade," he said, wiping his mouth with a linen napkin. "What would my congregation think of me if I let my daughter go to the Church of Scotland? We are Congregationalists."

"They sing hymns. It's boring," I bawled.

"Wilma, keep quiet," Mother said. "Don't upset your dad. He spent all day visiting the sick people in the hospital. Tonight, he leads the bible study and prayer meeting. He has two sermons to prepare for Sunday. He needs peace and quiet."

"I wanna go to the Brownies," I cried, thumping the table. "I'm never allowed to do anything."

"Wilma, don't answer back," Mother said. "Children should be seen and not heard. You need a spanking." As she hit my bottom with a wooden spoon, she continued, "This hurts me more than it hurts you." I did not think so.

"Mum, stop it. Wilma's had enough," Dorothy pleaded.

Father left for church. At bedtime, Mother read a chapter from *Uncle Tom's Cabin*.

"Wilma, are you sorry for your bad behaviour?" she asked, tucking the wool blankets around me.

"I really want to go the Brownies," I replied.

"You know your father won't allow it."

"I'm not allowed to play on Sundays. He's never here. It's not fair."

"Wilma, you're so stubborn. It says in the Bible: 'Don't let the sun go down on your wrath.'"

"I wouldn't have asked if I was going to be sorry."

"Oh, Wilma. What will become of you?" She shook her head, and with a deep sigh, left the room.

One day after school, Dorothy dragged me through the creaking door into the attic. Rain drummed on the skylight window. Surrounded by musty cardboard boxes and mildewed curtains, Dorothy showed me her bag full of chocolate biscuits.

"Where did these come from?" I asked. "Mother would never buy these. They're bad for our teeth."

"I bought them in the grocery store. Here, have some."

"Where did you get the money? We'll be in trouble if we're caught!"

"They won't find out," Dorothy said. I looked over my shoulder, checked that the door was closed, removed the silver paper, and sank my teeth into the sweet chocolate. Days later, mother discovered money missing from her purse and the remainder of the chocolate biscuits.

"You should both be ashamed of yourselves. Just wait till your father gets home," she threatened. That evening, Father sat in his big chair, his face red, his breathing laboured, and his dog collar askew. He held Dorothy over his knees and spanked her bottom with his slipper.

"Stop! Stop! I'm sorry!" Dorothy screamed.

I crawled behind the settee, curled into a ball, sniffled, and wiped my tears on my sleeve. I ached to escape outside, smell the earth, and hide under the weeping willow tree, feeling its rough bark support my back and the moist grass cradle my bottom.

As was common for the times, my parents believed that "to spare the rod was to spoil the child." The prevailing attitude was that praise made a young person swellheaded and proud—undesirable qualities in children.

The following week, too sick to go to school, I lay in my parent's mahogany bed. My mind was in a delirium, images of tall blank walls pressing on my chest. My throat throbbed as I struggled for breath. My bloated hands felt on fire. My mother's forehead furrowed as she placed a cold damp cloth on my fevered brow. "A poultice," she said in her soft Irish tongue as she lulled me to sleep.

From then on, I dreamed that a dark, unshaven, and angry-faced man had broken into our house. Shouting war cries, he chased our family around the living room with a red-hot iron. Sometimes he caught me and covered me with his fiery breath. I woke breathless and choking. Occasionally, I saved the family from his attacks. I imagined he lived under my bed ready to stab me in a moment of inattention.

In the summer, our family piled into our Ford Popular, which we had pack with suitcases. Father drove us away from the coal mines and polluted air of central Scotland and across the rolling emerald fields to Ardrossan on the Firth of Clyde. Ruth, Dorothy, and I squished into the back seat and sang at the top of our voices. Like a first kiss, sea air at the ferry terminal seduced me forever. Mother held our hands as we wobbled up the wooden gangplank into the cavernous ferry. With the tang of seaweed in our noses, we hung over the metal railing, watching crewmembers untie the ropes while the gap between the land and the boat widened. Followed by squawking seagulls, the ship crossed the silvery sea, chugging towards the distant mountains on the Island of Arran. There, Dorothy and I hung our heads out the car windows and yelled at the cows and sheep as we drove south past the hamlet of Lamlash to the holiday farm cottage that would be our home for a whole month.

Most days, laden with picnic baskets, buckets, spades, and towels, our family clambered down the steep hillside to the sandy beach that looked out to the Islands of Pladda and Ailsa Craig. On the beach, we helped Father collect wood and drums washed up on the shore. With a rope, he tied them into a raft.

"Come help me launch the raft," he called to us. "Take turns. Stay close to shore. I'm going to collect driftwood for the fire. Here... fill the tin drum with seawater to boil the potatoes."

Dorothy, Ruth, and I swam, bobbed on the raft, scrambled on the rocks, and threw purple jellyfish at each other while sausages sizzled in the wobbling frying pan. At lunch, we bit into the salty potatoes and devoured the sausages. In the afternoon, our family built an elaborate sandcastle that we decorated with white cockleshells. Dizzy with the smell of meadowsweet flowers, we squelched back to the cottage across peat bogs, the brown sludge oozing between our toes as the sun, rain, and wind embraced us.

Mother, Wilma, Ruth, Dorothy, and Father. Arran 1957

But even on holiday, Sundays were Sundays, and Father conducted the service at the local church. Dorothy and I brushed our salt-tangled hair and dressed in identical red homemade skirts, white shirts, and navy blazers. With only ten months between us, we were often mistaken for twins. Inhaling the aroma of cut grass, we walked along the field to the whitewashed church, which was surrounded by moss-covered gravestones. Inside on a wooden pew, Mother sat between Dorothy and me. After the hymns, she gave us one barley sugar sweetie to last the twenty-minute sermon. Father spoke fiery words: "The wages of sin is death." I heard that, if I disobeyed God, I would be condemned to hellfire and eternal damnation. While I did not understand what that meant, I knew it was not good. My focus drifted to the light streaming in through the red, green, and turquoise stained glass, while my soft fingers fidgeted with my mother's well-used hands and wedding ring.

Back home, I stood on the top of the high wall between our yard and my friend Linda's garden. The tall beech trees were alight with bronze and copper leaves.

"Scaredy cat," teased her brother in his white shirt. My stomach quivered as I looked at the pile of leaves far below.

"Jump," Linda shouted. With a yell, I soared through the air and landed with my bones intact.

Just before supper, Father clutched his chest and fell to the floor as if he was choking. Terror stabbed my heart. An ambulance rushed him to the hospital. Heart disease was the diagnosis. In those days, little was known about blocked arteries. That winter, Mother baked fat-free sponge cakes, while he painted watercolours after his pastoral duties.

February 1959
One snowy Saturday, Ruth, Dorothy, and I sat with Mother, eating lentil soup, wholemeal bread, and salad. Since his heart attack, my father took afternoon naps. Dorothy and I argued about whose turn it was to wash the dishes and who was to dry, chasing each other and cracking dishtowels in the air. To escape her torment, I ran upstairs.

"Mum, can I go play with Linda?" I asked breathlessly. I heard frightening rasping noises coming from my father's bedroom, his breath loud and laboured.

"What's wrong?" I whispered.

CIRCLING THE EDGE

"Dad is struggling for air," Mother said. "He'll calm down when he's rested. Go play."

I did. Linda and I somersaulted on her swing, skipped, and chased one another through the trees. Out of sight, behind the copper beech, we coughed and choked on her brother's cigarettes.

When I returned to our house, an unfamiliar man dressed in a black suit stood in our kitchen talking to Mother. "Is this the man who will take the church service tomorrow?" I asked.

"Father's gone to heaven," Ruth said as she hugged me. "This is the undertaker." I couldn't understand what she told me, but I knew that nothing would be the same again. That night, my sisters, my mother, and I crowded into her double bed and held one another.

The following morning, lashing sleet and wind battered the window. I thought, *Can I stop breathing and join Dad in heaven*? I hid under the blankets and held my breath, counting to ten until my cheeks puffed out and my mouth burst open. I repeated this until my brain spun, and I felt faint.

Before the funeral, Mother took Dorothy and me by the hand and led us into the parlour where the curtains were drawn. "Come and say goodbye to your father." I stood on my tiptoes and peered over the side of the oak casket where my forty-nine-year-old father lay in his suit. His ashen face looked unfamiliar, touched up with powder and lipstick. I touched him but recoiled from his cool, rubbery skin. My jaw and fists clenched.

"He's not here. He's in heaven," Mother said with a certainty that I did not share.

Why me? Why not Linda's father? I thought. *What will happen to us now? How dare he leave me?* I could not voice my anger. I knew what my mother would say if I did: *"Wilma, nice girls don't get angry. You should be ashamed of yourself."* I found it difficult to cry. Mother thought Dorothy and I were too young to participate in the funeral and cemetery burial, and so to protect us, we stayed in the manse and played. But that summer, I longed for him to

7

take us back to the beach on Arran.

Father's death catapulted us out of the rambling manse and garden into a cramped two-bedroom apartment in Edinburgh where the air smelled of coal smoke and hops from the breweries. But Sundays were still Sundays. Mother, Dorothy, Ruth, and I walked below the basalt Salisbury crags, returning from Hope Park Congregational Church. The autumn leaves fluttered like a million gold medallions.

"It's such a long walk," I whined. "My feet are sore. The service was boring. All the people in the church are old." In a photo from that time, my face is sad, my eyes hooded and lips clenched.

"I miss our Airdrie garden and Linda. I haven't any friends. My teacher Mr. McCaig has bushy eyebrows. Ruth, you would like him. He is a poet."

"He is one of Scotland's greatest poets," Ruth replied. "I read some of his poems for an essay I wrote at Moray House."

"That sounds boring," I said.

"Wilma. Stop it. Look at the beautiful swans. We'll be home soon," Mother coaxed.

Mother, Ruth, Wilma, and Dorothy 1960

Mother broadened her religious zeal to include attendance at the Baptist Chapel and the Church of Scotland. I gravitated to the bustling Baptist Church where they hoodwinked me into being born again, giving my life to Christ. One Sunday, I stood up at the microphone to confess my sins and looked out over a sea of people dressed in tweed suits, hats, and white shirts. What sins can a fourteen-year-old commit? I had broken some of the Ten Commandments. For example, I had played my French horn on a Sunday. I had admired the graven image of my neighbours' Iona Cross. I borrowed and did not return my sister's sweater.

I left the microphone, and in my angelic robe, I walked into the bath of tepid water where the minister in a black gown plunged me under. I arose as the congregation sang a rousing hymn: "At the Cross Where I First Saw the Light." Dripping wet, I did not feel their zeal, only a soggy silence and disenchantment that God had not reached down from the sky in a flash of light to comfort me and confirm my worth as a good girl. My disappointed face prompted my Sunday school teacher to warn me, "Beware of backsliding." I swallowed tears and gave her a blank look. I longed for a comforting hug, but those were unknown in that community.

Later in the spring, I sat with Linda on a gravestone in the Carlton Hill cemetery. The daffodils danced in the breeze as we looked over the tall tenements of the historic Royal Mile, Holyrood Palace, and the green hillsides of Arthur's Seat.

"I can't understand how I am supposed to be a dreadful sinner," I told Linda. "I could commit a heinous sin like underage drinking or even murder someone, crawl back and grovel for God's forgiveness, and then go and do it all again. That doesn't make sense. He can't be a God of fear *and* a God of love."

Yet underneath this crushing iceberg of fundamentalism, there was an unstoppable crystal stream that flooded into a torrent of defiance. After years of inner questioning and confusion, one

Sunday, I summoned all my courage and declared, "I am not coming to church this morning. I have too much homework to do."

Mother's face turned crimson and her jaw wobbled. "Wilma, you can do it later. You'll miss a good sermon by the Reverend Still." I was steadfast in my refusal. Stormy silences and sulking ensued as she pleaded and cajoled. "But what has Jesus done to you, Wilma?" she asked with her beseeching blue eyes. "We'll all be in heaven without you."

Mother never remarried. She thought that men were superior to women—their conversation more interesting. She told me in shocked tones that her friend had told her "cleavages are to keep men guessing." I learned that, to her, men were superior beings, useful as home handymen but with dangerous desires.

In my all-female household, I knew more about Bible stories than I did about human intimacy. I received no formal sex education from school or from my mother. For some reason, Mother did not include me when she told Dorothy some rudimentary information about periods. Dorothy furtively shared it with me. But the day my underwear was stained crimson, I stared in disbelief. I went to my biggest supporter, Ruth, for pads and a sanitary belt. For months, ill at ease, I hid my used pads under the mattress.

Sexuality and boyfriends were not topics for discussion around the dinner table or at any other time. However, as if by osmosis, I knew that men were only after one thing, and although the details eluded me, I knew it was wrong to give it to them. Nice girls were virgins when they were married to good Christian boys.

Academia came second to Scotland's Presbyterian God. Along with the religious destiny Mother mapped out for me, she delivered her powerful expectations on both her birthday and Mother's Day: "Good marks at school are the best gift you can give me." Hence, to escape washing the dishes, I often told her I had to study. Then, in my room, I curled up on my bed with a romantic novel by Georgette Heyer, or borrowed *Beautiful British Columbia* magazines, which tantalized me with spectacular waterfalls, misty trees, and snow-capped mountains.

In the stone building of Leith Academy Secondary School, in my science and math classes, twenty-five boys and four girls sat in rows at individual oak desks blotched with ink stains and engraved with initials. The unapproachable teachers dressed in black gowns.

Before my final year, Ruth accompanied me to my school guidance counsellor interview, which went something like this:

"I want to be a doctor."

"It's very hard to get into medicine. Have you thought of being a dentist?"

I repressed my laughter as I looked at the wobbling folds of skin on her aging chin.

"I see you do well in geography," she continued. "You could get a job as a technician or a bank teller."

"I want to study biology and physics," I said with my lips pursed and my jaw locked. "Both are programmed at the same time. Can I go to the physics class and study biology in my free periods?"

"You must see the rector, Mr. Drummond, about that. I don't know what he will say about your white lipstick," she said, taking the opportunity for criticism. Offended, I left her office and avoided her from then on, except when she summoned me for refusing to wear a school tie, and after the grad dance when she chastised me again for audaciously sitting on my boyfriend's knee.

That year, I surprised myself by achieving the highest marks in the advanced math class. At that moment, I proved to be as smart as the boys who strutted through the corridors in their uniforms and Elvis haircuts. They sometimes sneered, "You've dropped something." When we teenage girls ignored them, they taunted us, "Okay then, bleed to death." When we blushed, they guffawed. It was a joke of sorts but one filled with poison.

After my final state exams, in an unexpected turn of events, I found myself in the back seat of Mr. Drummond's car, appreciative as he and his wife drove me across Scotland to Benmore Outdoor Learning Centre. What a gift it was that he supported my initiative to study biology and encouraged my participation in the outward-bound course. There I found my passion for hiking, canoeing, climbing, and sailing. At the end of the year, I earned a prize for my success in maths and biology. I chose a photo book on mountains in distant countries—places I could only dream about.

I was the first woman in my family to have the opportunity for a university education, which was my route to a brilliant career and my ticket to travel the world. In comparison, my cousin's father—an eminent surgeon—thought his daughter did not need the university education he made available to his sons. My friend Linda married at nineteen and became pregnant at twenty. Ruth went to Moray House College of Education and graduated as a primary school teacher. Dorothy trained at the Royal Sick Children's Hospital as a nurse. By their mid-twenties, they had both married and had children.

Now and then, to keep the peace, I did accompany my mother to church. On one occasion, rainbow light streamed through the stained-glass window. For a fleeting moment, my heart opened up, not because of the minister's words or the singing of "The Lord is my shepherd" but rather because of an inexplicable essence, beyond the brown pews, my mother's presence, or the organ music. There was an exchange of something I had no name for… a beauty… an energy that did not come from this world. If I could have chosen only one word for it, I'd have called it joy.

CHAPTER 2
Scarlet Longing

"The feminine wound is created as we internalize the voices we hear at church, school, home, work, and within the culture at large suggesting (in ways both bold and subtle) that women and feminine experience are 'less than.'"
~ Sue Monk Kidd, The Dance of the Dissident Daughter

February 1969

A month into my second semester at Edinburgh University, I plodded up the hillside through the calf-deep snow. My ribs and calves protested as I panted for breath. Clouds blanketed the peaks. The men around me disappeared into the mist. My mother's warning rang in my ears: *"Hiking on a Sunday. You know better than that."* In my mind's eye, I saw her sitting on the hard wooden pew singing, "Onward Christian soldiers, marching as to war, with the cross of Jesus..." Now on the mountain, the wind tossed my straggling hair as a magnetic force lured me to the summit. There was no going back.

A week before, jostled by two hundred fledgling students, I'd stumbled out of a physics lecture into the cafeteria.

"I don't understand gravitational equations," I had complained to my new friend Morag. "Our hundred-year-old physics lecturer just told us, 'the good think about a bad lecturer is it makes your read the book.'"

"Don't take him seriously," Morag had said. "Why don't you come to Ben Alder with the Mountaineering Club this weekend?"

"What if I can't keep up with the boys?" I'd asked.

"Don't worry about it. You need a break. My friend and I went to Glencoe a few weekends ago. There were only four girls and twenty-eight boys. We need more females."

So on Friday, I'd clambered onto a bus filled with loud-mouthed boy-men and a handful of plucky girls from the Edinburgh University Mountaineering Club (the EUMC), and sat with Morag near the back. I'd listened with increasing apprehension to endless tales of being stranded on cliffs and getting lost in the impenetrable Scottish mist.

"There is a rickety three-roped bridge we have to cross," said tall, bearded Angus, chewing on his unlit pipe. "One strand for feet, two strands for hands. Last year, George slipped, dangled over the torrent, and almost drowned." He laughed.

"By the time we get there, it'll be dark and greasy from the rain," George said.

After we stopped for fish and chips and a beer, the entire bus erupted into traditional pub songs like "The Wild Rover" and some less savoury ones: "…bugger for his hole, there are none so fair as can compare with the likes of the EUMC." Uncomfortable with this overt sexuality, Morag and I raised our eyebrows. By the time we reached the road end, I asked myself, *Why did I come? I hope I'm not going to embarrass myself, or worse, kill myself falling off the bridge.*

Thirty of us lumbered out of the warm coach into the starless highland night and inhaled the earthy air. In the dark, I fumbled tying the laces on my climbing boots, then hoisted my pack onto my shoulders. Under the low clouds, I followed the boys across peat bogs. Pine trees loomed like ghosts as I tripped over roots and rocks on the eight miles to Ben Alder bothy, an old stone shepherd's cottage. While my flashlight faded, one young single-minded man with a ponytail and dark-rimmed glasses strode out ahead. He waded through the knee-deep river while the rest of us searched the darkness for the bridge, which I wobbled across. By the time we arrived, he was lying in his sleeping bag on the only bed. Later, I learned his name was Clive. The rest of us jostled for floor space.

"A sleeping bag is the best contraceptive ever invented," Angus informed us as he crawled into his feather bag. Exhausted, I lay on my mat too tired to feel any scarlet longing or worry about his urges.

In the morning, I stepped into the dazzling light bouncing off the loch. I gulped crisp air and peed behind the stone wall. Inside, the smell of bacon and paraffin filled the air. I battled with my primus stove.

"Wilma, are you coming with us?" Angus asked. "We're leaving in twenty minutes. Here's some hot water for your tea." I stuffed a Kendal mint cake, a sweater, mitts, and an ice-axe into my rucksack and set off with five young men on a narrow path that twisted through the heather. A relentless stream of mental chatter weighed me down. *Boys are much stronger than girls... I don't know how to use an ice axe... Maybe Mother was right...*

The leader, Angus, in britches and red gaiters, charged across the moors and upward to the snow. Behind him, I breathed heavily. We stopped by a boulder the size of a small house.

"You'll develop unladylike calf muscles walking through this deep snow," Angus said. A wave of irritation swept through my body as I threw him a silent dagger. My inability to come up with a cutting response annoyed me. Far below, George plodded upward while we waited twenty minutes for him. *Whew!* I thought, *I'm not last.*

My relief changed to silent frustration when I realized George was jeopardizing our chance to reach the summit. When George decided to retreat, the pace picked up. I trudged upwards, my muscles screaming, my ribs aching, and sweat trickling down my back. Not for the last time in my life, the shame of admitting I couldn't keep up propelled me forward.

Once on the airy ridge, which dropped five hundred feet on either side, I inched my way along. My hands crept over the snowy rocks, searching for the next hold as a gust of wind threatened to throw me over the precipice. I wondered why the whole world wasn't up there. Here was a magic that was incredibly alluring to me and inspired me much more than the pages of my university texts or Mother's church. Here, where the wind played with my hair, I felt the pulse of the earth electrifying my heart as I joined the laughter that rippled through the group.

Scottish winter trip with EUMC

"Can I sit beside you?" I asked Clive on the return bus journey to escape the unwanted attentions of Angus. He nodded.

"Where did you get your ring?" I asked. He wound it off his index finger and slipped it into my palm where it fell into a jumble of four linked rings.

"Can you put it back together?" he asked. I fumbled with the thin bands of silver but made no progress. With enviable skill, Clive manipulated and twisted the pieces into place. It reminded me of an interconnected Celtic knot.

"Last summer, I hitched through Bulgaria to Istanbul and hung out there for a month," he told me. "The bazaars are stuffed with jewellery like this Turkish puzzle ring, carpets, leather bags, and music."

Fascinated by his travels, I looked at him with wide eyes; my arms folded as I swallowed my inexperience. What did I have to talk about? I had never been out of Scotland. My previous summer adventure, hitch-hiking and camping on Skye, felt insignificant compared to his exotic trip to Turkey.

A few days later, I leaned on the sticky mahogany bar in Rutherfords Pub, the strong smell of hops and antiseptic in the air. On Wednesday lunchtimes, the members of the EUMC took a break from their engineering, veterinary, or medical studies to meet and reminisce on the weekend's activities in the Scottish Highlands and plan climbs to places like Glencoe, Ben Nevis, and Lochnagar. The wintry light illuminated the stained-glass windows and bathed us with a golden glow. Vibrant conversation buzzed over the tinkle of beer glasses. Dressed in a red suit and knee-high boots, with my fair hair curled over my shoulder, I chatted with my new girlfriends.

"Guess who asked me to the Valentine's Dance tonight?" I said.

"I saw you making eyes at Angus on the weekend," Morag smirked.

"I wasn't flirting with him!" I whispered as Angus stood close to us. "I know he fed me steak and mushrooms, but he can only talk about his engineering thesis. I told him going to the dance was out of the question. I have three lab reports due on Friday. Look at my Valentine's card. Do you think it's from him?"

Clive walked into the bar, his hair in a ponytail, his frayed jeans and sandals unusual in a Scottish winter. He came straight to me, his brown eyes dancing.

"Do you want to come with me to the Valentine's dance tonight?" he asked in a loud voice. I nodded. Angus never spoke to me again.

That afternoon in her kitchen, Mother looked at my purple T-shirt. "It looks like you're wearing your underwear. You'll arouse men's uncontrollable urges," she warned, wiping her hands on her apron. Just a few days before, after I'd searched high and low for my book *The Naked Ape* by Desmond Morris, Mother had admitted, as if she was doing me a favour, that she had burned it to save me from heretic evolutionary thought and the sin of comparing humans, created by God, to apes. That's the mentality I was up against. On one level, she encouraged education, but on another, she was threatened by theories that contradicted Genesis. With no time to argue, I rolled my blue mascara eyes, slammed the door, and ran up the road to meet Clive.

That evening in Clive's apartment, with a couple of friends, we drank his golden homebrew. Its high alcohol content made my head spin. Then we tumbled into his ancient A40 van to drive to the dance. Holding hands, we raced up the curved stairway of the George Street Assembly Halls. Under the crystal chandeliers, he pulled me close, and his tongue parted my lips. He pressed his fingers into the small of my back as my breasts thrust into his chest. An exhilarating eruption pulsated in every cell of my body, and I quivered with anticipation. That night we spun, whirled, jived, and twisted our bodies like dervishes to the loud beat of the "Na na na na na na… thousand dancers."

When the dance ended, Clive drove me to his local bakery, from which warm air, flour, and rays of light scattered into the sleeping city. We gobbled hot bread rolls and butter. Enroute to my mother's house, his van chugged up the sweep of the Mound, guarded by the floodlit castle perched on the basalt cliff.

"Pull over!" I said. "Look at the flames shooting into the sky. One of the big departmental stores is on fire!" A spectacular end to the evening.

Over the next few months, Clive and I went on movie dates and attended lectures about expeditions to the Karakoram, the Himalayas, and Patagonia by famous British mountaineers, all male, like Chris Bonnington and Hamish McInnes. Very few women had broken into the male-dominated mountaineering world. Clive picked me up at the end of our street. I wasn't ready to introduce him to my family, who would have judged a boy with long hair as not suitable for a "nice girl." On the other hand, on the long bus journeys with the EUMC to the mountains, the softness of each other's lips intoxicated us.

Each time we said goodnight, and we sat side by side in his van, his hands crept under my blouse, undid my bra, and fondled my breasts. I resisted as his hands wandered under my panties. With pounding heart and heavy breathing, I pushed him away.

"This is a mistake. I can't do that."

"Oh, come on. Stay longer," he said.

"Mother said I should be home at eleven." When I stepped out of his van, I took a deep breath, run my hands over my hair, rearrange my shirt, and hope Mother was asleep.

Once in my bed tucked under woollen blankets, I tossed and turned all night, my head filled with confusion and scarlet longing. *Should I follow the passionate desires of my body or the dictates of my mother's morality? Is it okay to feel the delicious sensations his touch arouses? Am I a whore because I want to go all the way before marriage?*

It was not only my mother and the Scottish patriarchal condemnation I recognized. I imagined that God with his long white beard, clothed in flowing white robes, was sitting on a cloud wagging an angry finger with one hand, while with the other, he wrote all my misdemeanours in a giant ledger: Talked in class. Refused to say she was sorry. Did not go to church on Sunday… He was particularly enraged if I was interested in my genitals. *Don't touch. Stuff of the devil.* He would be beside himself with wrath if I even thought of sex before marriage. I imagined my transgressions recorded for eternity and God's voice booming from the sky, "SINNER! SINNER! SINNER!"

Still, I longed to see Clive again, hear him laugh, and feel his gentle touch.

Then I stepped over the edge… into the unknown. "Mum, I am staying with Morag tonight. Her parents expect us back at eleven," I lied. In my uplift bra and pink mini dress, complete with a front zipper for ease of access, I rushed to a wild party with Clive. Steaming bodies gyrated, and we sang along to the Rolling Stones, changing the lyrics to "I can't get no sexual action." That night, in his flat, with help from Mother's demon drink and the insistent tug of my scarlet longing, my virginity became history, and I was consigned to everlasting damnation.

CHAPTER 3
Chameleon Summer

*"The beauty of the world has two edges, one of laughter,
one of anguish, cutting the heart asunder."*
~ Virginia Woolf, A Room of One's Own

July 1969

One morning, at the end of my second year, I opened the envelope from Edinburgh University and my mind went blank. I covered my eyes and gritted my teeth as my stomach tightened. No amount of re-reading changed the ominous word: "FAILED." At nineteen, about to realize my lifelong dream to travel to America, I had screwed up. Now I needed to stay and re-sit Biology 201. My thoughts churned like clothes in a tumble dryer: *If only I had studied harder. I shouldn't have gone to Skye with the mountaineering club the weekend before the exam. If only they hadn't asked the brainless question about how the dinosaurs had become extinct.* I blamed everyone who entered my mind, my mother and the zoology professor in particular. I recalled, with a little remorse, the hours spent lying with Clive on the lush grass under the cherry blossoms, kissing and fondling into a froth of desire until the most important decision at that moment was to seek the privacy of his flat and enjoy our bodies. Now guilt consumed me.

"Mum, I need to cancel Camp America. Clive has offered to drive me to London. We'll go to the office and get my deposit back."

"Oh, Wilma, you'll be the death of me. Where'll you stay? Do you think his old van will make it? What'll you do if it breaks down?" Her brow furrowed as she beat the cream and sugar for the cake faster and faster.

"His van is slow. We can stay with Clive's grandmother. She'll keep her eye on us. You have nothing to worry about."

She held her head in her hands. "How long will you be gone for?" I won my battle and left for London.

When we knocked, Clive's grandma—a tall woman with a hooked nose, high cheekbones, and a pronounced limp—welcomed us to her spacious ground-floor apartment. Colourful cushions covered her velvet couch and her oil paintings hung on the walls.

"Come in! It's good to see you. How was your journey? You can sleep here on the settee. Would you like some tea?" We nodded.

"Now, dear," she said, "sit down and tell me about yourself."

Unaccustomed to speaking out, and overcome with shyness, my brain froze, and so she began to talk, filling my awkward silence. "I have just returned from Israel. A trip I have dreamt of for years. With my bad hip, it was difficult to get on and off the coach. People were so helpful with my wheelchair. I loved the Wailing Wall, the Sea of Galilee, and the ancient churches."

"I read about those places in the Bible," I said. "I never imagined you could travel there."

"That's my painting studio at the end of the hall," she said. "My male model comes tomorrow. I do nude drawings." I drew a sharp breath.

After we retrieved my deposit from Camp America, and giddy with excitement, I photographed fearless Clive in his small van as he raced around Piccadilly Circus competing with the manic

London traffic. Meanwhile, my scarlet longing won, and Grandma turned a blind eye to our night-time lovemaking on the couch. At breakfast, she served tea as if nothing was out of line.

A couple of weeks later, back home in Edinburgh, I anxiously waited for stomach cramps. I visited the toilet every hour to examine my knickers. In disbelief, my mind spun. *This is not happening to me. We used a condom.* The nights were endless as I dreamt of the angry man who brandished a hatchet with the intent to end my life. Each morning, my pillow was soaked with tears, my jaw locked, and my shoulders rigid. I caught religion real bad. I implored God to intervene. I prayed so hard that Mother would have been proud, but it seemed that her patriarchal god was a deaf-mute, had his fingers in his ears, or was laughing hard: *"Ha! I will teach you who's boss."* As each day passed, the enormity of the growing realization that my period was not coming left me paralyzed.

My visit to the family doctor confirmed the worst. I left biting my lips, my hands shaking, and my eyes streaming tears.

A few days later, my sister Dorothy happened to visit the doctor. "It's really strange," she said to me. "He asked me if my feelings of depression had anything to do with you."

I felt my throat tighten and my mouth go dry. I lied. "What on earth can he be talking about? I haven't seen him in years."

Terrified of their judgement and disappointment, my mother and sisters were the last people in whom I could confide. I knew there was no help coming from them. Over a pint of lager, biting my nails and fearing his rejection, I broke the news to Clive. Despondent, we stared into our glasses. When the first shock wore off, as partners, we considered our options. I never entertained keeping the foetus, but I could not begin to contemplate an adoption. I refused to imagine the cells growing within me as a baby. To terminate a foetus was less cruel. I longed for this total disaster to disappear so that I could finish my degree and move on with my life. In 1969, there were no over-the-counter pregnancy tests, no birth-control clinics, and no abortion counsellors. The only person available to help us was the Pastoral Care Minister at the university. After a short dialogue, while I sobbed and blew my distress into tissues, he arranged an appointment at the hospital.

It was a summer of constant dread and double-dealing. Obsidian black, the colour of shame, blinded my vision as I worried about my mother discovering I was pregnant at nineteen. Alone, my mood darkened with the additional fear of her finding out that I planned to have an abortion. In her eyes, having sex before marriage, getting pregnant, and having an abortion would all be unforgivable sins. I did not know who I was, but like a chameleon, my colour brightened around Clive—my supportive confidant.

Six weeks later, about to go to the Royal Infirmary Hospital, the Pastoral Care office contacted me. Since I was not yet twenty-one, I needed my mother's signature for the anaesthetic. What was I to do? I needed man-sized handkerchiefs to soak up my incessant tears. I did not want to be responsible for breaking her heart and embarrassing her in front of her three indomitable Irish sisters. After a gut-wrenching week of deceit, another hospital that did not need parental consent accepted me. I lied again and told my mother I was visiting Clive's family. Once in the ward, I spent three days hiding under the covers in the hopes that no friend of my mother would see me.

Earlier that summer, I had followed the call of the wild to the Outer Hebrides with Morag. Behaving like a chameleon, I had not shared my predicament with her but pretended all was normal. My night dreams on that trip were haunted by a blue-skinned baby dead in my arms. Morag looked perplexed as I lagged behind her on our hikes, dragging legs that felt like lead through the heather to the highest point on the Island of Harris. Then at Hushnish, the hamlet at the end of the road, I hiked over a carpet of wildflowers and across the silvery sand, sat on the schist that sheltered pockets of sea pinks, and looked onto the turquoise sea speckled with white caps. Listening to the oystercatchers and herring gulls, I inhaled Atlantic sea-air as I dropped into a moment of release. A Celtic sixth sense told me not to stay in Scotland but to travel, explore, and search. For what, I did not know.

CHAPTER 4

Thumbs Up in the USA

"We delight in the beauty of the butterfly, but rarely admit the changes it has gone through to achieve that beauty."
~ Maya Angelou, American author and poet

Summer 1970

Mother imagined heaven in the afterlife, while I expected to find heaven in the United States of America. As I climbed onto the British Airways plane to Boston, my stomach tingled like fireworks. At last, I was escaping my studies, Mother's narrow attitudes, and grey skies to pursue my dream of seeing the world. A few days before, when I had hugged Clive—who left Edinburgh with a small bag slung over his shoulder to hitchhike to North Africa—my heart had splintered, but as the plane soared above the clouds, elation soothed my sadness. While most passengers slept, I glued my eyes to the window and stared with awe at Greenland's glaciated mountains far below and icebergs floating like tiny crystals on an indigo sea.

"Anything to declare?" the stern customs officer asked.

"I have two apples."

"Put them in the barrel," he ordered. Reluctantly, I threw away my mother's gift, given to ensure I would not starve on my journey to the land of plenty.

"Are you or have you ever been a member of the communist party?" he asked. I shook my head. When he stamped my passport, relief rippled out from my solar plexus. Heady with anticipation, I walked out of the airport to the promised land.

Our bus sped through the murky tunnels of Boston's freeways past billboards and flashing neon signs. Where was the glamour from *Gone with the Wind*? I arrived at the YWCA camp in Maine and took a deep breath of warm air, savouring the smell of pinesap and wood smoke. I stretched my head back to marvel at the shining stars above the fir trees. Then I heard the whine of mosquitoes—a new sound for me and one that I came to dread.

In my role as group leader, I slept in a cabin with eight teenage girls from a wide range of socio-economic and racial backgrounds, unlike predominantly white Scotland. All of us leaders, the girls, and Glen, our handyman and instructor, began our days standing in a circle around the flagpole. With our right hands on our hearts, we recited in unison, "*I pledge allegiance to the flag of the United States of America, and to the Republic for which it stands, one Nation under God, indivisible, with liberty and justice for all.*" I questioned Lucy, the camp director, about this ceremony.

"After the civil war, patriotism and national feeling were at a low ebb. The leaders in the government recognized that patriotic education needed to begin in public schools. A socialist called Francis Bellamy wrote this in 1892," she said, introducing me to American history and nation-building.

Each morning, with my group of enthusiastic girls, we walked through the forest scattered with log cabins to the lakeshore. Our swimming instructor and lifeguard, Sammy, was athletic and accomplished. She and Glen taught the girls how to balance on the rim of the canoes and to manoeuvre them into a star. Sammy had been coming to this camp for years. She radiated a sense of place and poise that contrasted my foreign unease and lack of skill.

On the other hand, large Peggy, my co-counsellor, made me grit my teeth. I did not like watching her fat legs jiggle as she waddled from one craft cabin to the other. Her focus on small details and order drove me crazy. After one frustrating camp craft class, unhappy with her method of teaching knots, I stomped back to my cabin and laid on my bunk, my breathing constrained as if my ribs had been clamped. I recollected that, in Scotland, obesity was rare and judged as a disgrace. Mother often cautioned me as I bit into a piece of cake, "A moment in your mouth and around your waistline forever." With my fashion-conscious sisters, we found guilty pleasure in gossiping about body size.

One day Lucy, a large short lady, asked how I felt about the deterioration in my relationship with Peggy. I replied, "Fine." This was the one word I used to cover all my emotional states. "Fine," with my teeth clenched, "fine," with eyes downcast and shoulders hunched, or "fine," with my lips curled and lightness in my heart. Lucy invited Peggy and me for tea to help us work out our antagonism, but I was inflexible. I hate to say it, but my distasteful bias revealed my belief that both Lucy and Peggy should have been ashamed of themselves, or at least covered their legs. Peggy and I avoided each other and worked side by side with little communication. As the summer progressed, I came to genuinely respect Lucy as she talked to me, encouraged me, and took time to help me see diversity from a more inclusive perspective.

An insatiable desire to acquire a suntan drove my short breaks. Because of Scottish rainy summers, a tan proved that I had travelled to sunnier climates. Most days after lunch, clad in my bikini and slathered in Johnson's Baby Oil, I walked down the gravel road and wandered between the fir trees to find a sunny spot on a rock by the lake. One day, I tiptoed through the scratchy underbrush and let out a piercing scream. To my horror, ferocious black-and-white-striped insects stung my ankles and calves. With difficulty, I brushed them off. My feet and ankles, injected with poison, formed red smarting bumps. In tears, I went to the nurse.

"Oh my god, those stings look painful. You stood on a hornet's nest," she said. "And that mosquito bite on your eye is almost the size of a tennis ball."

"We don't have mosquitoes or hornets in Scotland," I replied quietly. "I have never been stung before. We have tiny midges, no-see-ums, and they leave a small itchy spot."

"You need to go to the doctor for some antihistamine," she advised.

I scratched my bites until they bled. I cried myself to sleep. That night, a storm broke overhead, thunder cracking and drowning out the sound of wind moaning in the trees as the lightning lit up the forest. Raindrops the size of marbles bounced off the muddy ground. Irrepressible anger and prejudices fermented under my "nice girl" mask and sabotaged the recognition and acceptance I yearned for. I longed to escape to the mountains and into Clive's soothing arms.

That Friday evening, I sat with my group at the trestle table, which was scattered with cups and plates. Beside me, in floral bell-bottoms, Phyllis cupped her chin in her hand. Sarah sat behind her with her wild afro and the whites of her eyes and teeth gleaming in her ebony face. With plaits and rimless glasses, Paddy sat across from me. I waited for a lull in the conversation and then jumped in with my soft Scottish accent: "Paddy, can you pass the black biscuits please." Laughter erupted around the table. To my acute embarrassment, heat rushed to my face as if I should have known better.

"Oh, you mean the Oreo cookies?" she said. With relief, I grabbed one and took a bite.

"I like to break them up and slowly lick the white filling," Phyllis said.

"I like to eat them whole, just like you," Sarah said. "It's dance night. You like dancing?"

I nodded. To my surprise, I silenced the persistent Calvinistic voice in my head, reminding me that *"dancing is stuff of the devil."* Together, we moved the tables to one side. Jimi Hendrix, Janis Joplin, The Beatles, and Simon & Garfunkel's music boomed across the hall. The girls' eyes brimmed with joy as they rolled their shoulders and hips with fluidity and sensuality that made me feel stiff, like a tin man. Between dances, the girls massaged each other's shoulders. I envied the comfortable ease they had in their bodies. In my culture, we did not touch each other nor give back rubs.

My YWCA group of spirited teenagers

On one of our rare days off, Sammy invited me to climb a mountain in New Hampshire. We walked on a path through the woods, which was lined with emerald moss that looked like velvet. Fungi and lichens covered rotting deadfall and scrubby underbrush. Rays of sunlight lit up trees draped with strands of sage reindeer moss. Sporadic bird song and the buzz of flies interrupted any potential silence as we laboured upwards to the sound of our heavy exhalations, chatter, and footsteps. Unused to the heat, sweat dripped into my eyes. Near the top of the forest, we headed behind different trees to pee. Then we scrambled over granite boulders. Away from the stress of camp dynamics, I stood elated on the summit, looking at hazy blue ridges that stretched to the horizon.

Back at camp, I approached Lucy. "I'd love to take my group to the White Mountains."

"The trip you did would be too hard for them," she said. "I believe it's important that young women have successful experiences that they can build on."

"Hmm…" I said. "That sounds better than throwing them in the deep end to see if they will sink or swim."

The last week of camp, my group climbed into the back of Glen's pickup. Over the weeks, I hadn't had much to do with Glen. On this camping trip, he exuded mature confidence. He drove us to a spacious campsite in a forest by a lake. The warm weather, so different than Scotland's, made camping a joy. Canoeing on the river and hiking thrilled me. I walked up the trail with Paddy, who wore a sweaty bandana tied around her forehead. "What is the matter with Sarah and Phyllis?" she grumbled. "They never try hard, and they're always complaining. Why can't they just suck it up and be more like us?"

"Try to imagine what it is like for them though," I said, "with their mothers working all the time to try and make ends meet. They've had tough lives."

Further along on the track, I fell into step with Sarah. Sweat trickled down her dark cheeks.

"Paddy is always trying to get out of chores," she said. "She does as little as possible. She told me they have maids at home, and she's not expected to help with anything."

"I was jealous of a friend like that at university," I said. "Her wealthy life looked easier than mine. I always had to help my mother." Letting the conversation go, we raced to the summit, the expansive view of peaks and forests holding us all in its gentle embrace. We sat contentedly until the setting sun reminded us to return.

That evening, pleasantly tired, we sat around the campfire, toasting smores. As flames leaped into the darkness and sparks mingled with the stars, we sang camp songs together. I sang a Scottish song: "The summertime is coming…and the wild mountain thyme grows around the blooming heather…" We all held hands and finished with "We shall overcome." Back at camp, we embraced each other and said teary farewells.

With the camp over, Donna, the arts and crafts counsellor, and I put out our thumbs to hitchhike to Canada. Out on the road, her ginger hair fell over her shoulders as her sleeping bag spilled from her knapsack. Large Chevrolets, Buicks, and Cadillacs sped past. Two long-haired young men with bandanas around their heads and tie-dyed shirts, driving a yellow Volkswagen Beetle, pulled over. Donna and I squeezed into the back seat.

"We spent the summer working at a YWCA camp," I told them as we drove over the rolling hillsides of Vermont. "We're hitching to Montreal before I return to Scotland."

One fumbled in the dashboard and pulled out a thin reefer. He lit up and inhaled. The smoke curled into the air, and I experienced my first pungent smell of marijuana. Then he offered it to us. I did smoke cigarettes, but drugs frightened me. I took a small puff. The smoke irritated my throat. I was worried I'd do myself some permanent damage, or worse, lose control, and be taken advantage of.

As we chatted, the conversation turned to the Vietnam War as it often had that summer.

"My best friend from high school is in Vietnam," the driver said. "I'm at college, so I wasn't drafted. I hope to hell the Vietcong don't get him. Did you see the TV the other night? Explosions come from above and below in that goddamn jungle. Soldiers come home with their legs and arms blown off. It's time the government got out."

"Yeah, my brother's over there too," his friend said. "I can't wait till he comes back on leave. My cousin died there a year ago. I remember going to the beach with him in the summer as kids, playing on our bikes. I can't believe I'll never see him again. Man, he loved to party and make us laugh."

Chills ran down my spine. The Simon & Garfunkel song I'd been listening to all summer, "The Sound of Silence," with its reference to darkness, took on a solemn meaning. I couldn't begin to imagine my male friends from the mountaineering club in Edinburgh, or Clive or his brothers, being conscripted, and possibly dying in Asia.

We said goodbye in the middle of Vermont on a small road surrounded by lush green fields. A while later, a weather-beaten farmer hauling a trailer behind his truck stopped for us. "Where are ya headed? I'm not going far. I just picked up my cows from the market. It's getting late. You girls got somewhere to stay?" We looked at one another and shook our heads.

"Ya can stay with me. I see you have sleeping bags. Mind you, our farm is nothing fancy. But you're welcome." This man had an honest look, and we decided to trust him. As we bumped along between his fields, he warned us in his slow backcountry drawl, "Now don't you two girls be fighting over my son."

That evening, he showed us around his farm. Although I was thrilled to be hoisted upon their horse for a bareback ride, neither of us was attracted to his thick-set son in his muddy jeans. In the morning, we breakfasted in their small kitchen. A rickety table with the jam jar and milk carton on the top shattered my conviction that all Americans were wealthy. However, I do remember their kindness and friendship.

In Montreal, I hugged Donna goodbye as she headed to art school in Boston. I joined up with British students Colin and Diane, whom I had met on the aeroplane. In my mini dress and sunglasses that covered most of my face, I flirted with Colin as we wandered around Expo, drinking Coca-Cola, flying on the rides, and broadening our knowledge of the world in different pavilions. We boarded a Greyhound bus then and travelled through miles of forest to Toronto, Niagara Falls, and New York. Protected by the bus window, I stared at the busy streets of Harlem, astonished that there was not a white person to be seen.

After a night in a woman's hostel, Diane and I set out into a street with towering skyscrapers, its sidewalks filled with multicultural pedestrians. A bus bound for the Staten Island Ferry terminal pulled into the stop. While we fumbled for the correct change, the immaculately dressed gentlemen behind us paid our fares. After all the warnings on the news about crime in New York, I thought being mugged would have been a greater possibility than experiencing generosity. With an extra bounce in our step, we paid our nickel for a ferry ride to the Statue of Liberty, gifted by France to the USA in the late nineteenth century. The robed female figure represents Libertas, the Roman goddess of liberty. I read the inscription:

> "Give me your tired, your poor,
> Your huddled masses, yearning to breathe free,
> The wretched refuse of your teeming shore,
> Send these, the homeless, tempest-tost to me,
> I lift my lamp beside the golden door."
> ~Emma Lazarus 1876

The Hudson River flowed like quicksilver past the skyscrapers. Pulled by gravity, the water molecules swirled around one another and mixed with the Atlantic, just as indigenous people, former slaves, and immigrants from all over the world have intermingled to create both racial tensions and opportunities in America.

On top of the Empire State Building, the geometrical grid of Manhattan's skyscrapers lay below in contrast to the green rectangle of Central Park. The yellow taxis, like matchbox toys, scurried through the streets, and their horns and sirens pierced the rumble of the city. Here, at the arguable centre of the cultural world and automobile civilization, was a world full of unknown possibilities. My skin tingled with new vitality.

That afternoon, Diane and I stopped at a hospital. In America, unlike Scotland, blood was a commercial commodity. We signed the required forms, and the nurse showed us into a ward. I lay on the bed with a white sheet and watched a pint of my blood drip into a plastic bag. After a tea and a cookie, we clutched our blood money and rushed to buy tickets for *Hair*.

In the Broadway theatre, Diane's ponytail swung from side to side as we bounded up the creaking wooden stairs two at a time, as if climbing Led Zeppelin's "Stairway to Heaven." Once in my velour-covered seat, I stared at the stage, careful not to lean too far forward in case vertigo toppled me to the ground far below. "Aquarius" boomed out across the theatre; lithe muscular figures crawled out of the attic and slid down ropes with their hair streaming in the light. I was mesmerized by the eclectic music, wild physicality, explicit sexuality, fluidity between men and women, and the plea for "harmony and understanding." I did not want the show to end. Giddy from the music, or the lack of blood, we drank a beer afterwards in a bar in Times Square and chatted to a couple of young men.

"Have you seen *Hair*?" I asked.

"It's amazing," Diane jumped in. "The music is electrifying.

Claude is fighting his conscription. He needs to decide whether to resist the draft as his friends have done or follow parental and government pressure to serve in Vietnam. He is a pacifist and doesn't want to risk his life."

"Yeah, I was in the army. It was awful," one guy said.

"*Hair* shows everything that is in turmoil in America: civil rights, women's rights, free love, the cold war, and the Vietnam War." I shivered in the warm night, thinking, *I am not alone in my rebellion against my mother's Christianity.*

"Just think," Diane said, "one careless push of the button in the Oval Office, or the Kremlin, could create nuclear destruction across the globe. It would be the end of everything. It's terrifying."

In that moment and full of high spirits, I decided I did not want to be tied down to a permanent relationship with Clive. I wanted to be single and free to travel, and my university degree would be my passport to the world. Casting glances over our shoulders, worried about stalkers, we briskly walked through dark streets, and caught the overnight Greyhound bus to Washington.

On my last day in America, I held hands with Colin as we raced around grassy lawns, the White House, obelisks, and then to the grave of the Unknown Soldier. On the bus to the airport, within sight of the state buildings, the division of entrenched racial lines became stark with Washington's visibly underprivileged: black ghettoes or slums as we called them in Britain. *Where was the light promised in the inscription?*

CHAPTER 5

Overland on a Shoestring

"So many of our dreams at first seem impossible; then they seem improbable, and then, when we summon the will, they soon become inevitable."
~ Christopher Reeve, Speech at the 1996 Democratic National Convention.

A few days after I returned, the phone rang.
"Do you want to go for a walk up Arthur's Seat?" Clive's chirpy voice asked. For a moment, I reconsidered my recent decision to be single. "Yes. I'm dying to hear about your trip," I replied.

His tanned body jolted all reason out of my mind. With one electric kiss, our legs and arms entwined as we made love under a tree. At that moment, I knew with an unfamiliar certainty that *I must marry this man*.

In the summer of 1971, a year later, I strode down the aisle covered from neck to toe in my sister Ruth's white wedding dress. Clive wore a second-hand suit with a white carnation from the garden. Our traditional church wedding made Mother happy. I graduated from Edinburgh University with B.Sc. honours at the end of my new name and "Mrs." at the beginning. The promise of an overland trip with my lover, now husband, thrilled me.

We hitchhiked to London. In Hyde Park, Clive found a quiet spot behind some bushes, and we snuggled into our sleeping bags. In the early morning, a gruff voice interrupted our sleep: "Move along there." We weren't alone sleeping in the park. Longhaired hippies muttered curses as they collected their belongings, crunched over the gravel, and shuffled on their way. The policeman's heavy footsteps approached us, but tucked under a bush, we remained hidden. I pulled my feather sleeping bag around my chin. Ignoring the hard ground that dug into my hips, I attempted to snatch more sleep. *Have I made a mistake? What have I let myself in for?*

Hand in hand, Clive and I boarded the sleeper train to Southern Italy. Under his shirt, a safety wallet contained his parents' wedding present of 100 pounds sterling, earmarked for furniture. Full of curiosity, I hung out of the window to catch the essence of Paris, but it passed in a flash. In the darkness, I strained to see the Alps, then watched the dawn tinge Milan's grey industrial buildings pink. Out in the country, wizened olive trees peppered the parched fields. Enviously, I eyed the silvery beaches of the Adriatic, thronged with sun worshippers. After thirty-six hours, we arrived hot and sticky in Brindisi, on the heel of Italy.

As we wandered across the street towards the sea, Clive tugged my arm. "We'll buy ferry tickets to Patras in Greece."

"Can't we spend the night here? I want to look around."

"It's too expensive, sweetheart," he said. "You'll like Greece."

We jostled with the crowd at the ferry terminal. Men and women shouted in French, German, Italian, and Greek and elbowed each other to the ticket box. British style, I hung back to wait for a queue to form while Clive dove into the fray and emerged victorious, waving two tickets. On the ferry, thronged with tourists, we found deck space for our sleeping bags. We curled up under the clear sky and were gently rocked to sleep. As the next day warmed, we claimed seats by the packed pool, shed our clothes, and exposed our lily-white bodies to the Mediterranean sun.

At the Greek ferry terminal of Patras, we hitched a ride. The drive through the miles of suburbs and chemical plants shattered my illusions of romantic Athens, though I did catch a fleeting glimpse of the flood-lit pillars of the Parthenon. That evening, unable to catch a ferry to a Greek Island, we lay on the concrete benches at the ferry terminal. Every time I turned, my hips ached, and my stop-light red skin felt as if I was in the hell Mother's religion warned of.

"This is awful," I snapped in the morning. "My body's stinging all over. I need a wash. Let's go to a hotel."

"The hotels are too expensive. The ferry to Mykonos leaves in thirty minutes. You'll feel better out of the city." He put his arm around my shoulder.

"Ouch! That hurts!"

Sipping ice-cold Coke, I hung over the ship's railing, mesmerized by the ancient ruins of an island temple, its sandstone columns silhouetted against the cloudless sky.

At Mykonos, there was no jetty. Our ferry plunged up and down in the swell. We anchored in the bay, and a small boat tied alongside us. My hair blew wildly as I climbed down the ladder and grasped the strong hand of the tanned boatman who helped me into the open boat. In the town, tourists thronged the warren of narrow lanes, while the blinding sun bounced off the white houses squeezed around the harbour. We asked a young man with sun-bleached shoulder-length hair and cut-off jeans where we could sleep, and he directed us to the beach at Valdenachas. For a few drachmas, we boarded a rickety bus and squeezed in between people, chickens, and sacks of vegetables. It laboured over the steep hill, passing wrinkled men wandering up the road with their loaded donkeys. A row of white windmills, their canvas sails flying in the breeze, crowned the ridge.

As Clive had promised, this was fun. My toes curled around the silver sand, and my body floated in the warm sea. Later that evening, in a taverna filled with an international crowd of young people, I relished every mouthful of the cheesy moussaka, a welcome change from our staple diet of white crusty bread and tomatoes.

"We just arrived from Istanbul," said an American guy with his hair in a ponytail. "We took three months to travel from India."

Then an English woman with the darkest tan I had ever seen chimed in. "We came from Santorini. You have to go there. It's amazing."

"The ruins of Ephesus and Troy are *incroyable*," added a Frenchman.

An elegant three-masted schooner sailed into the bay and anchored as the golden sun slipped into the Mediterranean. The full-bodied moon gleamed on the black water as we meandered, arm in arm, along the water's edge to our sleeping spot on a rocky promontory. Our limbs entangled, we lay awake under the Milky Way.

Clive and I in Greece

These new places absorbed me. On the other hand, for Clive, a seasoned traveller whose parents loved adventurous holidays, the East was magnetic. He dreamed of Afghanistan—a country I had not learned about in high school geography, my mother's Biblical stories, or headlined in the world news. Following the information gleaned from the previous night's conversation, we took the overnight ferry to Samos enroute to Turkey. Rain and spray lashed the decks as the boat pitched and rolled across a dark sea streaked with foam. The wind roared around the funnel above our sleeping spot. Nothing was still in this watery world. While my stomach heaved, an ingrained Bible story dominated my thoughts. Would I, like Jonah, be swallowed by a whale and spewed up on a desolate beach?

On the island of Samos, shuttered stucco buildings with wrought-iron balconies were crowded around the bay. In brightly coloured fishing boats, fishermen coiled their nets and stacked lobster pots. In one of the many cafes that hugged the water's edge, we lingered over coffee.

"Pythagoras came from here," Clive told me.

"In a right-angled triangle, the square on the hypotenuse is equal to the sum of the squares on the other two sides," I said, reciting my high school geometry while pondering his life thousands of years ago.

Meanwhile, the clouds disappeared, and the sun shone, turning the sea into a kaleidoscope of blue and turquoise. On the small launch to Kusadasi, Turkey, we climbed over ropes to sit on the bow. The boat frolicked east over white caps, and salt spray sprinkled my face. As we left Europe, I had no idea what lay ahead.

Once through the Turkish Customs, we heard the impatient shouts from the driver of a *dolmus*, shared taxi: "Efes, Efes! You go to Efes?" Efes is the remains of the ancient Greek town of Ephesus. *"Cas para?"* Clive asked, meaning—how much? The answer came back in a torrent.

We looked blank, and the driver repeated the price in English. When no more people could squeeze into the minibus, the driver took off at breakneck speed with Turkish music blaring. His hand was stuck on the horn as he raced past donkeys, bicycles, cars, and buses.

"This driving is crazy. I hope he doesn't kill us," I said, gripping Clive's arm.

"Maybe Allah protects him, but I wish he'd slow down," Clive said.

At Ephesus, sweating under the scorching sun, we meandered up the dusty road to the deserted ruins. "Ephesus used to be a port. The sea is now five kilometres away. The area is filled in with sediments that are now fields," Clive read from the display board. "It was greater than Athens. This immense ruined amphitheatre held twenty-four thousand people."

In awe, we strolled past the flattened ruins of the temple of Artemis, one of the seven wonders of the ancient world. On the marble paving of the Arcadian Way, I walked along the grooves left by the chariot wheels. Then under the shade of an acacia tree, I sat on a broken column and wrote down a scene as I imagined it two thousand years ago:

I hear shouts from the wharves as cargoes of olives and grain are loaded. The air filled with the fragrance of spices and herbs. The ropes creak as the boats rise up and down on the gentle swell. I listen to the rumble of chariots, the clatter of horses' hooves as they haul their loads to the town. The merchants swish past in their long white robes. The town bustles with activity.

I held my ear to the warm stones of the brothel's crumbling walls to hear bawdy stories and learn their wisdom but heard only the rustle of leaves and song of a skylark. Over its long history, this now quiet ruin had experienced waves of peace and violence, construction and destruction. These ruins piqued my interest more than any of my high school history lessons.

After studying our map of Asia, torn from a school atlas, we boarded a bus to the south. We passed orchards of peaches, olive groves, and cornfields. I thought of Scotland's water-laden moors and understood why this fertile land had been fought over since the beginning of time.

In the modern city of Anatalya, several men approached us and asked, "You want cheap oteli? I have a nice oteli, very clean, not far from here." We followed Ahmed through the Bekir Akbodak, past the shop fronts with peeling paint, a slender minaret, and stray cats to the Armagan Oteli. For six lira each, we stayed in a simple whitewashed room with a shared shower and an eastern toilet that stank of urine. I held my nose and squatted over the hole. Concerned that the sheets had been used, I inspected them for grit and hair. Still, grateful for a real bed, I curled into my sheet sleeping bag and did not move all night.

In the morning, Ahmed brought us tea in elegant, bulbous glasses on saucers with two sugar cubes and a tiny teaspoon with holes in it. When he discovered we were just married, he rushed to tell his wife, Kari. She wore baggy pants and a knee-length tunic, and a white scarf covered her head. She placed my hand in hers and examined my gold ring. She smiled and made some approving comments in Turkish that warmed my heart. To celebrate and introduce us to the delights of eastern big-heartedness, Ahmed bought us breakfast in a nearby café: Turkish coffee, white toast, butter, and jam. He paid eight liras. In return, he asked, "Please tell all your friends about my oteli!"

While Clive wanted to keep travelling, I needed a diversion. We swam in a Mediterranean cove surrounded by dark volcanic rocks and framed by palm trees and magenta bougainvillea. The turquoise sea soothed my sun-burnt body as I gazed on the nine-thousand-foot mountains. Like ghosts, snow-covered tops hovered in and out of the thick heat haze.

That afternoon, we caught a bus east to Alanya, where we walked through the old streets, watching barbers in their spotless white jackets and blacksmiths in their open-fronted shops. I became aware of the men. There were men mending shoes, men selling bread, vegetables, and meat, men mending clothes, and men fixing punctures. I sensed their brown eyes gawk at my bare legs. Then I noticed an absence of females, let alone any in shorts. Violated by these invasive stares, I wanted to disappear. I clutched Clive's arm and rushed to the protection of a nearby hotel. I stuffed my shorts to the bottom of my pack where they stayed for the rest of the trip.

Outside our hotel, people caroused all night. In the early dawn, buses revved up their engines, and men shouted as they loaded their luggage. Bleary-eyed, we packed our few belongings and walked out of town to try our luck hitchhiking. In the morning heat, my T-shirt stuck to my back, and I sat at the side of the road, short-tempered. It felt as if we were waiting for Godot. Clive read poems from the *Oxford Book of Poetry*. I flicked through a Denis Wheatley book, picking my cuticles as I stared at the ants scurrying in the dust.

Finally, I looked at the empty road and grumbled, "This is useless. Let's get a bus."

"Last year, I waited twenty-four hours for a ride in the south of Spain. We've hardly been here an hour," Clive said with single-minded determination.

Then, miracle of miracles, a car stopped. The driver was unshaven, with an olive complexion, and greasy hair that stuck straight up. He launched into a stream of questions that became more familiar the further east we travelled:

"What is your country?"

"What is your name?"

"Where are you going?"

"Are you married?"
"Where have you been in Turkey?"
"You like Turkey?"
"What do you do?"
"Where is your family?"

Between his questions, we learned that Mustafa, a commercial traveller from Izmir, was married with two children. The road along the south coast of Turkey wound its way high above the azure sea. The bottle-green pine trees clothed the hillside that swept down to inaccessible golden beaches tucked into coves and guarded by rocky promontories. It was breathtaking. At a roadside stall, Mustafa purchased a watermelon from a child. Under the welcome shade of a silky pine tree, I sank my teeth into the pink flesh of my first-ever watermelon; the sticky juice ran down my hands. It was delicious. However, when Mustafa put his arm around my shoulders for a photo, my throat and torso tightened, and I squirmed out of his reach.

When the road descended to a sandy beach, he asked, "You want to swim?" With beads of sweat on my forehead, I couldn't refuse, but I was shocked by the fully clothed women splashing in the water. Once in the water, when Mustafa's eyes devoured every curve on my bikini-clad body, I shivered in the sunlight and bit my lips. Back in the car, we drove a couple of miles down the road.

"Oh my god! Where's our wallet with the passports and papers?" Clive exclaimed.

"Did you leave them on the roof?" I asked. He wound down the window, stretched up his hand, and snatched them. The spasms in my shoulders melted, and I almost cried with relief.

Mustafa stopped to do some business at the market in the town of Kalediran, and I wandered past stalls laden with peppers, tomatoes, onions, strings of garlic, and scaly fish that I had never seen before. He kindly bought us a local delicacy: "ayran," a type of salty buttermilk, which I politely tasted, but so many new tastes and smells tied my stomach in knots.

As we continued our journey to Anamur, Mustafa muttered in a mix of Turkish and English. After a foreign-language struggle, we deciphered that he wished to pay for our hotel room, meaning all three of us would be in the same room. We parted company at the next petrol station, where a hoard of children swarmed around us.

"Where are you from?"

"Where are you going?"

"What is your country?"

"How do you like Turkey?"

"*Cok guzel,*" very fine, became our standard reply.

In an hour, an old grey *deux cheveaux*, a Citroen, pulled up. The petrol-pump attendant called us over. He'd asked the German couple to give us a ride. Embarrassed but grateful, we crawled into the small, overloaded car, and bounced east over the rolling hills to Silifke on the south coast. A crusader fortress dominated the town.

"I can't imagine soldiers walking from Northern Europe to here and on to the Holy Land," I said.

"I read somewhere that, back in the twelfth century, the pope told his Christian armies that if they died in the war they would be rewarded with virgins in heaven," Clive said.

"Thank goodness, in this heat, we can use cars and buses."

We haggled over the price of a hotel room. On our tight budget, staying in the cheapest place was a matter of principle. In the morning at the chemist shop, Ilker Unluselek befriended us. Like many Turks, he had thick hair, a mustache, and his white shirt hung out over his trousers. He ordered chai for us, and we chatted.

"You come and stay in my motel? It is beautiful down by the beach. You can swim and camp there."

"How far is it?" asked Clive.

"Not so far. Maybe twenty minutes. You can be my guests."

"How do we get there?"

"We go by dolmus." More chai was served at the bank, where we changed one of our treasured five-pound travellers' cheques. As we bumped along the rough road in the dolmus, to my amazement, a scooter carrying five people and a sheep passed us.

The "motel" was a fly-infested one-roomed restaurant in a shady olive grove beside a sandy beach. We enjoyed the afternoon swimming and sunbathing, keeping to ourselves. Too embarrassed to share our meagre fare with anyone, we ate our stale bread and tomatoes alone. Unhappy with us, Ilker rattled out some words in Turkish and then English.

"I invited you to come to eat and share food."

"We are students and don't have much money. We can't pay for a fancy meal."

"I understand, but I invited you." He nodded his head. "Come and join, my friends."

I pulled my T-shirt over my bikini and moved to sit around a wobbly table with a plastic tablecloth. The local army captain, a tall man with a barrel chest, bull neck, large jaw, and swarthy complexion, swigged beer.

"You like beer or Russian vodka?" This was followed by the standard questions in English. Then he called his aide, an awkward youth in an ill-fitting uniform.

"My pistol. You know this gun?" My heart sank; I shook my head and cowered into my chair as he brandished his weapon.

"See how it works. Here are… What do you say? Bullets?"

When the food arrived, I sighed with relief as he returned the gun to its holster. A whole fish with shrivelled eyes stared at us as its tail sagged over the side of the platter, which held other seafood.

"You have had crab?" He showed us how to crack the legs and suck the delicious sweetmeat.

The moon shone on the sea. Without thinking, I pulled off my T-shirt. In my bikini, I ran down the beach and joined the men for a swim. They were drunk and fooling around. I was alarmed by the captain's invasive stares, lingering on my breasts. Although nothing bad had yet happened, I was on my guard. I walked up the beach and covered myself with my towel, then sat on the sand, jealous of their freedoms. I hated how the men, never blinking, looked at me. They were nothing like my male mountaineering friends. My mind was in turmoil about my role as a woman in this Islamic country. This was so different from my American experience.

After the soldiers left, we retired to the flat roof and tucked into our sleeping bags. A cool land breeze fanned us. In the absence of street lights, the night sky glittered, but the continual buzz of mosquitoes disturbed my sleep.

In the morning, we shook hands with Ilker Unluselek and offered our profuse thanks for his goodwill. Scratching our numerous mosquito bites, we hitched east to the large city of Mersin and arrived in time to catch the train to Erzurum, located on the Anatolian plateau in the northeast of Turkey

The wheels groaned on the rails as the ancient steam train trundled east across the fertile plains. In our creaking third-class compartment, a young woman with her hair covered in a headscarf, looking like she was still in high school, cuddled a small baby that was tightly swaddled in white bandages with only its wrinkled blue face visible. She thrust her tiny bundle into my arms. With troubling memories of my abortion, I stiffened, shrank into the seat, and worried this fragile creature might die as I held her. When she started to squawk, and my awkward rocking did little to soothe her, I passed her back. The smiles over, we sank into silence and stared at the passing fruit trees. I sat with my arms tightly crossed, trying not to think that I could now have been the mother of a two-year-old. Had I committed an unforgivable sin? I did not share my thoughts and swallowed my self-judgments.

Darkness fell as the train stopped in a town. Bored, we wandered through the grimy corridors and chatted to some vivacious male students from Istanbul University who asked us to have drinks with them.

"No, thank you." Clive shook his head.

"Why not?" I asked. "At least it would help the time pass. We can't watch the scenery in the dark."

"Believe me, it's not a good idea," Clive replied. I rolled my eyes, clenched my lips, and marched along the half-lit platform back to our carriage and read my books.

The night lingered on and on, sleep impossible in the hot, crowded compartment. In the bleak dawn, the train stopped at a dilapidated village nestled at the bottom of grey cliffs. Ragged children stopped to stare. From our map, we calculated we were only halfway to our destination: Erzurum. A commotion on the platform distracted us. Police surrounded the students who had asked us for a drink. They were staggering around, supporting one drunk who was bent double, his hair brushing the concrete.

"Just as well we didn't join them. They'll rot in a Turkish jail for years," Clive said.

"What a close shave!" Shivering, I grabbed his arm. "How did you know not to join them?"

"I had a bad feeling about drinking with them." Clive's street smarts impressed me.

The train rattled on through deep ravines, over plains covered in golden wheat, and valleys filled with apple trees. The clatter of the wheels on the rails masked the sounds of the countryside. Acrid smoke stung my nose. Much to our frustration, we had underestimated our position in the morning and only arrived at the halfway mark at five in the afternoon.

The second night, there were fewer passengers and our mood brightened as we stretched our sleeping bags out along the slatted seats. While the train rattled through the eastern Turkish steppes, pinpoints of lights from isolated hamlets and shepherds' fires shone under a myriad of stars as I imagined they had done for centuries.

CIRCLING THE EDGE

The following day, one of the ticket collectors, asked, "You come with us for chai?"

We followed him, leaning our arms on the walls and lurching into the second-class coach, which was adorned with shiny wood panels, big windows, and worn leather upholstery. We answered the usual questions as we sipped our tea.

"Would you like to ride in the engine?" they asked.

"Yes!" We replied in unison, and at the next stop, we climbed up a couple of stairs into the engine where the driver polished the brass. The stoker, his body glistening with sweat, shovelled coal into the fiery furnace. We stood on the step, clinging onto the shiny rail with the wind in our faces, smiling and waving to people working in the fields.

To our surprise, the train halted in the middle of nowhere. Everyone climbed down to the track and set out through the willow trees to fill up their water containers from a mountain stream. We enjoyed the rest of the journey, interacting with some friendly soldiers, our age, who taught us some Turkish.

"*Bir, iki, uc, dort...* one, two, three, four."

"*Balu...* bear"

"*Cok guzel.*"

The wide plain that stretched to Erzurum was scattered with several army camps. High barbed-wire fences enclosed row upon row of tanks. The close proximity of the Russian border, the threat of the Cold War, the dread of communist domination, and nuclear devastation became real.

After forty-nine hours and eight hundred kilometres, the train ground to a halt in Erzurum, and the Mediterranean sun was replaced with dull grey weather. It was as if we had reached the end of the earth. Scruffy boys besieged us, shouting,

"Where are you going?"

"What is your country?"

"Mister, what is your name?"

"Baksheesh, mister?"

Several young westerners in jeans and T-shirts reminded us that we were back on the main overland trail to India. Before Clive disappeared with some Italian students to the Turkish baths, we had a heated conversation.

"What do you mean it's not ladies' day?" I asked. "You can go get clean, and I can't? It's not fair." In an effort to tolerate my unwashed body and console myself, I ate a yellow custard pie.

Later in a café with photos of the symmetrical cone of Mount Ararat, we sipped cold Tekel Birasi beer and swapped stories with travellers. I was thrilled by their adventures. A New Zealand couple heading west told us how they had journeyed on buses all through Thailand and India. A Turkish mountain guide gave me the impression I could be climbing up the slopes of the Biblical Mount Ararat the next day. A French student with a guitar accompanied Ferhad, the Turkish bus-ticket vendor, on his elegant twelve-stringed guitar. We sang, "It's Been a Hard Day's Night," "Yesterday" and "The House of The Rising Sun." The power of music as a social lubricant united us in our diversity and opened up the world. Distant countries that seemed impossibly far from Scotland were now within my reach.

The party ended at midnight. Ferhad, with another display of Turkish bigheartedness, offered us free sleeping space in his office, but there was no shower or toilet. As if to protect his office, Ferhad locked the door as he left. The custard pie fermented in my guts. I did not sleep. With no choice, I emptied my erupting bowels into plastic bags. Clive's guts were fine. Respite came in the dull dawn when Ferhad opened up for business, and we rushed out to find a toilet.

In contrast to the slow train, we sank into comfortable seats on the modern bus to Tehran, sipped cold Coke and Fanta, and raced over the high mountain passes of eastern Turkey. Here, boys with vicious-looking catapults slung on their belts guarded flocks of sheep. My nauseated search for toilets—stinking holes in the ground surrounded by rickety wooden boxes—dominated each stop. On entry, I held my breath, and retched as my bowels exploded as never before.

In Tehran, I lurched off the bus weak, hungry, thinking of Mother's homemade treacle scones and my comfortable bed in her house. In the budget hotel Amrikabir, recommended by other travellers, I snuggled under the sheets, grateful to escape my misery in sleep, though it was interrupted by frequent toilet breaks. Healthy Clive disappeared on daily explorations of the city and cheered me up with sterile Coca-Cola and interesting tidbits.

"There's a guy here who's cycling around the world. His route is mapped out and attached to his bike. Each place he visits, he contacts the newspapers."

"Riding a bike sounds impossible. How does he carry enough water to cross the deserts? I am so ill," I said, staggering to the toilet again.

CHAPTER 6

Crossroads

*"Only those who will risk going too far can
possibly find out how far one can go."*
~ T.S. Eliot, Preface to Harry Crosby, Transit of Venus (1931)

Two days later, I stepped outside, my legs like jelly, into a cacophony of car horns and the smell of incense, cigarette smoke, and diesel fumes. My eyes smarted in the bright sunlight. Tehran was a hectic city packed with modern buildings and old markets. We entered a ceramic-tiled teahouse, like an Asian male clubhouse. Under harsh fluorescent lights, the photographs of the Shah, and Empress Farah in a sumptuous evening gown, looking nothing like the local women. As the only woman, surrounded by men who sipped green tea from Chinese bowls, I avoided eye contact. One man noisily cleared his throat and spat into an aluminum spittoon, as others sucked on hubble-bubble pipes or hookahs. Clive pointed out the opium addicts: old men with their harsh lives carved into their wrinkled faces. Men scraped their chairs along the dusty floor as they left the smoke-laden atmosphere.

We hailed a taxi. The reckless driver, with one hand attached to the horn, raced between pedestrians and hand-pushed carts piled high with carpets, vegetables, and sacks of rice. I clutched my rucksack and stifled screams when twice, at the last minute, he swerved to avoid head-on collisions. Shaking all over, I climbed out happy to be alive. As we walked across the square to the new railway station, for the first time in my life, someone pinched my bum—a man I presumed. Outraged, I spun around but whoever had violated my body had disappeared into the crowd. I walked closer to Clive.

Iranians crowded the marble railway station, like an ancient temple with its high ceilings. I watched the women who wore makeup, high heels, and western dresses. A long filmy length of material covered their heads and shoulders. Struggling to carry babies and parcels, this impractical covering frequently fell around their ankles. A few women wore tent-like black burkas. Families squatted in clusters around overflowing plastic bags and boxes. Clive purchased tickets to Mashad in eastern Iran.

Although people crowded every carriage, we enjoyed the spacious buffet car with large scenic windows. I drank Coca-Cola to settle my growling interior. To my bewilderment, in the middle of the desert, a man appeared on a bicycle.

"How does he survive in this arid land?" I asked.

"I guess biking is better than walking." Clive shrugged his shoulders and shook his head. "Look at the moonlight reflecting off the sand." Coming from cloudy Scotland, the clear night skies delighted me.

In the cool of the morning, I hung out of the train window, straining to catch the first sight of the golden dome of Mashad's mosque. I knew about zoology and microbiology, and now I was learning about different religions and cultures.

Even covered with long-sleeved shirts and jeans, the mosque was forbidden to us. We peered through the railings that surrounded the magnificent, turquoise-tiled mosque. The wide courtyards were crowded with white doves and tidy rows of men bowing in unison, chanting to Allah. At the wooden door of the museum, a man with downcast eyes handed me a black headscarf. From the dog-eared black-and-white photos, I read that this mosque was dedicated to Shia Muslims and contained the sacred remains of the founding Iman.

"Why should I have to cover my head, and you don't?" I asked.

"Sorry. We must respect their customs," Clive said. "We have our Afghan visa. Let's get the bus to the border."

Once through Iranian customs, the twenty-kilometre road through no man's land to the Afghan border was surrounded by rolls of barbed wire. With the absence of public transport, we walked into searing emptiness, where not even the smallest blade of grass grew. After five minutes, sweat trickled down my spine, my heart thumped, and my throat burned. When a couple of Germans offered us a ride in their Volkswagen camper, I swallowed tears of relief. In Islamqala, policemen with straight faces directed us through maze-like buildings to four different offices. The last official smudged a strange script in purple ink over a page in our single passport for a married couple. With a sense of accomplishment, we set off to find transport to Herat.

Word of mouth replaced the absence of timetables or a bus terminal. In the shade, an old bus sat empty.

"If the bus is full, I'll leave at two o'clock," the driver said. Since it was only eleven in the morning, we began bargaining for a ride on a beaten-up oil tanker.

"Can you take us to Herat?" The driver nodded his head.

"When do you leave?"

"Soon!"

"How much for two of us?"

When the first bus driver overheard our conversation, he screamed at the truck driver, who shook his head and withdrew his offer. The sound of more angry voices interrupted our quest for transport. An Afghan shopkeeper and a Frenchman, clutching a map, bellowed at each other in their own languages. I heard the rasp of material rip as a soldier grabbed the Frenchman's shirt and pushed him hard. Talking non-stop in French, he punched the soldier. His girlfriend stepped between them and was roughly shoved aside. The brawl ended when the Frenchman, in his torn shirt and with a black eye, walked away still holding his crumpled map.

"I have never seen men fight like this. I don't feel safe," I said, shivering in the heat.

"Don't worry. We'll be okay," Clive reassured me, but I was not convinced.

When a rumour spread that a bus was leaving, and we picked up our packs, the driver from the two o'clock bus shook his fist at us as we squeezed into the second bus, crowded with Westerners and Afghans. The bus bumped over the rough corrugations along the gravel road, throwing us around on the hard seats. In a cloud of dust, we drove into Herat as the sun set behind leafy trees, crumbling minarets, and the remains of an old madrassa or theological school. Herat turned the clock back on the modern age like nowhere I had been.

On the main street, we selected the tourist Beyhad hotel. The simple, white-washed room with spotless sheets was a sanctuary. And with hot running water in the washroom, I closed my eyes in delight as the hot water ran in rivulets over my dusty, sweaty body. Clive and I caressed each other, his soft touch burning my skin, his bearded face brushing my shoulder, and my body quivering. I wrapped my legs around his waist, our breathing heavy with desire. He moaned and I sighed with waves of orgasmic pleasure.

After a breakfast of naan, delicious wholemeal bread hot from an earthenware oven, and a kilo of sweet grapes, washed down with pots of green tea, we walked down the tree-lined main street to discover Herat's rich history. The city lies at the crossroads of trade routes that once led from the Middle East to Central Asia and China. In the old city, we explored a warren of alleys lined by small open-fronted shops. Each shop had two shopkeepers who were often accompanied by a couple of children. Western industrial culture has not reached Herat. In the blacksmiths' lane, we heard hammering and wheezing as young pale-faced boys, who looked about nine years old, worked the bellows that blew air on the red-hot coals. The covered carpet bazaar offered a welcome relief from the blazing sun. It disturbed me to learn that it was children, whose small hands could tie tiny knots, who made the finest, most expensive Persian carpets.

Afghani craftsmen

Blacksmith's shop in Herat

Five times a day, the metallic cry of the muezzin called the faithful to prayer. Men stopped their activities, laid out their intricately designed prayer carpets, removed their shoes and turbans, faced southwest to Mecca, raised their hands to the sky, and bowed low, kneeling as they murmured prayers. This open display of devotion astonished me.

After a couple of rest days, we continued our journey east on an overnight bus along the southern road through Kandahar to Kabul. Naively, I believed that, motivated by benevolence, the Americans had built this tarmac road while the Russians had constructed the road north from Kabul to Mazar-I-Sharif, only forty miles from their border.

Defying gravity, flat-roofed, mud-brick houses clung like limpets to the hillsides that overlooked Kabul. In the height of summer, the fetid green waters of the Kabul River trickled through the city. The dried mud banks left behind by the spring melt were strewn with rubbish. The waters reeked of rotting vegetation and turned my stomach. In contrast, brightly coloured carpets and *kelims* with striking geometrical patterns, all for sale, covered the concrete walls along the riverside.

With a pot of green tea, we sat in our hotel restaurant, writing postcards to our families.

"What's that putrid stink?" I asked with a hand over my nostrils.

"I've no idea. It's awful."

"Look." I pointed to the stairs. Two men appeared, carrying a purple bloated body not even covered in a sheet. They disappeared to the ground floor while the rotten odour hung in the air.

Horrified, we looked at one another in alarm. On inquiry, we learned that the young male traveller had died in his room from a drug overdose and lay undiscovered for a week.

"That's terrifying," Clive said. "I need to get out. Let's go for a walk."

In the city, which was a complex mix of old and new, we gravitated to the bazaar, a maze of narrow twisted lanes with shops filled with vegetables, spices, cloth, and silvery pots, and packed with people. In front of bales of colourful cloth, I stared at two faceless women hidden underneath their flowing chadris—black tent-like garments that covered them from head to foot, with only a small-embroidered grill for their eyes. I couldn't envisage wearing these prison-like garments, which looked uncomfortably hot. I longed to see their animated faces and hear about their lives.

From a street vendor, we purchased Afghanistan's fast food: a peeled cucumber dipped in salt. In a public park, resting on the grass under a Tamarisk tree, we enjoyed the cooler evening air, and a student, dressed in a white baggy shirt and trousers, befriended us.

"My name is Mohammed Osman Ammi. I am studying English at Kabul University. What is your country?" As soon as we answered, he was ready with another question.

"Are you students and what do you study? You come to my house?"

Deeply honoured, we followed Mohammed through the poorly lit lanes of Kabul, avoiding mud, garbage, emaciated cats, and rats that scuttled into dark holes. Mohammed opened a creaky wooden door in a mud-brick wall, and we crept along an even darker passageway. At last, he entered a doorway, which led to a small courtyard with brightly lit windows. He exchanged a torrent of Farsi with his mother. Her hair was covered in a loose headscarf. Her smiling brown eyes welcomed us while two younger boys peered around her flowery pants. She showed us into a whitewashed room. A solitary light bulb hung from the ceiling. According to the custom, we sat cross-legged on a red Turkoman carpet with octagonal designs.

"Where are you going? How long have you been travelling?" Mohammed's older brother asked us. Even though the conversation was laboured, they generously shared their mutton and rice. In Scotland, I would never have invited strangers into my home. Their gracious hospitality invigorated me. As I left, I looked into this woman's eyes and bowed my profound appreciation. Alone, glancing over our shoulders, Clive and I returned through the dark alleys to our hotel. For five Afghanis, five cents, each, we slept on the roof on wooden charpoys under a canopy of stars.

At three in the morning, under a deep red sky, we climbed onto a bus whose windows were caked with grime. We squeezed between women, children, and luggage. Soon the bus departed for the fabled Bamiyan Valley deep in the Hindu Kush Mountains. After half an hour of heat, dust, body odour, and squirming, I wanted to scream. "This is unbearable," I said. "How will I last for eight hours?" Clive put his arm around me and nodded.

After two hours of intense discomfort, we scrambled off the bus at a roadside village framed by tall chinar trees and surrounded by waving wheat fields. At the teahouse, a boy sprinkled water on the ground to keep the dust down. In the cool morning air, he lowered a rope attached at one end to a large wooden framework and the other onto a bucket, made from an old tire, into the well. We filled our water bottles with cold water.

"I can't drink this," I said. "It must have bugs. I don't want more gut rot. Coca-Cola might dissolve my teeth but at least it's sterile."

"There is no Coca-Cola here," Clive said. "You can buy one of these local green or red drinks. I remember bottles like these, with wire and a round glass ball for a stopper, when I was a kid."

I wiped the top and grimaced as I sipped the sugary liquid, then pointed to the roof of the bus. "Those guys are sitting on the luggage. Do you think we can join them?"

"I don't think that's legal. It doesn't look safe," he said. Just as the bus left, we clambered up the iron ladder to the roof and edged our bodies in amongst goats, chickens, bags of rice, and bedding rolls. In an instant, our moods changed. The fresh air brushed our skin. With my eyes wide open and my body alert, we enjoyed a panoramic view. We shared our rooftop with dignified Afghan men who did not ask intrusive questions.

Natural air-conditioned Afghan bus

The overloaded bus laboured up steep switchbacks. My neck strained upwards beyond the towering cliffs to a strip of blue sky. The bus descended into a green irrigated valley that contrasted with the desiccated mountain. At the edge of the village, nomad caravans camped in crumbling *caravanserais*, fort-like structures enclosed by high walls. Enthralled, I watched nomad girls fill their goatskins with water from the stream and balance them on their shoulders. As they ran away, their red dresses swirled around their ankles. Tall men with their heads covered in fine yellow and blue turbans stood and watched us. In the sunshine, their life looked idyllic, but I knew nothing about the hardships of an agricultural lifestyle dictated by the seasons.

At one stop, we watched a noisy transaction between a policeman and our bus conductor. Money exchanged hands. Our friendly conductor told us he'd paid a bribe to avoid the fine for carrying people on the roof. Shocked, we decided this was corruption, but he laughed as if it was a big game.

The rock walls of the final gorge retreated, and the bus emerged into the fertile Bamiyan valley, fringed by the snow-capped ranges of the Hindu Kush. The evening light bounced off the colossal Buddha statues carved into the cliff.

Fuelled by a rare western breakfast, we walked along a path up a hillside pocked with caves, some occupied by families grinding corn. We puffed up the staircase that tunnelled through the mountain to the top of the Buddha's head, about fifty meters high. Barking dogs and melodic voices wafted upward.

"Wow, the fields look like a patchwork quilt," I said. "The people look like ants."

"These statues were once all covered in gold leaf and jewels," Clive replied

"Look at that piece of female fresco. Too bad most of it has been destroyed."

"I had no idea we'd find anything this sophisticated and majestic," he said.

"This is mind-blowing."

The smaller Buddha statue - 125 feet - built in approximately 550 AD. The niches hosted pilgrims and monks.

From Bamiyan, most tourists returned to Kabul. Exhilarated by our discoveries, unknown mysteries enticed us. We travelled west on the bus through nomad country to the five lakes of Band-e-Amir. Our first glimpse of the blue waters, framed by sandstone cliffs and nestled in beige hillsides, was breathtaking. Below rugged limestone cliffs, we hiked beside the lapping waters on the white calcite deposits and wild camped in scrubby bushes. The first night in this unfamiliar wilderness, I slept restlessly, haunted by the atrocities performed centuries ago by Genghis Khan. However, each time I awoke, it was not to a person of murderous intent but to the dazzling kaleidoscope of stars dancing across the sky.

The dramatic honeycomb cliffs to the west beckoned us, and a short bus ride took us through more spectacular gorges and fields of ripe grain that rippled like a Van Gogh painting. Local warlords protected the families who lived in tribal forts that dotted the landscape. In the hamlet of Panjau, we installed ourselves in a *chaikanna* or teahouse. For twelve afghanis, we ate our evening meal of rice and mutton and slept for free.

As darkness fell, the outside temperature dropped. Inside the white-washed room, the air was warm and friendly. We sat on rugs, grateful for the company of three French travellers.

"You like hashish?" asked our bus driver Zahir, a wiry man with sparkling eyes.

"Yes," we replied cautiously, hesitant of smoking with the Afghanis. We had heard rumours of westerners who, when stoned, had all their belongings, passports, and money stolen. Zahir brought out his clay chillum. In stillness, as if participating in a religious ceremony, he filled it, then nestled the pipe between his cupped hands, and resting his lips on his thumbs, he closed his eyes and took one long inhalation.

"Ah, this is maybe… number-two hashish," he said. With his eyes still closed, he passed it around. Inexperienced at inhaling, I coughed and spluttered as the smoke stung the back of my throat. Clive rolled a joint with the small amount we had purchased from a street vendor in Kabul and passed it around the circle.

"This is no good hashish," Zahir said with his mouth turned down. He put his hand in his breast pocket and pulled out a small piece, which he sniffed and fondled with care before passing it around for our inspection.

"This is also number-two hashish," he said, plunging his hand into an inside pocket. "And this is number one. You try," he announced like a magician. The group grew mellow.

"You can have this," he said. As we crawled into our sleeping bags, Clive stuffed the pebble-sized piece into his breast pocket. With the smell of grass exuding from our clothes, we slept well that night, more from the friendship than the hash.

Our atlas map showed a thin black line, called the Middle Road, dissecting Afghanistan's mountains all the way to Herat. There were no guidebooks, no timetables, no phones, and no signposts. Our parents had no idea where we were. Wary of the unknown, I was both irritable and excited. In the morning, we walked along the gravel road amongst goats, chickens, and children but no vehicles. Uncertainty hung in the bazaar. We established that there were no buses and that a truck might show up today or tomorrow or maybe next week. *Will I ever get home?*

Three physically strong nomad women, whose embroidered black skirts spun around their loose-fitting pants, approached me. They wore carved silver jewellery and long shawls over their hair. Unlike the village women, they did not cover their faces, which were tattooed with dark-blue symbols. They wore sturdy leather shoes with turned-up toes, which to me looked like something out of a fairy tale. One woman pulled back her sleeve. Under dozens of plastic bracelets, she pointed to a rash on her dry skin as if she expected me to fix it. But I had no medical knowledge and only a minimal first-aid kit. I rubbed on some Vaseline. These resilient women who lived in tents, their routines dictated by the seasons, riveted me. Since some Islamic women believed that photography stole their souls, I kept the camera in my pocket.

The next day, out of nowhere, a truck driver appeared and agreed for a small price to take us to Chaghcharan, about one-third of the way to Herat. With no idea how long it would take to get there, we climbed into an open compartment on top of the cab. The truck cab, panels, and spars were artistically painted with girls, birds, aeroplanes, sunsets, palm trees, and flowers. We shivered until the sun rose. The Afghanis uncoiled their turbans and covered their faces, while we used bandanas to protect us from the dusty, unsealed road. At a snail's pace, our truck was labouring up a hill when an oncoming truck forced us to the edge of the precipice. In fear for my life, I watched the driver's assistant jump down. He kicked loose gravel into the abyss as he forced big wooden wedges under the wheels to prevent us from running back as the other truck inched past. A second time we ground to a halt and leaned at a precarious angle. Careful not to upset the truck's delicate balance, we scrambled out. This time a bald tire was flat.

Me with Afghan nomads

By the end of the day, stiff and covered in dust, we thankfully stopped for the night in the remote village of Lalosarjanjal. The village street curved up a gentle hill. Cowpats dried on the walls of the mud houses. We stayed in a busy *chaikanna* with many families. Outside in a bamboo cage, small yellow birds sang. The owner told me the birdsong made him happy.

Although the locals slept outside, they instructed us to sleep inside. They were concerned that, if anything happened to us, the villagers would be punished by the authorities. With our three French friends, we settled down for the night. Later, semi-comatose, I started to scratch as I drifted in and out of sleep, then I heard a muffled shout. The itching became more insistent. Something was crawling over my body. I heard some scuffles. My throat, shoulders, and stomach muscles froze. When I opened my eyes, a solid blackness enveloped me.

"I'll try the door," someone said. I heard mumblings in French. Clive stumbled to the door and rattled it.

"It's locked from the outside," he announced. I struggled to breathe. Seconds and minutes passed.

"Has anyone got a light?" someone with a French accent asked. I heard a match strike. For a moment, faces appeared out of the dark. The flame flickered and went out. The night became more intense. Clive hammered on the door. I heard someone outside mutter in Farsi as he unlocked the door. We rushed out, into the welcome cool of the night. After a jumbled conversation in French, English, and Farsi, we found *charpoys* outside.

Under an oil lamp, I lay down and squashed at least thirty bloated bedbugs that I found in the creases of my sleeping bag. My blood squirted everywhere. Then I cuddled into the warmth of the feathers, but sleep was impossible. As I watched the multitude of stars, distant footsteps became louder. A figure in a heavy greatcoat with a rifle slung over his shoulder loomed out of the night, calling the hour as he passed. The town crier returned at regular intervals until cockerels crowed and a peach light ate the darkness.

In the morning, curious about bedbugs, we inspected the teahouse walls. The roof was made of branches, and the walls were of mud plastered over a wooden frame, creating endless hiding places for creepy crawlies. Beside a wall of rickety shelves, a three-foot brass samovar boiled water. Barefoot men sat on the carpet, enjoying tea in the morning peace.

After sitting on the bucking truck for a couple of hours, my search for a toilet became urgent. I walked away from the main street and peeped behind a crumbling wall to ensure it was not occupied, then picked my way between the irregular piles of turds. Overwhelmed by the stench, I held my breath and wretched. When I looked up, staring children surrounded me.

At one chai stop, under the shade of trees, we sat on a platform that straddled a rushing stream, providing natural air conditioning in the heat of the day. I watched a man with a long beard, lines etched on his face, and a calm demeanor serve tea and naan to a small boy. When the boy turned his small turbaned head and I saw his white, sightless eyes, tears flooded my cheeks.

Mother and child, young bride, and boy

Our roller-coaster journey continued over high plains scattered with clusters of black tents. Among the aromatic sage bushes, small boys guarded grazing goats and sheep. Spellbinding nomad caravans with their animals and families walked along the roadside. Exquisite handmade carpets with long tassels and shells decorated the backs and necks of their camels and horses.

Nomad women on a decorated camel

As our truck stopped near one nomad camp, a handsome, white-turbaned passenger climbed down with a large bedding roll tucked under his arm. A slender woman walked up the road to meet him. Since I was on my honeymoon, romantic-movie images cluttered my mind. I imagined this young woman was his wife. Would it be a Hollywood greeting? Would they embrace with passion? With a slight nod of his head, he dumped his bedding roll into her outstretched arms and continued up the road, no kiss, no hug, no outward display of affection, and no small talk. Whether or not she was his wife, his disregard shocked me. I moved closer to Clive.

At Chaghcharan, it was a local holiday. In a field like a parade ground, we watched the soldiers in their sun-bleached uniforms and school children in white shirts march past a group of local dignitaries. A lively demonstration of the national sport, a competitive polo-like game called Buzkashi, followed. Two teams of riders on glossy horses chased a stuffed goat's head around the field, displaying their expert equestrian skills. Enthusiastic spectators cheered the teams.

Bhurka clad woman and her kids

These Afghan women turned back their burkas and agreed to be photographed.

On our last night on the Middle Road, we stopped in the village of Farsi at an elegant low-domed adobe building. Inside, the graceful arches and vaults made interesting shadows. The thick walls kept the interior cool. What a privilege to experience this spotlessly clean teahouse, with gracious people and no trace of bedbugs. As I fell asleep in this tranquil space, I reflected that there are many diverse ways to live on this earth.

After our remote travels, the city of Herat now appeared like the heart of progress. Tired and hot from the truck journey, we hailed a horse-drawn carriage to take us to our hotel. When the driver lashed the skinny horse on its shoulder blades, something in me broke down.

"I can't watch this!" I cried out.

"It's not far," Clive said, his voice lost beneath another crack of the whip.

"Do something. Tell him to stop."

"He needs the money," Clive said as I was already climbing down. Clive paid the driver and caught up with me. "What's the matter with you, Wilma?"

"Nothing," I groaned as my backpack dug into my shoulders. My feet dragged along the dusty road. We walked in silence.

In the tiny bathroom, I showered and scrubbed off the caked dust. Clive appeared at the door.

"Maybe you're not cut out for this," he said.

I glared at him, thinking that, if he really loved me, he would know what I needed. Even after long hot showers, we continued to snarl at each other. I wiped my eyes with the towel.

"I don't know if I can keep going."

"You haven't written in the journal since Bamiyan," he said.

"You said you'd keep the journal up to date. It's useless," I said, with an intensity that shocked me.

"How dare you say that!"

"I'm going shopping!" I slammed the door.

I walked along the main street, fascinated by stalls that looked like Aladdin's cave, full of carpets, hand-blown turquoise glassware, and silver antique jewellery. I dried my eyes. I saw an embroidered sheepskin coat, complete with a few twigs and goat poo. It fit perfectly.

Then, sitting in a teahouse, I wrote in my journal and unravelled myself. I recognized that Clive had a fierce determination to explore, but my foray into this wild, foreign world exposed raw feelings I did not know how to manage. While I loved the gorges and the nomads, I needed time to recuperate from sickness, bedbugs, and dust. I was at a crossroad where my outer and inner worlds met. While part of me wanted more, I missed my predictable home comforts. But more importantly, in this predominantly Muslim world, where women were hidden by burkas or stayed home, my options were restricted. When I returned to the hotel, we acknowledged our mutual exhaustion as Clive tenderly unbuttoned my new coat.

After a good sleep, together in the carpet bazaar, the patient salesmen served us tea as we flipped through piles of carpets. We haggled for an old carpetbag and a red Afghan rug. The transactions, unlike our first experiences at the border, were peaceful and respectful.

To begin our long journey home, Clive collected our visas from the Iranian consulate.

"I saw a van with two English guys outside the consulate," he told me. "I wanted to ask them for a lift to Mashad."

"It's not worth the trouble," I said. "It's not far, and the bus is cheap."

The next day, we retraced our steps to the border town. Once on the Iranian side, we worried when the official drove us into the village for further investigation. From our dusty packs, the custom's official pulled out our smelly T-shirts, shorts, and sleeping bags. I trusted that the thimble-sized piece of hashish, a present from Zahir, which had disappeared, would not turn up in a side pocket and cause us major trouble.

"Ha! A few hours ago, we inspected a van driven by two Englishmen. They told us they did not have any drugs," the official said. "Just as I was about to allow them through, I noticed a small piece of hashish on the dashboard." I raised my eyebrows in shock. "I searched them," he continued. "Two of us pulled their vehicle apart and discovered a false floor filled with two hundred and fifty kilos of hashish. That's the biggest haul we have had at this border."

He pointed to the rusty bars on the window of the small cell that was holding the men until they were taken to the jail in Mashad. Their confiscated van was parked in a compound behind barbed wire.

"That's the one I saw in Herat," Clive whispered. I shivered.

"If they were Iranian, they'd be shot," the official continued. "But as Europeans, they will probably get a life sentence and their vehicle donated to the Red Cross. You can go. Have a safe journey home."

We walked to a café and sat in a shady courtyard where pink roses grew up the walls. We savoured an ice-cold Coca-Cola as we collected ourselves and thanked our lucky stars.

Clive wanted to hitchhike. Agitated, I sat at the edge of the gravel desert road, worried that something awful might happen. A pickup truck zoomed by, and the driver waved. About thirty minutes later, he returned, the back of his truck piled up with more melons than I had ever seen.

"*Salam alaikum*," he called out as he stopped.

"I'm sorry, we don't speak Farsi," I said. With sign language, we indicated that we were going to Mashad. He handed us a couple of melons. His gift dispelled my gnawing dread, and I looked in hope at the empty road. In time, a Canadian couple in a Volkswagen picked us up.

Back in Turkey, speeding buses overtook hand-pushed carts, donkeys, and wobbling bicycles. As if to confirm our worst fears, on the side of the road to the Black Sea we saw several deceased passengers covered in black cloths by the jagged remains of a bus. We hitched on quieter back roads. A BMW picked us up. The driver worked in Germany and was home visiting his family. When he dropped us in the village of Merzifon, a mob of boys and men ogled us as if we were celebrities. The locals ushered us into a teahouse where the owner barred the crowd from entering. They gazed at us through the window while the owner relayed our every action. How different from Afghanistan, where people rarely lifted their heads as we passed. A boy ran in to tell us that there was a truck at the garage that was heading west and would give us a ride.

We sat on a load of bricks, and whenever the truck stopped, the locals offered us a bounty of fresh apples and cucumbers. In this fertile land, a mosque with a minaret dominated each village. That night, our current truck driver treated us to dinner. Then, in one town, we visited a small restaurant for some yoghurt. Out of place in our grubby jeans and T-shirts, we sat amongst smart Turkish businessmen who spoke in perfect English and worked in London. To our embarrassment, they paid our bill, teaching me again about generosity. My fears of the unknown, violence from others, and concerns about my physical safety were unfounded. Kindness after kindness followed us home.

When we reached Uskudar, we left Asia and crossed the Bosphorous on a ferry to Istanbul. As we approached the European shore, the sky turned orange and pink over the minarets of the Blue Mosque. With our final fifty pounds, exactly what we had spent in the previous eight weeks, we purchased two student rail tickets to London. The train rolled out of the station and followed the Bosphorous. At the window, I relished the smells and the warmth as I watched the lights of the fishing boats scurrying across the water to Asia. The city lights faded as the train chugged west through Europe.

Back in London, it was a luxury to drink tap water and indulge our cravings for fish and chips, Mars bars, and beer. For the first time on the trip, Clive's cast-iron stomach revolted. I appreciated walking in the streets without intrusive male attention. For the final leg, we hitched to Edinburgh. On our first ride, the driver, who had been on nightshift, asked Clive to drive. Thankful for orderly British traffic, we sat in style in the front seats while the driver curled up and slept in the back. Our next ride dropped us at my mother's front door.

History – in a nutshell
For centuries, land-locked Afghanistan was the meeting place of east and west. It has attracted conquerors and empire builders from all sides of the globe: Alexander the Great, Genghis Khan, Tamerlane, the British colonials, the Soviets in 1979, and the Americans in 2001. In the first century AD, Buddhism spread from the east and fused with the Hellenistic tradition left by Alexander the Great's descendants, and Greek and Indian art flourished in the Bamiyan Valley. Invaders came in waves, with the first being the white Huns in the fourth century.

In 623 AD, when the Chinese priest Hsuan-Tsang visited, there were at least ten Buddhist monasteries and more than a thousand priests who lived in caves carved out of the soft rock. As a town on the Silk Road that connected China to Rome, it grew rich.

In the seventh century, Afghanistan felt the eastern thrust of Islam. In the thirteenth century, the Mongols from central Mongolia invaded. The thunderous pounding of horses' hooves announced the arrival of Genghis Khan's warriors. In a rampage of destruction, they pulled out tent pegs, massacring residents and animals. Their screams echoed through the valley.

There were three conflicts, 1839–1842; 1878–1880; and 1919, in which Great Britain, from its base in India, sought to extend its control over Afghanistan and to oppose Russian influence there. After many bloody battles, the final peace treaty was signed in 1919. In 1921, the Afghans signed a treaty of friendship with the new Bolshevik regime in the Soviet Union and initiated a "special relationship."

In the early nineteen seventies, their infant tourist industry was beginning to bring prosperity. The Russian invasion began in December 1979, while anti-communist rebels garnered support from the United States. After nine years of a fierce guerrilla war, Russian troop withdrawal began in 1988. Out of the remaining chaos, the repressive Taliban rose to power in 1995. In 2001, they destroyed the Bamiyan Buddhas. That same year, the attack on the twin towers in New York by the Al Qaeda, led by Osama Bin Laden, initiated the American invasion and Afghanistan became headline news. The Americans withdrew in 2021, and the Taliban regained power.

CHAPTER 7
College Interlude

*"This is my country, the land that begat me, these windy places
And those who toil here in the sweat of their faces
are the flesh of my flesh, bone of my bone."*
~ Sir Alexander Gray

In a photo from the fall of 1971, taken at Edinburgh Airport, my hair hung on the tangled wool of my smelly Afghan coat, my eyes are bloodshot and my lips tight. Although his face is downcast, Clive looks handsome in his blue shirt and denim jacket. We hugged. He flew off to work to the southern deserts of Oman on the Arabian Peninsula for a three-month-on and one-month-off contract, on the all-male crew of a seismic company. For him, his dream of science and adventure had come true, but for me, it felt like a life sentence. For nights, I cried myself to sleep waiting for Clive's return. Then one day on an Edinburgh bus, with my chest caved in as the conductor's comment shook me: "Dinna worry, hen; it's nae say bad."

After that, I stopped wishing my life away and signed up for trips with the university mountaineering club. New Year found me with friends hiking in Glen Affric. Still pining for Clive, I looked at the stars of Orion and imagined him six thousand miles away in the sand dunes of the Arabian Empty Quarter, staring at those same stars.

Winter hiking in Glen Affric

Without much thought for a brilliant career, I had enrolled for a one-year teaching diploma at Moray House College of Education in Edinburgh even though, when I saw hordes of adolescents milling outside a high school, my belly froze, and a lump formed in my throat. I convinced myself that teaching, like an insurance policy, was a good skill to fall back on.

With my palms damp with sweat, and my eyes fixed on the grey, bubble-gum-stained pavement, I entered the door of the stone-built high school for my six-week teaching practice. My science mentor had taught me how to plan my lessons. However, when I asked him how he commanded respect when he entered the classroom, his tongue-in-cheek advice dumbfounded me: "Treat them like wild animals."

On my second teaching practicum, I followed the religious education teacher, a middle-aged woman, along the bright corridors of a new Catholic Secondary School that enjoyed a park-like setting. In a classroom with bare walls, thirty boisterous teens sat in tidy rows of oak desks with their catechisms, which as a

Protestant, I had never seen. According to Presbyterians, only the King James Bible was the true word of God. The teacher began her tirade:

"Sit down and keep your mouths shut. Jimmy, wipe that smile off your face. Can't you keep your face straight for five minutes? Well, I suppose your mother loves you. Marie, you haven't brought your jotter? You'd forget your head if it wasn't screwed on. How many times do I have to tell you that a good workman always brings his tools?"

Only a few years older than the students, I cringed and wanted to disappear into the floor while another part of me felt outraged. With no escape route, I listened as she continued her rant.

"This is Mrs. Rubens. She is taking the class. Don't dare make any noise, or you will have me to deal with. Start reading your catechisms from page thirty. I will test you next week."

She turned sharply, marched out, and slammed the door. Within minutes, the boys whistled at the girls, paper aeroplanes flew across the room, and girls combed each other's hair. My voice imploring them to be quiet and settle down was drowned by the uproar. When the bell finally rang, I was lucky not to be crushed in the stampede.

One February day, I walked down the cobbled street and dropped my pile of fifty envelopes into the red letterbox. As I heard them clunk, I hoped they would find me a job in the Himalayas. After all, my married sister Ruth had just moved to Africa. It was my turn now.

Towards the end of the college year, on a kayak expedition that was part of my outdoor education course, I enjoyed paddling down the River Tweed. Then the current, like teaching, caught me unawares. Held under the kayak, I gulped mouthfuls of cold water as I fumbled to remove my spray-skirt and ease my legs out of the cockpit. Back on shore, shivering, I towelled my body and struggled to pull my jeans over my goose-pimpled legs. Back in the minivan, our group talked about our plans after graduation. Having tasted the fruits of travel, I wanted more.

"I'm looking for a job in the Himalayas," I announced.

"My next-door neighbour works in Kalimpong. He'll find you a job," replied our instructor. I felt a spark of excitement flood my chest.

"Where is that?" I asked.

"It is near Darjeeling in the foothills of North East India."

Several weeks later, I stood in the phone box at Moray House College, dialled my mother's phone number, and ecstatically announced, "Hi, Mum. Guess what? You'll never believe it! My outdoor education instructor has found me a job teaching English in Kashmir."

"Where?"

"You know, it's in North India."

"Oh, that's nice, dear," she whispered.

A month later at Edinburgh airport, beside myself with anticipation, I strode across the runway and barely turned to wave goodbye to my mother and Dorothy. Once on the aeroplane, unable to conceal my enthusiasm, I announced to a middle-aged man beside me, "I am going to India for a whole year. I have a job teaching English in Srinagar."

"Do you speak Urdu?" he asked.

"Oh no, but I'll figure it out," I replied, sitting up tall and shutting out my niggling self-doubt.

CHAPTER 8

Mountain Madness in Kashmir

"It is the tremendous experience of becoming conscious, which nature has laid upon humankind, which unites the most diverse cultures in a common task."
~ C.G. Jung

July 1972

I jostled my way through a vivacious crowd of Indians towards the customs desk in New Delhi airport. The men wore spotless white turbans, and their wives wore shalwar and kameez, loose ankle-length trousers and knee-length shirts, or silk saris in shimmering red, blue, and orange. My blouse stuck to my skin as I waited for the customs official behind the smeared glass to stamp my passport. The air hummed with unfamiliar languages and a mildewed smell. On tiptoes, I peered over the sea of brown faces to look for Clive. With no sign of him, panic twisted in my abdomen. When I spotted his bearded white face, I pushed through the crowd into his welcoming arms.

"How was the Aeroflot flight?" he asked.

"I stopped in Moscow," I said. "The airport was drab and depressing. The Russian air-hostesses did not smile once. We ate caviar. I don't know why it's a delicacy."

"I've been here for a couple of hours. There's a flight just about to leave for Kathmandu. We can go trekking. What do you think?" he asked.

"Nepal would be fantastic, but isn't it the monsoon season?" I said, my mind spinning from jet lag and culture shock.

"Let's go. You stay here with the rucksacks, and I'll buy the tickets," he said, disappearing into the crowd.

Hand in hand, we left the chaos, stepped into the clammy heat, bounced across the tarmac under the burning sun, and up the metal steps to board our Air India Flight to Kathmandu.

The plane landed in Agra. With escalating alarm, we watched a pool of fluid accumulate beneath the aeroplane. A bevy of white-coated technicians with spanners inspected the fuselage and scratched their heads. Although eager to see my first glimpse of the Himalayas, the leaking plane fed the fear in my stomach. A crackling announcement came over the loudspeakers: "The plane has a mechanical fault. Passengers travelling to Kathmandu will be transported by bus to the Hotel Shiraz in Agra." Disgruntled at this unwanted detour, we whined about this incompetence, but of course, it could have happened anywhere.

Our mood lightened as we stepped into a spacious marble-floored hotel lobby that opened onto a courtyard framed by tall trees, red hibiscus flowers, chirping bulbuls, and a tinkling fountain. We climbed the elegant staircase and walked along the creaking floor to our air-conditioned room. Our sweaty bodies revelled in the comfort of warm showers and cool cotton sheets. We kissed with mounting fervour; Clive's beard tickled my skin, our bodies hungry for one another, tongues, lips, legs, and arms interlocked with wild craving. Afterward, melting with pleasure, we snuggled until the mysterious sub-continent of India called us to action.

After three long months of separation, I sat with my love, arms linked, in a bicycle rickshaw pedalled by a skinny Indian through the shadowy streets of Agra. I enjoyed the sultry air. An aroma of spices, dust, and garbage assaulted my nostrils. Dogs barked, children cried, and people scurried into the shadows. While it troubled me to be moved by a human being whose gaunt muscles glistened with sweat, the rickshaw protected us in this unfamiliar world.

Neither my British education nor my mother's interest in missionaries prepared me for the majesty of the white marble domes and minarets of the Taj Mahal. Gleaming under the full moon, it sat like a celestial angel on the edge of the ravine, overlooking the river that twisted across the plain. In less than twenty-four hours since I left Edinburgh, India's beauty pierced through my armour of erroneous expectations and superiority.

The next morning, we peered out of the plane window to catch a glimpse of a few mountain summits that floated like boats on a sea of mushrooming clouds. Once in Kathmandu, rain splattered on our jackets as we wandered wide-eyed through streets filled with antique palaces, stupas, and temples.

"The wood carvings are so intricate," I said

"Look out. Watch your feet. That garbage stinks," Clive said.

"It is like the stories of the old Edinburgh when tenement dwellers shouted 'gardy-loo' before they threw their rubbish onto the street," I replied as warm rain trickled down my neck.

"We can't trek in this rain," Clive said. "Let's go to the Chinese-Tibetan border. We'll get out of the city and maybe see some mountains."

Away from the hectic streets, my eyes feasted on the green paddy terraces that climbed into the mist. Greedy for views of the snow-covered mountains, I twisted all around, but only pockets of mountainsides peeped out between the monsoon clouds. I expected poverty; however, the villages charmed me with substantial houses and happy healthy children.

That evening, our mouths on fire from chicken curry, we walked past sleeping urchins tucked under doorways and alleys. In a temple, surrounded by halos of incense, wrinkled men in ochre robes sat cross-legged, playing stringed instruments and chanting. The altar, displaying a brass Buddha strewn with marigolds and rice, triggered my deeply implanted Presbyterian suspicion. The Old Testament commandment circled into my awareness: *You shall not make for yourself a graven image for I the Lord your God am a jealous God.* If I obeyed these commandments, my status in the afterlife was assured—heaven for Christians and hell for everyone else, with no exceptions. As a child in Sunday school, I used to sing, "Hurry little penny, though you are so small, help to tell the children Jesus loves them all." Thus, according to Christianity, Hindus, Muslims, Buddhists, and Catholics were damned. Now I questioned it. *Is it possible that their gods and rituals are valid? Or are they destined for hell? How could a God of love do that?*

The elders stopped chanting and passed around a clay chillum, which they nestled between their cupped hands, and inhaled the pungent hashish. I thought that any religion must pursue *the* truth and quest toward higher principles. While I'd experimented with marijuana, I did not think it had a place in religion.

With the mountains out of our reach, the only climbing we did was up the rickety wooden stairs to the government hashish shop. Plastic candy jars filled with dried green leaves lined the shelves. "There are different qualities. Rub a pinch between your fingers and smell the various strengths," the shopkeeper instructed. But to me, they all had the same stringent aroma. Clive was more experienced, so I left him to choose. The young man weighed out our order and packed it into a polythene bag just like candy. Later in a cafe, we rolled a joint to share with other travellers. Unlike my experience in Afghanistan when I just slept well, this time I inhaled more. In no time, ordinary people climbing the stairs, even dogs sniffing in the street, caused uproarious laughter.

Even with our Scottish heritage of wet weather, the tropical rain thwarted our goal to trek in the mountains. Through the traveller's grapevine, we learned that Kashmir in the northwest region of India was less affected by the monsoon. We returned to the airport, flew to Delhi and onto Srinagar, the capital of Kashmir. Once on the tarmac in Srinagar, the view of the snowy mountains that surrounded the sun-drenched valley made my heart tingle. As we left the airport bus, a mass of men selling their services hounded us.

"Mister, you want houseboat? I have very nice houseboat at good price."

"Mister, you want hotel?"

"Mister, you want shikara?"

"You want taxi?"

Hot and overwhelmed, we edged away from the horde to the nearby government tourist hotel, a remnant from colonial times situated in a beautiful garden with tall chinar trees, chattering mina birds, lush lawns, and colourful flowerbeds. In the coolness of our airy room, its floorboards covered with a threadbare Persian carpet, we collected our thoughts. How would we find a mountain to climb or trek amongst these giants? It was impossible to buy a map as they were government classified information. I knew very little about Kashmir and its surroundings.

We took a taxi to the Tyndale Biscoe Boys School and the Mallinson's Girls School belonging to the Church of North India where I was to teach. We walked off the crowded street through a gate into the spacious compound of the school buildings and playing fields.

"The English principal Mr. Rae and his family are on holiday. You can stay tonight in the boys' hostel," said friendly Minister Matradas as he bobbed his head from side to side.

"Can you tell us where to go trekking?" I asked.

"Ah, Mr. Rae, he knows so much about the mountains. You'll

have to wait for his return," he replied, his head tilted skyward. He showed us to a room with two single beds with horsehair mattresses. I woke in the dark, my body itching all over. With my flashlight, I discovered bedbugs crawling over my skin and clouds of mosquitoes devouring my body. After one torturous night, I didn't know how I would survive a year.

In the morning, we caught a bus to the mountain town of Phalgam. On arrival, there was no time to appreciate the mountains as a mob of men in tattered clothing surrounded us, competing for our business.

"You want horse? I have very fine pony."

"You want hotel?"

"You want porter?"

To escape these persistent salesmen, we battled through the crowd to a cheap hotel. After a long hot night, I rubbed my bites while dogs barked and people yelled to each other as they loaded their possessions on and off buses. Loudly revving engines made sleep impossible. Early in the morning, Clive answered a knock on our door. As I lay half asleep under the sheet, I heard, "Mister, you want a very fine pony?" I heard the sound of fast footsteps as an irate Clive chased the pony wallah down the hall.

Watching a cross-legged Sikh, in a spotless turban, cook chapattis on the walls of an adobe oven, we ate breakfast and chatted to a French couple wearing hiking boots.

"Have you been trekking?" I asked.

"Not yet. Later today we're going on a five-day pilgrimage to Amarnath Cave. We don't need to carry tents as there are camps set up for the pilgrims along the way. We'll leave at noon if you want to join us," Marie-Pierre said.

"It's not climbing mountains," I said to Clive, "but it's a start."

"Sounds fun. We'll take our rain jackets and sleeping bags. We can leave some stuff in the hotel," he replied.

That afternoon, happy to escape the town, we hoisted up our rucksacks and hiked along the sandy path through cornfields littered with free-range chickens, mangy dogs, and a welcoming committee of bright, brown-eyed children. As always, my invisible baggage weighed me down: self-doubts about whether I was tough enough to complete the trek. Given my desire to escape Christianity, the religious aspect of a Hindu pilgrimage confused me. I thought, as a pilgrim, I must give my will to God, deny my desires, and receive a revelation. I just wanted to be a tourist and travel for pleasure.

Over several weeks, this annual pilgrimage attracted as many as one hundred thousand people. One legend told that Shiva, a living Hindu god, revealed to the goddess Parvati the secret of creation in the Amarnath Cave. A pair of mating doves eavesdropped on their conversation. As a result, the doves, which are reborn again and again, made the sacred cave their eternal abode.

That evening, in a canvas tent, we ate dahl and rice at a rickety table surrounded by the Sadhus or holy men, their hair matted in dreadlocks, some in bare feet and others wearing leather sandals. The red dots below white-chalked foreheads, between their deep brown eyes, added to their unusual appearance.

"These men look like hippies," Clive suggested.

"They're so different to the ministers and priests back home with their short-cropped hair and dark suits," I said.

"They only carry a blanket and a bowl. Everyone respects them."

"And only wear a thin cotton cloth," I said. "Are they immune to physical discomfort? I'm wearing all my clothes and feel cold."

"They're smoking dope. I don't think that's holy."

"Do they have the secret to life? Do they have *the* truth? Are they enlightened?" I mused.

Each day on the trail, whenever we rested, smiling Gujar children hovered in the background asking, "Hullo, mister, *backsheesh?*" These nomadic people spent their summers in the high mountain pastures. At a tea stall, sipping milky chai, a tall gujar with a weather-beaten face and wearing exquisite leather shoes with curled-up toes was accompanied by a couple of barefoot girls who wore hand-embroidered hats, decorated with silver trinkets and shells.

Holy sadhu on Amarnath Pilgrimage

"Where have you come from?" I asked.
"From the plains," he replied.
"How do you carry your tents and bedding?"
"On our horses. We herd our sheep and goats."
"What's in the pouches around the girl's necks?" I asked.
"Prayers to Allah." I fell silent, thinking about how their lifestyle, in tune with the seasons, was poles apart from mine.

On the third day, panting for breath with my lowland lungs about to explode, I hiked over the Mahagunas Pass at 14,100 feet. *I'll never make it. Will I get enlightened in the cave?* My calves and thighs strained; my monkey mind flipped from resistance to enthusiasm. Around the next corner, the sublime views of the jade-green waters of Sheshnag Lake jolted me out of my wayward thoughts. The lake was fed by the glaciers clinging to 23,000-foot Nun Kun Mountain. The summits, shrouded in cloud, filled me with a hunger for the expansive sensations I associated with hiking on ridges and mountaintops. The French couple disappeared while we covered our blisters before descending the muddy trail to the tents and shacks at Panchtarni and a welcome sweet milky chai.

That night, ice formed on the tent walls. In the early morning, we hiked six kilometres up a valley to the cave: a hole in the honey-coloured limestone cliff. Inside, the sacred ice lingam, which poured over the rock like a frozen stalagmite, was sprinkled with marigold petals and smoking incense sticks. The Indians prostrated themselves and chanted Sanskrit mantras. When I touched the ice, much to my disenchantment, the heavens did not shift. I did not experience a blissful makeover.

Opposite the cave, a naked yogi with a shrivelled penis beckoned us as he covered his body with a light cotton cloth. He lit a fire, and in a short time, offered us chai.

"I am here to help the people, meditate, and pray," he told us in perfect English.

"How can you survive at such cold temperatures with nothing on?" I asked.

"It is not so cold," he said, laughing. "I am used to it."

"Where do you go for the winter?"

"I walk to the Punjab. It is warmer there."

"Who do you pray to?"

"I ask the Divine Mother to give me strength and happiness so that I can serve the people."

As I walked back down the valley, my inner being warmed by his good humour and kindness, I said to Clive, "How could he be so happy with so little? What did he mean by the Divine Mother?"

Two days later, on the final pass, framed in white monsoon clouds, the trail plunged into the forested valley. Brilliant sunlight bathed a barefoot sadhu and lit up his orange robes, which fluttered like angel wings. Exuding peaceful, self-assurance, he strode towards the plains.

After another week of exhilarating trekking, once again I choked back my tears as I hugged Clive goodbye. His month's leave over, he boarded a flight to Karachi, enroute to Dubai and the Oman deserts. Heading to the Mallinson Girls School, I caught a bus to the city. I pushed my worries about the hazards I faced as a lone woman to the back of my mind.

The English headmaster Mr. Rae and his wife welcomed me into their comfortable home. After a British meal of stew and potatoes followed by apple pie and custard, Mr. Rae walked me across the compound under the chinar trees, not to the boys' hostel but to a gracious colonial house.

"In the days of the British raj, the headmistress lived here. Now it is divided into four apartments. The deputy principal lives downstairs and teachers from South India rent the other rooms," he explained. We entered the dark hallway, climbed the creaking stairs, and knocked on a door.

"This is Debbie from Hertfordshire," he said when a woman answered. "You are taking over her position as the English teacher."

"Come in and I'll show you around," she said with a warm smile. Dressed in a silk sari, she appeared to glide across the carpet to the veranda, while I stopped to stare at the photographic poster above the fireplace. My attention was riveted by the voluptuous bare-breasted women entwined with naked men, carved out of solid rock, joyfully participating in sexual pleasure.

"I bought that last winter when I visited the temples of

Khajuraho. They were built about a thousand years ago. It is a genuine spiritual place," Debbie explained. She confused me. I thought that this open display of eroticism had no place in religion and that simmering female sexuality belonged to a certain type of "bad" woman, whom I had been taught to look down on.

I continued to the veranda, which was furnished with a table and chairs and a bed covered with a mosquito net. It overlooked a garden filled with roses and marigolds.

"This is so beautiful," I said. "So much better than I expected." Over a cup of tea, I learned that Debbie had been here over a year, had Sikh friends in the Indian army, spoke Urdu, and had had jaundice. She told me she had learned that people were more important than places. How I envied her graceful confidence.

The first night, I lay in my single bed longing for Clive's reassuring presence. I awoke to a loud scuttling noise that drowned out the buzzing mosquitoes. I froze in terror, my pulse pounding. What could it be? Bedbugs never made that kind of noise. Rats? What if they jumped onto my bed and infected me with the plague? After a sleepless night, Debbie assured me, "Don't worry. The rats live in the ceiling, but they never come into the room. There are no bedbugs in here."

A couple of weeks later, when Debbie left for England, my childhood nightmare of the dark unshaven man startled me. I woke, struggling for breath, my mind filled with apprehension. I had never lived alone. I did not speak the language. Removed from everything familiar, had my hunger for travel blinded me to the perils of India?

Many nights, one dog's bark invited a response from the packs of stray dogs that roamed the streets. Over this cacophony, people shouted, children sang, and distant wedding music played, sounds that echoed through my night-dreams hour after hour. Each morning at four, from the nearby mosque, a spluttering cough followed by a guttural amplified voice, called people to pray.

Awake, I smacked whining mosquitoes, their dead bodies and blood splattering on my hands. Near dawn, I dozed; then the mosque started again and competed with the dogs. Just as the mullah built up to a fervent crescendo, the dogs quietened, the cocks crowed, the birds began their dawn chorus, rhythmic thumps came from the family in the cabin out back, the wedding drums started again, and somewhere a baby cried. As the pink dawn coloured the eastern sky, all hope of sleep gone, I scratched my mosquito bites. I heated water for the pail in my makeshift shower. Unsure how I'd keep awake for my classes, I poured cups of warm water over my sweaty body.

At lunchtimes in the staff room, I chatted to my Hindu colleague Jasvinder, who was decked out in gold necklaces, earrings, and a flowing sari. Even as I made friends with her, I judged her bare midriff as fat, as if to confirm to myself that there was a right and a wrong way for a woman to have a body. Back home, women's magazines, TV, and movies had convinced me I'd be more desirable skinny.

"In Britain, there is a popular model called Twiggy, who is thinner than a stick. I wish I looked like her. I don't want to put on any weight," I said, running my hands over my waist and thinking of Clive.

"Fat is beautiful," Jasvinder told me, obviously comfortable with her body and challenging my flawed beliefs about body image.

Although the British Empire ended in 1947, the Indian education system continued to use English. I had been employed to teach English. After a few weeks, Premi, the principal—a soft-spoken woman in her late thirties—asked me to teach general science. I welcomed the change. She showed me into an old room that looked as if it had not been painted since partition. It contained five science benches, a few rusty tripods, Bunsen burners, and a pile of tattered physics books. While I did try to learn Urdu and to pronounce the names of my students—Padmani, Sarabjit, Fatima,

Musrat, and Sharaz—I struggled in English to explain the subtleties between upstream and downstream in physics problems.

In this multicultural society, life revolved around Hindu, Muslim, and Christian religious holidays. These provided time for treasured excursions outside school.

One Saturday in September, unable to find any women to hike with, I met up with Nick from England and Rashid from New Delhi, who were both teachers in the Tyndale Biscoe boys school. We laboured up through the pine forest on a steep track to the high meadows below Haramukh Mountain. Marvelling at the chunky glaciers that clung to its rock walls, while the aquamarine waters of Gangabal Lake gently lapped, we hiked across a flower-filled meadow to an Indian army camp, a solitary canvas tent in this forbidding landscape. The mist hung in the rugged pass that led to Pakistan. The soldiers welcomed our visit and hospitably shared their food with us. I wrapped my hands around a tin mug of chai and listened to their stories.

"We are protecting the pass from the Pakistani soldiers," one said. We looked at them in disbelief. There was no sign of any big weapons, only a few handguns.

Another continued. "Last year, the Pakistanis came and infiltrated a valley near here. They were discovered after someone found a huge pile of sheep carcasses." Between mouthfuls of potato and cauliflower curry, they told us a tall tale:

"A few years back, near Baramullah, an Indian army patrol was attacked one night, and a fierce battle ensued. When the dawn broke, they found, to their horror, they were shooting at fellow Indians."

We pitched our tents in a craggy cirque that overlooked the Sind Valley, five thousand feet below. Perched on a rock, we soaked in the golden light that shone through clouds across the valley onto the snowy summit of Kolahoi. Later that night, lightning flashed around my tent. I peeked out the door to see the mountains illuminated momentarily and then vanish into the dark. My distressed shouts to Nick and Rashid disappeared into a thunder crack that almost burst my eardrums. In minutes, hail hammered on my tent, which vibrated like a drum. I pulled my sleeping bag over my head, held the rib I had bruised in a fall, and longed for the morning.

Porters returning from Pakistan border

Lucy, Caddy, Nick, and me, with Indian soldiers close to the Pakistan border

The hardships of my troubled night faded as the pink light of dawn ignited the mountain ridges. Reluctant to leave this explosion of natural beauty, I followed the others on a path that contoured high above the valley through the yellow-leaved birches and deodar forest. Then we descended a steep trail to the road. To our dismay, we had missed the last bus to Srinagar.

"What are we going to do?" I asked, biting my lips.

"We'll have to get the morning bus. It will get in at eight thirty," Nick replied.

"I have a science class at eight. I can't miss it," I said.

A shrill voice rang through the darkness. "Anyone want a ride to Srinagar?"

This was a change from the regular shouts of *"Balu!"* issued from the farmers to chase the bears away from their cornfields. The offer came from a wizened Kashmiri, Mr. Noake. In a country where there were few private vehicles, a ride to Srinagar felt like a gift from the gods. After he changed a flat tire, we piled into his Land Rover, which must have been one of the original models produced in the early fifties. We bumped over the potholes back to Srinagar. When Mr. Noake dropped us at the school, he kindly invited us to his houseboat for dinner some time.

A few weeks later, I was the only woman on a trip with Mr. Rae, Nick, and three Indian teachers: Rashid, Shafi, and Leo Telang. The drive to the mountain on Friday night reminded me of my Scottish adventures. After the car exhaust, dust, and rotting organic matter of the city, the moonlit clouds, mountains, and smell of pinesap energized me. On Saturday, we hiked twelve miles and four thousand feet to Konwat Lake nestled in the Pir Panjal mountains, which shielded the Vale of Kashmir from the plains.

On Sunday, Shafi and I set off up an un-named peak of about fifteen thousand feet. Because my climbing boots had rubbed up blisters, I slithered over the snow-covered rocks in baseball shoes. My breath laboured in the thin air. Nothing could hold me back.

Like an obsession, the summit pulled me upwards. With each step, an ever-widening view unfolded before me, with some mountains now familiar, like Kolahoi and the three tooth-like points of Nun Kun. From our summit, the massive twenty-six thousand foot Nanga Parbat towered to the north. The jagged peaks of the Pir Panjal range stretched in waves beyond the fertile Kashmir valley. To the south, Himalayan giants disappeared into the horizon. We had no time to linger. Slithering down through knee-deep snow, my feet and hands froze. Back at the hut, the others waited for us to hike the twelve miles back to the road end. My aching feet and general weariness were a small price to pay for my fulfilled dream of sitting on a fifteen thousand-foot peak. Unexpectedly, at the road end, we met Mr. Noake.

"You didn't come for dinner," he said, reproaching us. "When are you coming?"

Later that week, Nick and I took a bus to the Dhal Lake and found *Tit Willow,* Mr. Noake's tourist houseboat. He showed us along a narrow corridor to a dining room laid with a white table cloth and silver. To our delight, we were served a banquet, a mouth-watering array of Indian curries and European dishes. From then on, I became a welcomed guest on his houseboat, and I grew to value his friendship.

One October afternoon, under his wooden canopy, he and I sat content in the warmth of the autumn sunshine surrounded by the melodic noises of everyday life on the lake. Soft voices called to each other as locals paddled their boats or worked on their floating gardens of reeds and silt, which produced bountiful crops of melons and cucumbers. *Tit Willow* creaked as it rocked on its mooring. The wind moaned through the reeds. We sipped chai with whole cardamoms floating on the surface as we chatted about our shared love of the mountains.

The conversation changed. "My wife is not doing well," he confided. "She's been in bed now for a couple of weeks. Her stomach is bloated."

"It sounds like she is in pain," I said.

"She is not eating much, and the doctors are not sure what's wrong." He talked about her with so much tenderness that I was touched.

"Did you have an arranged marriage?" I asked, seeking to understand our different cultures.

"Yes. We have been married forty-eight years."

My twenty-three-year-old self was bewildered. More than his words, the heartfelt tone of his voice, and above all, the warmth in his eyes left me mystified as to how an arranged marriage had turned into compassionate love.

On my walk home, I puzzled over the lack of choice in marriage in traditional Indian culture. That my mother might have chosen my spouse was inconceivable. I couldn't imagine not knowing Clive before marrying him. Many times, when I raised the topic of arranged marriages with Indians, they would say, "In the west, you have a high divorce rate. In India, only a few couples divorce."

Missionary Mr. Rae liked to point out that western culture was degenerate. "Look at the crime rate in the British streets. The rampant sexuality in Hollywood movies is shocking. The west has lost its moral compass. It's high time it returned to Christian values." I did not know who was right.

Towards the end of November, the weather deteriorated, dense clouds replaced the clear skies of autumn and curtailed my weekend adventures. I missed Clive's energy, the comfort of home, and my friends. I relished letters. Unfortunately, the government censor opened them, and the pages were stuck together. Frustrated, I pored over them trying to decipher interrupted sentences. What political violations were they searching for? In my return letters, I did not tell Mother how I missed her homemade scones and hot water bottle in my bed, and fearing her criticism, I wrote only of my positive excursions, not my challenges.

My visits to the market were fraught with tension, fending off men who assumed my body was for public consumption, to be handled without my consent.

One Saturday evening, lonely, I walked along the crowded Bund—the path by the Jellum River. My eyes weepy and lips tight, I looked over the crowd of male faces strolling arm in arm, speaking Urdu and Hindi. I ached to see a familiar face and hear a friendly greeting: *"Wilma, how nice to see you. How is it going?"* I did not know how to cross the insurmountable walls between us and build the connections my soul longed for. I felt abandoned in this sea of humanity.

One day after school, I found my courage and strode down the street with its red streaks of spit from chewed Betel nuts. I glowered at any man who attempted to grope my body. I walked into the bookstore that was lit by a single light bulb. A poster with an emerald background showed a bejewelled goddess with a bare midriff, riding a gold-and-black-striped tiger while her multiple arms held symbols of Hindu Divine Power. On another, a bright-eyed man Ganesh had an elephant trunk draped in jewels. Then Kali, the goddess of destruction with her necklace of skeletons and her foot on a demon, looked petrifying. The staring-eyed gods and archetypal demons depicted in the Buddhist mandalas illustrated the cycles of death and rebirth. All were beyond my comprehension.

The complexity of Hinduism's polytheism made no sense to my brain, which had been heavily imprinted by patriarchal monotheism. Reincarnation intrigued me, offering the possibility that, if I was good enough in this lifetime, I might be elevated to male status or become a holy cow in my next lifetime. But failing that, I might return as a cockroach or a mouse.

I looked for English books amongst the Hindi and Urdu ones piled on the trestle tables. The plain navy-blue covers were dull in comparison to the colourful paperbacks at home. I picked one by

CIRCLING THE EDGE

Sri Aurobindo of Pondicherry, whom I had never heard of. Back on my balcony, reading his words confronted the murkiness of my sacred cows: "*Know that the Mother's light and force are the Truth, remain always in contact with the Mother's light and force, only then can you grow into the divine Truth.*"

Who is the mother? I wondered. *Is it his birth mother?*

I could not imagine a female aspect of God. Although Catholics had Mother Mary, no Presbyterian would have dared suggest that their authoritarian male God had a feminine aspect. This was blasphemy. Yet the possibility of the sacred feminine stirred up something deep within me and opened an inner crack.

Homesick, pondering the meaning of my life, I sat on my veranda marking exams papers. My eye caught sight of a bird with a long, flowing white tail and an iridescent blue head, darting through the trees like a graceful angel. The Paradise Flycatcher's exquisite beauty appeared not of this world. As if caressed by its wings, with answers on their tips, I felt elated as warmth rushed from my chest, and joy spread through my body.

In December, the school closed for two months. Excited that my three-month separation with Clive was over and bursting with anticipation, I boarded a bus to the airport. The bad news that a blizzard had cancelled the plane to Delhi filled me with frustration. I sent Clive a telegram. Then with three men, we hired a taxi to drive through the mountains, over the Baramullah Pass to Jammu on the plains. After dark, treacherous landslides and snow forced us to stop, I asserted myself and refused to share a room with one of the men. In a cupboard-like room, under a broken window, I tucked into my sleeping bag and slept with the security of a padlock on the door. In the morning, we continued through the mountains to the warm air of Jammu and arrived just in time to catch a plane to Delhi. My legs shaking, I sank into my seat. After a short time, the air hostess called me to the cockpit to talk with the captain.

"You want to go to Delhi?" he asked.

"Yes. I only have a boarding pass to Chandigar. I am meeting my husband there. He flew in from Oman yesterday," I replied.

"What have you been doing?"

"My husband is on a bachelor's contract. I have been teaching in Kashmir."

"You can have a seat to Delhi. Do you want to see the plane land?"

"Yes."

I stood, my knuckles white on the back of his leather seat, with a fleeting fear that I might be catapulted through the window. Surrounded by a dashboard of dials, he moved a lever, nosed the plane down, and screeched to a halt on the runway. Invigorated, I returned to my seat. When the plane stayed motionless, I fidgeted, anxious to know if Clive had received my messages. The air hostesses brought cups of tea and cookies and explained, "There is a shortage of sugar and spoons. We must drink while the plane is on the ground." Twitching with this further delay, I resisted my urge to scream. India's lesson was patience, and I, a reluctant apprentice.

I arrived in Delhi twenty-four hours late and flung myself into Clive's arms. As if on a second honeymoon, wildly in love, we headed to Nepal. In Kathmandu, I walked in dignity with no fear of being touched. Unlike our summer monsoon experience, on our flight to Pokhara, Himalayan peaks dazzled us. We trekked towards Annapurna, puffing over mountain passes and down into valleys carved deep in the earth. Alongside Tibetan traders, we soaked our aching muscles in a sulphurous hot pool under the full moon—its light bouncing off the snowy summits far above—thrilled to be alive.

When Clive's two-week leave was over, I returned with him to Oman where we house-sat for a couple of months, and whenever possible, explored this wild country. We loved it.

At the beginning of February, I flew back to Kashmir with an overnight stop in Bombay. My frustrations began in my five-star hotel when a man followed me down a dark corridor and attempted to enter my room.

Back at the Mallinson Girls School, the mountains continued to call me. One Saturday, I headed for Phalgam and the Windrush Hotel, situated by a roaring river in a mountain meadow. On the bus, I sat surrounded by Kashmiri families. The bus rumbled onto the streets of Anantnag, the last town in the valley. A mob of men stopped us. At first, I paid no attention and sat, shaking my legs, full of my western impatience.

"What is happening?" I asked the man next to me.

"Oh, it is only a riot," he replied. "Nothing to worry about."

The crowd appeared to disperse, and a policeman waved the bus on, but progress proved impossible. Then a young man with a red face, tight lips, a cape over his shoulders, and a baton in his hand, jumped on the bus. He raved in Kashmiri. I watched with rising alarm as the men filed off the bus, obeying his orders. The women, children, the man sitting next to me, and the bus driver remained seated. Then the rioter noticed my fair skin and hair.

"You!" His spit splashed my face. "You're a Christian and worship that god of yours." He leaned towards me and shouted a loud tirade in his dialect followed by, "You get off the bus! Get out! Get off!" Never had anyone looked at me with such animosity. A thin pane of glass separated me from fierce men with long truncheons who crowded the closed door. They might pull me from limb to limb. I pulled my rucksack into my churning stomach and attempted to stand up.

"You stay here," said the bus driver as he shook his head and pointed to my seat. The man next to me and the aggressive rioter engaged in a loud dialogue while I attempted to disappear into the seat. I wanted to tell the rioter, *My Mother is mad at me, because I am not a Christian. Now you are accusing me of being a Christian?* I recognized that he was not the listening kind. After more ranting, which I interpreted as curses, the bully climbed off the bus and disappeared into the crowd.

When the bus turned down a side street, I left. I jumped onto a tonga and asked to go to the mission hospital. To my horror, a man who had been on the bus climbed up beside me and attempted to put his arm around me. I pushed him away and screamed at him as I pressed my rucksack between us.

"You must be so thankful for me," he told me. Gratitude was the last thing on my mind. "I saved you. The man beside you protected you. He told the angry student you were his wife."

Relief swept over me as I entered the guarded entrance of the mission hospital. Peaceful, Irish nurses dressed in their starched white uniforms welcomed me. Between sobs, I told my story. These nurses appeared unaffected by the mayhem in the town. A solitary policeman watched over their compound.

That afternoon, along with two other westerners seeking asylum, the sisters assigned us the task of measuring the badminton court while outside the chaos continued. That night, I woke up choking, as once again the dark man of my childhood dreams attempted to strangle me.

On Sunday evening, along with the Europeans, I returned to Srinagar where all was quiet. Tuesday, some rioters attacked the school bus, and the broken glass cut one of my students. School was cancelled. All the Europeans in the school complex, Nick, two young English students, Mrs. Ray, her children, and I left the compound out the back gate to avoid the main street. Nervously, we looked over our shoulders as we walked to a side street. The school Land Rover drove us to a suburban garden. There on the lawn, we spent a quiet day reading. At twilight, we drove back along the main street, alarmed to see many shops with broken windows. Unsettling rumours spread that the police had used tear gas to disperse the mob, while ten western travellers were beaten up and several people killed.

The political upheaval continued, and all the schools and

colleges closed for three days. Thinking we'd be safer away from the city, Nick and I decided to go trekking.

"I heard that politicians can pay a person called the 'sumpet man' a certain amount of money to create a riot," Nick told me on the bus.

"Really? I don't believe you!" I replied.

"Yes. This was specifically an anti-Christian riot. Politicians fuel people's devotion to their Islamic beliefs. A student in the Anantnag college library found a picture of the prophet Mohammed in Arthur Mee's *Book of Knowledge* printed in 1897. The Islamic religion forbids any images of the prophet."

"That's why the anger was directed towards me?"

"You're Christian to them. The picture was a convenient excuse to inflame people and cover up the political intentions behind the violence. It's like Rent-a-Riot!"

On the outskirts of Anantnag, we saw a house on fire, boarded up shops, and a crowd of men. I could not believe how stupid I was to return to the town from which, only a few days before, I had escaped with my life. The bus driver signalled that we should hide. We crouched down while someone covered us with a coat. Curious as ever, I peeped out to see a few people and a herd of helmeted policemen. After the bus left the bazaar for the paddy fields, we sat up.

As we expected, all was quiet in the tourist town of Phalgam. The Windrush Hotel down by the river was full of missionaries. I shared a room with two of them who did not miss a chance to push their religion. Unable to say no, I was cajoled into joining their Bible study. I thoroughly resented their proselytizing.

The next day, Nick and I shouldered our backpacks and sweated up the steep track. After the missionaries and the chaos of the city, the lush forest of Himalayan Pine with soft green tips and translucent new leaves soothed me. At the treeline, the unoccupied nomadic Gujar huts that circled the meadow were filled with snow. Beyond the huts, the valley narrowed and held Tulian Lake with its floating icebergs. We pitched the tent in this idyllic spot. For the next few days, far from the rioters, we ate porridge for breakfast and mountains for lunch. We climbed peaks and glissaded down snowfields. In the long evenings, as distant ridges were consumed by the sun, we sat by our campfire under a starry canopy and absorbed solitude. However, ignorant of the dangers of the rarefied atmosphere of the high alpine, I sunburned my face. On my return to school, my red skin turned into yellow pus blisters. It was as if the sun, like the Indian subcontinent, had peeled off a layer of my prejudices.

Tulian Lake

Scrambling in the mountains above Tulian Lake

Near the end of my year in Kashmir, laden with precious gifts of Dutch gouda and marmite, my mother came to visit for six weeks. She enjoyed my south-facing colonial apartment, the garden of tall trees and lush flowers that attracted golden orioles, bulbuls, and a paradise flycatcher. She struggled with the poverty and dusty overcrowded streets. She resisted eating freshly cooked bagels, because they did not come wrapped in a clean plastic bag. Many times, she and I collided over my rejection of her fundamentalist beliefs, my tentative explorations into polytheistic Hinduism, and my intense anger at the unwanted male touch.

On an excursion to the mountain village of Gulmarg, I bargained hard with the pony wallahs who pestered us to ride their horses. I thought Mother would be delighted to be on a horse: a dream come true for her. But the trail that clung close to the mountain precipice terrified her. To add to her physical discomfort, the pony man in his ragged clothes told her a sad story about how hard it was to support his six kids. At the end of the ride, she pleaded with me to pay him extra money. I was on a local salary.

Upset that she did not recognize my hard-earned bargaining skills, I paid up.

At the back of my house, the school cook, his wife Lakshmi, and five children lived in a two-roomed cottage. This family came from Ladakh, an area with close cultural similarities to Tibet. In her early thirties, Lakshmi had Mongolian features, dressed in flowery pants and tunic with her long black plaits swathed in a flowing scarf. Her ten-year-old daughter carried the four-month-old baby around like a rag doll. There were no Pampers for her. I rarely heard the baby cry as she was passed from one sibling to another.

Me, Lakshmi, my mother and Lakshmi's six children.

One hot Saturday afternoon, my mother and I took the family on their first trip to the Dal Lake on a *shikara*, a Kashmiri gondola, with brightly painted canopies and comfortable cushion seats. We sat back in style while the shikara man paddled us through the waterways of the valley. We watched iridescent kingfishers snatch fish from the brown waters and people tend their floating gardens. At the lake, Lakshmi watched as my mother, the children, and I jumped in and out of the warm water. On the return trip, I helped paddle as we raced with another boat. Laughing, Mother and the children all cheered and yelled at me to go faster. When the time came for my mother to leave, Lakshmi came with a gift: two pairs of hand-knitted woollen socks, one pair for Mother and one pair for her first grandchild.

At the end of June, thirty-six schoolgirls, several teachers, two English volunteers, my mother, and I set off for the annual school expedition to climb thirteen thousand-foot Mahadeo, the peak that Clive and I had climbed on his spring visit. My students, aglow with enthusiasm, chit-chatted up the trail. Under the shade of their umbrellas, three Kashmiri teachers hiked at a steady pace. Halfway up the valley, some Gujar women squatted around a fire that supported a cauldron filled with strawberry-pink noon chai, made from tea leaves, bicarbonate of soda, salt, and milk. This and fresh *rotis*, bagels, provided a snack for our group.

I brought up the rear, following the trail of girls puffing upwards along the mountain stream to the tree line and the Gujar hamlet of Lidderwat at ten thousand feet. We happily pitched our tents on the rich pasture and wildflowers. Later that evening, Principal Premi and her brother unexpectedly walked out of the forest. She looked calm and serene in her yellow sari. She joined us around the campfire as Gujars sang and danced.

The following morning, while Mother kept Premi company at the camp, our large party set off. We admired the furry marmots scurrying around the rocks. In my element, I encouraged my pupils over the rugged ground.

On the summit, the mist shrouding the mountaintops cleared and revealed tantalizing views in all directions. To the north, at almost eighteen thousand feet, Haramukh floated above the cloud in the Sind valley and captivated us. I regretted not bringing my mother.

Back at our camp, the two English volunteers and I decided to stay for another night while Mother, the teachers, and pupils hurried down the valley to their home comforts. I walked across the meadow barefoot to bathe in the icy river. As I dried myself in the hot sun, barefooted Gujar children watched my curious ways then stood stiffly for a photograph. We followed them through the pines to visit the cluster of huts. Their mothers sat on the sun-baked ground. A handsome woman, whose face was lined with cross-hatched wrinkles, greeted us with a warm smile and told us her name was Fatima. We communicated by sign language and a few words of Urdu. She massaged white fat into her daughter Shaheen's thick long hair and combed it into separated sections. Her practiced fingers formed many fine glistening braids, which she crossed over the crown of Shaheen's head. To my surprise, they allowed me to photograph this elegant hairstyle.

Gujar hairdresser

Three generations

My turn

"Are you married?" Fatima asked. I nodded, pointing to my gold band. They looked puzzled. With my limited language skills, I could not explain that my husband worked in the Middle East. "Have you any children?" she asked. When all three of us shook our heads, they looked at us sorrowfully. Shaheen, at about twenty, cradled a baby in her arms and pointed to her three toddlers, whom we admired. Fatima offered us a hairdo. With my fine hair, I hoped the rancid fat might work a miracle. Fatima made me a few skinny plaits. In this Gujar women's world, we were not impressive, with no husbands, no children, and almost no hair.

We toured their log huts, which were open to the elements. Red-paint circles decorated the roof and fresh pine branches lined the floor. I inhaled the aroma of fresh bread mingled with the smell of burning pine. Squatting in front of a small fire, covered with a box-like clay oven, Shaheen mixed water with maize flour that had been carried up from the village five thousand feet below. She patted small rolls of dough into flat circles and placed them on the inside wall of her oven. Her *dechi*, saucepan, with noon chai sat in one of two holes on the top. With her copper ladle, complete with a dragon carved on the handle, she poured tea into bowls that had come all the way from Shanghai. We sat cross-legged and dipped the hot chapatti into the pink liquid. I thought about all the luxuries such as a gas oven, washing machine, and kitchen sink I needed to make a good life at home. Here on the mountain, a good life looked more modest. Outside, bathed in the warm evening light, Shaheen's husband looked like the picture of peace as he puffed on his hubble-bubble pipe.

As the sun sank below the distant mountains and stars penetrated the expansive sky, I felt profound gratitude for this blessed connection that transcended age, skin colour, and culture.

At the beginning of July, my pupils dressed up in colourful outfits from the many regions of India and gathered for the school concert. They adjusted their makeup and giggled among themselves. Even after I'd been a year in India, their self-assurance, beauty, and diversity dazzled me. I recognized we were more alike than different.

My elegant students dressed for the school concert

Later that week, another drama unfolded. I was sitting on my veranda, correcting exam papers, and became aware of boys and girls cheering and shouting outside. Tight jawed, I walked to the staff room, trying to ignore the derogatory boos from my ninth-grade class.

"School is closed for two days. Some teachers are on strike," a teacher calmly informed me. Then, the following day, the strikers made rude posters and shouted slogans at us. The police occupied the school grounds. In response to this aggression, the school officially closed until autumn term.

I walked to town to deliver some letters for Mr. Rae. On my return, some boys harassed me. "Darling, do you fuck?" one mumbled as another hit me on the back. My hands knuckled into fists, and my eyes narrowed as I glared at them. With a loud sigh, and eyes filled with tears, I entered the sanctuary of the school grounds and returned to my treasured veranda.

That evening, my mother and I visited my student Sarabjit's family for a farewell meal. As western women, we sat uncomfortably surrounded by her father, uncles, and brothers while her mother and aunts stayed in the kitchen. With downcast eyes, Sarabjit served us delicious homemade curries. This gulf between my freedoms, the inequality of men and women, and the invasive touches were unacceptable. No matter how broad-minded I tried to be, Kashmir was more patriarchal, more repressive of women, than my own culture.

Yet within its wealth of cultures, poverty, and chaos, India embraced a cornucopia of enchantments, snake charmers, rainbows of colour, luxuriant aromas, exotic birds, religions, sensuality, and gracious people. As I packed my bags, heading to Britain and the man I loved, I wore the star ruby gold ring I had haggled for. When the sunlight shone on the translucent purple stone, it revealed a six-pointed star, reminding me how my inner darkness had been illumined by India's ancient light.

CHAPTER 9
"Two Mrs and no Mr?"

"Twenty years from now you will be more disappointed by the things you didn't do than by the things you did."
~ Mark Twain

In Oman, the tough heat of summer settled into the sultry fall while the oil crisis of 1974 showed no sign of resolution. Clive worked for Seismograph Services, a contracting company to Shell. We had lived together for a year. I worked as a laboratory technician at the Shell Medical Hospital, having replaced the English technician who drank the lab alcohol between testing urine and blood samples for tropical parasites.

On his rare days off, Clive borrowed a company Land Rover. Lured by shimmering mountains, we bounced over the corrugated dirt roads away from the coastal strip to the interior adobe villages, surrounded by irrigated fields of wheat and date palms. The dusty streets swarmed with colourful children sparkling with antique silver necklaces. Their fascinating way of life, unchanged for centuries, was untouched by western culture. However, the lack of tarmac roads frustrated our need for recreational adventure. One evening, strolling on the cliffs and gazing over the

Arabian Sea, I suggested, "We can't buy a four-wheel-drive vehicle here. Why don't we go to London, buy a Land Rover, and drive it out overland?"

"You know I have no holidays for three months. You can't go alone. A single woman driving through Middle Eastern countries isn't safe," Clive replied.

"I survived in Kashmir. Maybe I could find someone else to drive with."

"I'm not comfortable. What if you broke down? It's far too risky."

The idea refused to die, and we chewed it over most days. One day at my laboratory, Shell's exploration manager came in for a blood test. In awe of his advanced position near the top of the hierarchy, I hesitantly asked about his wife, Gloria, who taught me pottery. She created elegant vases, while I made stumpy ashtrays.

"She's in England," he said, "taking the kids to boarding school."

"I want to drive a Land Rover from London to Oman," I said. "Do you think Gloria would come with me?"

"I am sure Glo would be interested. I'll write to her immediately," he replied to my astonishment.

When I heard by snail mail that Gloria wanted to come on my trip, I enlisted my father-in-law's help to purchase a Land Rover in Britain. Then I studied maps to figure out routes from London to Oman. The obvious way was across Europe, Turkey, and the Middle East to Saudi Arabia. I phoned the consulate.

"Do I need a transit visa to drive through Saudi Arabia?" There was silence at the other end of the phone. I tried again, "My friend and I want to drive across your country in a Land Rover to Oman. Can I get a visa?"

"Yes, but you must take your husband."

"He is working and can't come," I said.

"You have a brother? You must take him."

"I don't have a brother. We are two women on our own."

"You must take your husband or your brother."

Without a male to accompany us through Saudi Arabia, the alternative route was across Iran, over the Persian Gulf on a dhow to Dubai, and on to Oman.

One hot afternoon, I drove into the nearby town of Muttrah to visit the Embassy of the United Arab Emirates. The aristocratic Arab, dressed in his long robes and a white headdress held in place by a black headband, answered my question.

"No. I can't give you a visa. You can get one in London. For two women, it won't be a problem," he assured me.

Then one evening after dinner in the expatriate club, I overheard a woman gossip to her friend, "What does that young girl think she is doing driving through those dangerous countries? Her blonde hair will be an open invitation for trouble. Men in those countries are not to be trusted. It's foolhardy." Yet with my experiences in India, Pakistan, and Afghanistan, I knew that, at a grassroots level, people were friendly and helpful. But as I broke new ground in the complex world of regulations, borders, and visas, I wondered if the naysayers did know better, and the obstacles were too great.

I flew to London. After an enervating Omani summer, the cold blast of damp British weather made my feet bounce. Gloria and I visited the United Arab Emirates (UAE) Embassy.

"We'd like a transit visa please," I told them.

"You don't need a visa if you are in transit. When you enter the country, they will hold your passport until you leave," replied the young Arab woman.

"But we are driving through the country, entering and leaving at a different place. We will arrive in Dubai, then drive to Oman," I explained.

"Yes, you need a visa and a letter."

"A letter? What for?" I asked.

"A letter from your company," she said.

"But I don't have company," I said.

She shrugged her shoulders, rolled her eyes, and looked at the queue building up behind us. We walked to the Bulgarian embassy. They accepted our request and instructed us to pick up our passports in a few days. Gloria's husband obtained the required letter from Shell, and we purchased the UAE visa.

In the North London dealership, I inhaled the new car smell as I inspected my brand new short-wheel-based Land Rover. The salesman sat in the passenger seat while we went for a test drive.

"Have you driven one before?" he inquired.

"No." I did not disclose a vivid memory of myself in Oman, at the wheel of the company Land Rover, snaking violently on a gravel road. In the London rush hour, I maneuvered around a corner. "You're on the wrong side of the road," he said. I gritted my teeth, clenched the steering wheel, and swerved to the left.

For two weeks, I turned my mother's house into a warehouse of household items that Clive and I needed to set up house in Oman. Mother never complained and regularly baked her delicious treacle scones. I understood her silence and her prayers as support. On departure day, a November morning in the south of England, Gloria and I crawled along with hundreds of commuters.

"Can you believe they will repeat this commute twenty times in the four weeks it will take us to drive to Oman?" Gloria said.

"I can't imagine being a commuter. So boring." Biting my nails, I asked, "What's the time?"

"We have to be at the hovercraft terminal in twenty minutes. Geez, all this traffic slowed us down."

"Remember, your husband said, 'Catching the hovercraft will be the hardest part of the trip.'"

Twenty-five minutes later, my stomach tension eased as I handed our passports to the customs officials and answered the usual questions with unusual answers.

"Where are you going?"

"How long will you be out of the country?"

In the duty-free, we purchased a couple of bottles of whiskey and stashed them between the trunk and suitcases. Thrilled to have achieved our first milestone, Gloria captured a photo of our vehicle, as we left British soil and disappeared into the bowels of the hovercraft. We sank into the comfy seats and looked out the small windows as the hovercraft bumped over the heaving channel.

"We must remember to drive on the right-hand side of the road," I said as we landed in Calais.

"It will be awkward with our left-hand drive vehicle. We'll both need to pay attention," Gloria replied.

"Oh no! We forgot to fill the tank before we left England. I didn't bring any French money. We can't run out of petrol on our first day!" I exclaimed as we struggled to read the map and figure out our route.

"I bought some Belgian Francs. Belgium's not far," said Gloria. I breathed again, grateful for her foresight.

On the autobahn, the flow of traffic swept us along. In the pouring rain, we battled through the Brussels rush hour to find our downtown hotel. Then we celebrated our progress of two hundred and thirty-four miles of our six-thousand-mile journey in a busy restaurant before enjoying a stroll around the historic Town Hall Square surrounded by floodlit buildings.

Desperate for sleep, I fell into bed. Gloria fell asleep in an instant, and eventually, her loud snores jolted me awake. In my imagination, storms and monster trucks crashed into us, our bodies bloodied, torn, and broken. All night, these technicolour nightmares flashed through my busy mind. Was it foolish to do this trip without a male protector who knew about engines and could fend off rapists? By morning, I had driven at least halfway to Oman in my night dreams.

I wiped sleep out of my eyes as I sank my teeth into a crisp croissant. I inhaled the aroma of coffee as the caffeine woke me up. In wet weather, through endless road works, we battled with German juggernauts for road space.

"What should we do? It's dark so early. We said we wouldn't drive in the dark," Gloria said in the gathering gloom of the late afternoon.

"It's only four o'clock. It's still two hundred miles to Salzburg. There are only industrial towns here. Where would we stay?" I replied, rubbing my eyes.

"Let's keep going. It should take about four hours max. With a short stop, we'll make it by nine," Gloria replied, stretching her arms above her head. "I feel so stiff."

The traffic eased. We took turns at the wheel. We buzzed along until thick fog slowed us to a snail's pace. I sang Beatles and pub songs to keep myself awake. At midnight, I rested my pounding head on a soft pillow. Once again while Gloria snored, my legs twitched, and in my mind, I re-drove the entire trip embellished with garish dreams.

The weight of the night dropped away as I pulled back the curtain to reveal crystal mountain air, glittering sunshine, and clear skies. I gazed at the mountains in their winter plumage, framed in a canopy of golden autumn leaves.

"Let's go and see Salzburg. I was here a few years ago," Gloria told me.

"Thank goodness we don't have to drive today," I said.

Surrounded by tourists, we walked past Mozart's birthplace on Getreidegasse and strolled up the cobbles to the dominating stone walls of Hohensalzburg Castle. In the market, we lingered over the stalls of trinkets and purchased edelweiss ornaments. In a cafe, we sipped on coffee and munched Black Forest gateaux. Out on the street, well-dressed Austrians with an air of solid prosperity sauntered past.

The next day, exhilarated, we drove across sun-sparkled alpine meadows, past rushing streams, and through gorges framed with orange larch trees. The buggy—our nickname for the Land Rover—romped along the tarmac strip. At the top of one pass, banks of snow flanked the road. High in the mountains, we stopped in a hotel. The crisp air, glimmering snowy mountains, white moon, and brilliant stars were uplifting. I treated myself to my own room, allowing Gloria to snore alone.

In communist Yugoslavia, our exuberance evaporated. The sky was overcast as we passed flat mile after flat mile of dry, limp cornstalks. We stopped in a muddy field and ate a quick lunch of cheese and crackers.

"We're stuck, Gloria. How do I use the four-wheel drive?" I asked, clutching the steering wheel. She pulled the lever. We chugged out and turned into the traffic.

"Look at those wayside memorials. There's one every kilometre," I said.

"I can see the photos of the dead stuck in the bunches of dusty plastic flowers. So scary," Gloria said. Just then, a car raced over a narrow bridge on the wrong side of the road, swerved, and missed us by inches.

"God, that was close. The monster trucks rule the road. I don't think they see us," I said.

"I am sick of looking at bloody corn," Gloria said.

"I am sick of looking at this truck's arse."

"Watch out. There's another handcart with no lights," she said.

"There's a signpost for a motel. Let's stop."

We escaped the frenetic driving to the seedy Motel Spacva Vinoci. As if inconvenienced by our appearance, the receptionist replied to our questions in guttural grunts. At least we had a room for the night. Over our pre-dinner whiskey, we commiserated.

"We have only covered 1300 miles of our 6000 miles."

"That's depressing. Today was difficult," Gloria said.

"I don't suppose trips are always scintillating," I said.

"I have found that most things in life have a downside," Gloria said. "We'll hang in. We can't drive back to London."

We arose with a fighting spirit and headed out with renewed persistence. In the early morning light, the traffic was less intimidating. By mid-morning, we reached the Bulgarian border. Even with our visa, we lined up in five different queues to stamp our passport, to import the Land Rover, to buy compulsory car insurance, to change money, and to purchase petrol coupons.

The road signs in the Cyrillic script challenged our translation skills. "Someone warned us of dangerous bandits who stopped and robbed foreign vehicles in Bulgaria," Gloria reminded me.

"Clive's parents have a good friend in Sophia," I said. "A couple of years ago, they flew here, hired a car, and drove to Istanbul without any problems."

But once again, as darkness approached with nowhere to stay, we had no choice but to drive on to the capital, Sophia. When we plunged into dense fog, our visibility decreased to a car length and reduced our speed to a crawl. The headlights illuminated a sphere of white moist air. I strained to see vehicles, hand-drawn carts, and to follow the edge of the road, which did not have a white line. Without warning, we found ourselves shuddering over potholes and onto a gravel road.

"Oh God! We're off the highway."

"There are no lights or signs. We can't see a thing. The map is no help."

"How do we know if we continue that there will be an on-ramp? We might get even more lost."

"Let's reverse back to the highway. There's not much traffic."

Terrified, we peered into the fog and backed up to the main road. Vigilant, we continued through the murk to Sophia. Once in the city, we drove on dim cobbled streets with no signposts. We asked for directions to the town centre, which was difficult as no one spoke English. After several wrong turns, we pulled up outside the Balkan Hotel in time for supper. In the brightly lit dining hall, we sat at a table covered in starched linen and listened to the classical pianist over the buzz of Bulgarian conversations. We welcomed the goulash and potatoes and celebrated our accomplishment with a glass of Bulgarian wine. After dinner, we wandered around the square, admiring the old buildings and the elegant onion domes of the Russian church.

"You must wait. Your passport is away!" the morose receptionist told me as we checked out of the hotel.

"Away where?" I asked anxiously.

"To the passport office." I worried I'd be sent to a sordid Bulgarian jail. After thirty minutes, a different woman thrust my passport into my hand without a word, and we left.

In the early afternoon, we arrived at the Turkish border. Custom officials inspected long queues of Turks returning from Europe, their vehicles spilling over with washing machines, fridges, TVs, and other household goods. Taking a deep breath, I asked some men for directions. As they pointed us to the customs building, they interrogated me:

"Where are you from?"

"Where are you going?"

"Are you married?"

"Where is your husband?"

"Is that your mother?"

Needless to say, this upset Gloria, but I felt some comfort, as if her thirty-five-year-old presence gave me, at twenty-five, some protection from eastern men. Jostling with Turks, we lined up, and in a couple of hours, we emerged triumphant with my passport stamped with a little car and inscribed in Turkish. Jubilant to have crossed another border, we thought it must be all downhill to Istanbul.

How did I know I was back in Turkey? The language and people dressed differently, but in our first hotel at Edirne, the receptionist directed us to a room down a dark corridor. As I carried my overnight bag, a man followed and dared to put his arm around me. I growled and shook him off. Meanwhile, Gloria discovered that there was no hot water in our room. We returned to the receptionist and demanded a room with hot water and closer to the lobby.

At dusk, we visited the Selimiye Cami, the Mosque of Sultan Selim. Leaving our shoes in the marble hallway, we entered along with Turkish worshipers. Under the stone arches, I walked over thick rugs, soaking in the aura of tranquillity that permeated the space. I knew nothing about formal meditation, but I lingered on the floor, absorbing a strong feeling of harmony with the past and the present. The pressures of the journey fell away as my body and mind rested in this stillness.

In the morning, we continued beside the calm Sea of Marmaris and over golden hills towards Istanbul. Approaching the city, with no lane discipline and unclear rules, crazy streams of traffic swept us along. We concentrated on following the signs. At one major intersection, I slowed to stop at the red lights only to find that the other cars honked and raced past on either side. A lone policeman stood in the middle blowing his whistle and waving his arms. It appeared he overruled the red light. As we hurtled along, the minarets of the Blue Mosque came into view. I assured Gloria that the hotel Clive and I had stayed in on our shoestring budget, only a few years ago, was good. When I saw her discomfort with the basic green room, I questioned my choice. Still, we celebrated that Istanbul was one-third of the total distance to Oman.

For a couple of days, like tourists, we visited the Aya Sophia and the Blue Mosque. We enjoyed sitting in a cafe and writing postcards to our families. We toured the Imperial Harem of the Topkapi Palace with its labyrinth of rooms decorated with artistic tiles, gold, and carved wooden shutters. This luxurious building, called the Golden Cage, imprisoned the Sultan's wives and eight hundred concubines, who were selected for their beauty from all over the Ottoman Empire. We walked along the musty corridor that housed the eunuchs, who were considered safe to look after the women. The powerful mother of the Sultan reigned over the harem.

Very appreciative of our modern freedoms, we headed to the covered bazaar called the Kapaci Carsi, which had been built in 1461 but destroyed many times by fire and earthquakes. As we wandered through the labyrinth of fluorescent-lit alleys, Turkish music blared, and the smell of spices hung in the air. Shopkeepers hassled us to buy their bags, carpets, jewellery, and food. I bargained for two suede jackets for Clive and myself. When the lengthy transactions finished, it was time to pick up our Land Rover, which was in the garage for a service.

"My cousin will drive you to the garage if you pay for the petrol," said the man who had sold us the coats. Old enough to be my father, he sat in the car with his arm around Gloria. We nicknamed him Sugar Daddy. He continually asked, "How do you like Istanbul?"

"*Cok guzel,*" Gloria replied. "We have driven from London. We are very tired."

"Tonight, you sleep. Tomorrow, you come, and we all have lunch," he said. Then flashing his eyes, he continued, "Tonight, you sleep. Tomorrow night, you come and see Turkish belly dancer." We burst into peals of nervous laughter and departed with promises to return.

However, in the morning, Gloria and I agreed to tackle the intimidating drive to Eastern Turkey and Iran. We wove in and out of road works, crossed the new Bosphorous Bridge, and stopped at a petrol station. I pulled the brass knob on the bathroom door. The odour of stale urine overwhelmed me as I tiptoed around the brown deposits on the floor. I held my nostrils with my left hand, as I struggled to pull my jeans down with my right hand and then squat over the white porcelain hole. With my bladder relieved, my brain screamed, *"Get out of here!"* With my jeans half up, I tried to undo the lock. Envisioning death by toxic fumes, I fought with the lock, all logical powers drowning in the stench. What an inglorious end, to die in a Turkish toilet. Just as I was ready to faint, the attendant opened the door.

"Why didn't you come and help me?" I challenged Gloria.

"You were only gone for a few minutes. I was looking at the guidebook," she said.

"I've just had a near-death experience!" Gloria rolled her eyes. "My legs feel like jelly."

"We should have tried to find a phone in Istanbul and contact John and Clive," she said.

"We told them not to expect any communication from us," I said in a rasping voice.

"Nobody knows where we are. We must send a telegram from Iran."

At dusk, we spotted a motel beside a lake. After the noise and dirt of Istanbul, this pastoral setting was an oasis. The fresh air soothed my seared lungs. As the sun set, the reeds, and the rocks of the shoreline lit up with burning reds and pinks as if promising us a safe drive.

Our adventure continued at six thirty a.m. on the busy road to Ankara. With two thousand miles of experience, we drove with confidence around the ring road, following the signs to Samsun on the Black Sea. We sped across quiet roads over the spacious hills of Anatolia.

"Thank goodness the driving has calmed down. The guidebook mentions an ancient Hittite city at Bogazkoy. It's on our way. People have lived in these hills for seven thousand years," I read.

"Who were they?" Gloria asked as she drove.

"The Hittites had a powerful empire in Anatolia and northern Syria in the eighteenth-century BC. The ancient capital of the empire was at Bogazkoy and called Hattusas. It was destroyed by the Phrygians in 1180 BC," I continued.

"If we're lucky with the traffic, we'll have time to visit and still drive to Samsun before dark," Gloria said.

"It would be more sensible to keep going. We've driven enough in the dark."

When we arrived at the intersection, the buggy turned right on its own accord. The ruins demanded our attention. In the fading light, I imagined ghostly shadows from past millenniums floating around the large earthenware storage pots. They had been shattered by the passage of time but pieced together by the painstaking hands of the twentieth century. The Hittite ghosts vanished when two Turks shouted at us, "We will show you the Lions' Gate!" Despite our wariness of Turkish males, we agreed that these men looked harmless and accepted their offer. They squashed in beside us. Gloria pulled on the four-wheel drive and headed up the steep dirt-track road.

Mehmed waved us to stop at a hole in the hillside. He told us to bring a flashlight. To our astonishment, the crude hole was the entrance to a long tunnel, built for defence purposes. Our flashlight lit up the V-shaped roof, corbelled with chiselled rock slabs.

In the gathering dusk, we drove to the Lion's gate, one of the entrances to this Hittite citadel. The ancients believed the lions protected the city from outside evil. Three damaged lions carved out of solid basalt towered over my head. The only intact lion was silhouetted against the soft pink sky. We enjoyed the smell of herbs as the first stars twinkled, as they must have done eons ago when the city had been alive with activity. Bewitched, we reluctantly turned around. Back in the car park, we bargained for an ancient memento. Pondering on our clay Hittite elephants, we wondered if there had ever been elephants or lions in the middle of Turkey. Neither of us knew the answer.

That evening in the hotel, we found ourselves the only women in a restaurant full of businessmen. We avoided eye contact and ate fish fried in thick corn flour and eggplant. We mused on what life had been like for women in that hilltop fortress two thousand years ago, the battles fought, and the rise and fall of empires that had occurred on these desirable fertile lands.

The next day, the tobacco fields around Samsun gave way to a rugged coastline carved with river gorges and views of the Black Sea. Further east, terraces of tea plants clung to the mountainsides. In the sunlight, the russet and orange leaves gleamed like jewels. We climbed over the coastal mountains through a thick forest on a gravel road. When I misjudged one corner, our vehicle lurched out of control and snaked across the road towards a precipitous drop. Adrenalin fired through my chest. When I regained control, I continued with caution, aware of the tense silence between us. A few kilometres later on, on a sharp corner, we encountered the flattened remains of a Volkswagen. "That could have been us!" Gloria said. I clenched my teeth.

Mid-afternoon, we stopped for a short walk on the pass, soaking in the beauty of interweaving mountain ranges that stretched crest after crest like ocean waves to the horizon. Overhead a raven soared. On the final stretch of road to Erzurum, the evening sun lit up the wheat fields, and the mountains blazed like gold. We wanted to drive forever.

That night in the hotel, I lay on my single bed, longing for sleep, but soon started to scratch. In my dozy state, I realized that I was not alone in the bed. My nemesis, the tiny bedbug, had caught me in his monstrous razor jaws. All thought of sleep gone, I crawled all over the bed on a murderous search while Gloria remained fast asleep. Did her snoring somehow afford her special protection?

Erzurum was not a place to loiter at any time of year and certainly not in November. The overcast sky stole our high spirits

"Look at all these men in grey suits. They don't look at all friendly. There's not one woman around," Gloria said as we drove east through the small village of Horasan.

"Let's lock the doors," I said.

"Thank goodness we don't need petrol."

The menacing clouds added to our foreboding as we ascended the muddy road that twisted and turned like a serpent over the mountains. On this twentieth-century trade route, Mercedes raced past us. We hung behind lumbering TIR trucks, as safe passing places were nonexistent. With relief, we reached the Tahir Pass, at 7,844 feet, and slowly descended before the approaching storm that hid the elegant cone of Mount Ararat. Eager to cover the last few kilometres to the Iranian border, I hit one of the numerous potholes, and Gloria's head hit the roof.

"Ouch! Wilma, slow down before you break the axle and my skull," she said.

"I'm sorry. I want to get out of Turkey. Iran is friendlier with better roads."

At the Turkish-Iranian border, there were long line-ups of trucks, but as a private vehicle, we did not have to wait.

"You have a carnet?" asked the customs officer as he stared at my passport.

"No," I replied, aware of a dull ache between my shoulders. He sighed and filled out thirteen forms while Gloria and I crawled over the Land Rover to answer his demands.

"What is your axle number?"

"Your engine number?"

"You must buy Iranian comprehensive insurance."

I nodded, handed him twenty-three hundred rials, about fifteen British pounds, and thanked him for the signed papers.

The low clouds and rain dampened our elation at crossing another difficult border. I scratched my bedbug bites. One look at the motel in the small town sent us searching for something better. Although it was late afternoon, and despite a headache, we decided to drive another one hundred and seventy miles to Tabriz.

The rain lashed the windscreen. The wipers droned on and on. The buggy followed a wet strip of asphalt. Trucks, lit up like

Christmas trees, loomed out of the murk. It was hard to tell if they were coming or going. The beams from our headlights reduced our world to the sodden wayside. As we doubted the sanity of our decision, the lights of a cafe materialized out of the darkness. We gobbled hot fries and tea. Four huge trucks crunched to a halt on the gravel. We heard the unexpected sound of English voices. Four British truck drivers walked in cursing the weather.

"And where are you girls heading?" they asked, eyebrows raised as if taken aback to see two western women in the middle of nowhere.

"Tonight, Tabriz, but we are driving to Oman near Dubai in Arabia."

"Are you on your own?"

"Yes. Thank God we crossed the Turkish passes before the storm hit. We have had no trouble so far. Touch wood and fingers crossed," I said.

"Gosh, you are lucky. We've just spent three days at the border. We can tell you a few stories to make your hair curl." With my body already tense like a violin string, I did not need to hear horror stories.

"Let's hit the road," Gloria said.

With another eighty miles to a warm bug-free bed, my knuckles tight on the steering wheel, on the edge of my courage, I drove into the night. On the final pass before Tabriz, the rain turned to slush and then snow, and we almost decided to pull over until morning. We changed drivers. Gloria's arms were stiff as she maneuvered along the slippery road. When the lights of Tabriz appeared, we both sighed with relief.

In a modern hotel, hot showers soothed us, and we welcomed spotless sheets. In the morning, my bites subsided, and we agreed to a rest day and some retail therapy. Under the elegant domes and arches of Tabriz's ancient carpet bazaar, we looked over piles of exquisite Persian carpets with beautiful designs, which were out of our price range. By the end of the afternoon, we both purchased *kelims*, woven tapestry rugs, of mellow rusts, blues, and gold.

In the early morning, driving through the sprawling city with the bare trees ready for winter, it was difficult to imagine that Tabriz, Iran's fourth-largest city, with a 2,500-year history of natural disasters and invaders, was believed by some to have been the original site of the Garden of Eden.

Out of the city, the sun burst through the clouds onto plains that were framed by mountains covered in fresh snow.

"It looks so peaceful," I said, cruising past adobe villages.

"The Shah modernized this country," Gloria said.

"Yeah, but he rules with the help of a brutal secret police force, Savak, created with the help of the CIA," I said.

"We don't want to upset anyone."

Close to Tehran, the road became a suicidal racecourse with the most aggressive driving we'd encountered. The trucks sped past, cutting in a few inches from our bumper. My fingernails dug into my palms, and I prepared to take evasive action. By the time we arrived in Tehran, four lanes of rush hour traffic were squished together like sardines. The first hotel we stopped at was fully booked. With dread, we launched ourselves back into the frantic traffic and waited at a red traffic light.

"There's a hotel in a couple of blocks," Gloria told me as she thumbed through the guidebook.

"Let's hope it has a room and parking. I'm exhausted," I replied, yawning.

When the light turned green, I edged to the left and heard a loud crunching noise.

"Oh, God. What have I hit?" An angry taxi driver jumped out and appeared at the window. I sat with my head in my hands before climbing out to inspect the damage. Some men bumped the taxi off our solid aluminum bumper, leaving a tell-tale patch of red paint. A long scrape on the red door of the Toyota did not look so good. I clambered back in, shaking all over, and waited. Behind us, the traffic plunged into chaos. A policeman arrived with a schoolboy interpreter. He declared it was my fault, and I must pay. I waved the comprehensive insurance policy I had purchased at the border.

"You can go to the office and pay the day after tomorrow. Tomorrow is a holiday," the boy translated.

"But we won't be here. We drive to Isfahan tomorrow," I explained.

"Then you must pay four hundred Rials."

"But I have insurance. I will only pay two hundred Rials," I replied. Unimpressed at my offer, the driver shook his head. With massive resignation, I took out four hundred Rials and waved it towards the taxi driver.

"No, I want five hundred," the reply came through the schoolboy.

"Hurry up," instructed the policeman. "Show me your driving license." I gave him my international one and kept my British and Omani licenses hidden.

"Come to the police station," he said. We followed him to the other side of the road, but there was no police station. Another policeman who spoke English arrived. He listened to Gloria's re-telling our side of the story.

"You pay five hundred," he commanded.

"But at the beginning, they asked for four hundred," I explained.

"You pay four hundred," he said. I paid up and drove to the nearest hotel. Drained and teary, we fell into the room and sipped whiskey out of our Turkish tea glasses.

"I'm mad. What was I thinking to challenge their authority? I should have paid up and left," I said.

"I thought the insurance we bought at the border was supposed to cover an incident like that," Gloria said.

I remember reading that, at some point, a journey goes from bad to worse, to ridiculous, and finally, to the tragicomic. The next morning, I opened the buggy's back door, creasing my brow as I smelled a pungent odor. To my dismay, my bags and suitcases sat in a viscous liquid, which I gingerly touched. When I withdrew my slimy fingers, they dripped with oil.

For the second time in twenty-four hours, tears trickled over my cheeks. I picked up our spare gallon can of oil. Its lid was tight, but it was empty. I noticed a small hole near the bottom of the can where it had rubbed on the lip of the door. Dejected, we removed our Turkish overnight bags, three suitcases, and a trunk, and wiped up a gallon of oil with old rags provided by the hotel staff.

By midday, we headed to the post office. With great determination, we waited in a long line up to send a telegram to our husbands. This was the first and only time we contacted them. We said we missed them and were well. As we walked down the post office steps, Gloria slipped and sprawled in the mud. My overwrought body didn't know whether to laugh or cry.

As I helped her up, I asked, "Have you broken anything? Do you need to go to the hospital?"

"I'm fine," she said. "I need to get out of this city."

Gloria, tight-lipped in her muddy jeans and turtleneck, walked slowly to our vehicle. I eased into the traffic, battling with double-decker buses and Mercedes.

"Watch that bullock cart," she said. "We need to turn left somewhere. Look for a sign to Esfahan."

"Look at that car. Those eyes painted on the trunk are mocking us."

"Careful of that three-wheeled-scooter. Heavens, it's stacked with four boxes. The man sitting on top looks as if he's about to fall off. Geez, those black exhaust fumes are gross. Yikes, lookout for the man on the donkey. God, this is crazy."

We left the chaos of the city, the traffic thinned, and we purred over excellent roads across the desert. Because of the delays in Tehran, we were forced to drive in the dark. Then on the dashboard the red ignition light came on. Together, we groaned as we pulled off the road.

"This happened to us in Oman. I am sure it's the fan belt," Gloria announced as she pulled out the handbook and thumbed through the pages to find a description of the problem. Her superior mechanical knowledge impressed me.

After studying the manual, I declared with more confidence than I felt, "We can fix this." I lay on the cold gravel, under the engine, fiercely resolute to use my physical strength to loosen a bolt. I pulled my Afghan coat around me as my freezing fingers pulled on the spanner. After forty-five minutes, I realized my efforts were futile. I battled with my principles, my fears of asking for help, and my terror at revealing our female vulnerability in the pitch dark of the Iranian desert. I looked at the twinkling sky, wishing that the problem would go away.

"This is impossible. We need help, Gloria," I said.

"We are miles from anywhere," she said. "I'll stay inside for the moment. Nobody will know we are two women travelling alone. I'll be ready to help you if necessary."

Petrified, I stood by the road and stuck up my thumb at the next set of headlights that loomed out of the night. A huge truck roared past. My heart thundered as I pulled my coat tighter against the bitter blast of air. The third vehicle stopped. As soon as I saw a woman wedged between two men, my panic subsided. Maybe we would not be raped, or murdered, or have our vehicle stolen. The men jumped out and scurried around their pick-up truck for a container and a pipe.

"No, no, we have petrol. It's the fan-belt," I said in English. He did not understand. I shook my head and pointed to the engine and the fan belt. This man did not use the spanner, but with simple brute strength, he yanked the cog into the appropriate place. Within five minutes, we were back on the road to Isfahan, the red light off, and our new guardian angels following us.

CIRCLING THE EDGE

An hour later in Isfahan, we slunk into the most expensive hotel in town. The staff indicated that we could park in a space beside the front door. We grabbed our overnight bags, took the elevator to our luxurious room, and soaked in steaming hot baths.

For two days, we revelled in Isfahan's long distinguished history at the crossroads of Iran. We slipped back in time as we explored shady boulevards across covered bridges and past the blue-tiled domes of the mosques and minarets. We lingered in bazaars filled with the crafts of skilled artisans: jewellery, coffee pots, and carved brass plates. As if in a Persian miniature painting, we enjoyed the vaulted galleries decorated with blue tiles. We sipped tea in the gracious serenity of the hotel's walled garden. On the second afternoon, the hotel staff asked me to move my vehicle. I discovered, because they did not like where it was parked, that someone had let the tires down. I demanded to see the manager.

"How dare they let down my tires? Why couldn't they have told me? They are so ignorant!" I ranted to Gloria. A man showed up with a hand pump that he attached to the tire. I told a noisy male bystander to shut up, which triggered a stream of abuse from him.

"Iran best-est country. All British girls are loose."

"I am *not* loose! I am angry!" I yelled as I checked the tire gauge.

"More!" I shouted. He pumped the tires up until they looked like balloons. This mild-mannered Iranian was not about to argue with me, a raving white woman. Meanwhile, Gloria discreetly disappeared to the hotel room. Then, to my utter humiliation, I realized I'd misread the tire gauge, reading thirty-five kilograms rather than thirty-five pounds per square inch. I cried as I slunk down the road to the garage.

Back on the road, the Land Rover hummed over mile upon mile of empty desert road. Gloria listened to me as I explained my outburst, blaming the hotel staff and worrying about the next calamity. "Rather than interfere, I thought it best to leave you to sort it out," she said. I nodded. Our next overnight stop was in the town of Yazd.

"Two Mrs and no Mr?" the puzzled receptionist repeated as she read Gloria's passport upside down. As we walked to a local restaurant, I watched the earth's shadow grow over the moon, captivated as it turned a dull red colour. We sat in the local restaurant under fluorescent lights, enjoying Iranian *abgoosht*—a kind of stew with lamb, chickpeas, potatoes, and delicious spices. I kept peeking out the window to watch the progress of the eclipse.

"I read that Yazd was an ancient centre for Zoroastrianism. The founder of this religion believed that you could follow the good Lord Ahuramasda or the bad Lord Ahriman," I said.

"He thought that, if humans worked with the earth, we could create heaven here."

"What a concept: heaven on earth. My mother believes that heaven is in the afterlife," I replied.

"Who knows? Apparently, the kilometres of water tunnels or qanats are about two and a half thousand years old," Gloria read from the guide book.

"Too bad we haven't time to visit the town. Who knows what will happen in Bander Abbas?"

"I have the name of a shipping agent. They'll help us find a dhow. It will work out," Gloria, ever the optimist, assured me.

"I'm ready for bed. Let's see how the eclipse is doing," I said. The earth's shadow had moved on, leaving a mysterious aura around the full moon.

Bandar Abbas, the home of the Iranian navy and a major shipping port, had a long history of coastal trade with India, Arabia, and East Africa. Without a regular ferry to cross the Persian Gulf to Dubai in the United Arab Emirates, we needed to find a Dhow. Dhow was the generic name of traditional sailing vessels that were around five hundred tons, with one or more masts and lateen sails, replaced in modern times with engines.

Without a doubt, we were on a journey and not a guided tour. We phoned the shipping agent Gray Mackenzie. Someone replied,

"Come to the office, after *qailulah*, at four o'clock this afternoon." Gloria recognized this word to mean a short mid-day nap, like a siesta, which was a practice embedded in Muslim culture. We phoned again at three-thirty. No answer. We set out to look for the office, which we found locked. We phoned again at seven o'clock, and a Mr. Kardooni answered. "I will come to your hotel at eight o'clock tomorrow morning."

"*Inshallah*." God willing.

The following morning, to our joy, Mr. Kardooni arrived on time, dressed in a smart suit. We exchanged greetings in Arabic:

"*Kayf Haalak?*" How are you?

"*Bi-khayr, al-Hamdu lillah.*" Fine, praise God.

With his translator, a businessman from Tehran, we drove to an office building. When Mr. Kardooni disappeared for forty-five minutes, we sat discouraged with nothing to do. On his return, we drove to the docks to look for the "launch" as he called the dhows. On the dock, Arabs wearing *dish-dashes*—long traditional robes—passed hessian sacs onto the wooden deck of the forty-foot boat. Mr. Kardooni talked to the captain in his brown dish-dash and spotless turban. Reluctant to take us as passengers, the captain suggested we leave the Land Rover with him while we flew to Dubai. We shook our heads. Through the translator, we learned that the weather could be stormy, but he agreed to take us if we did not rush him. With the impression that the boat might leave that afternoon, but it may take two or three days to get to Dubai, we returned to our hotel to wait on the whim of our captain

The following morning, the wind blew hard, and we worried that the weather might take days to clear. At eleven, Mr. Kardooni drove us to the docks.

"Bring your vehicle at two p.m.," the captain told us.

With our departure out of our control, and with nothing else to do, we walked along the litter-strewn beach, as the dust-filled wind whipped sand in our faces. Time dragged as uncertainty ate into us.

At two o'clock, we found our way to the docks. Again, we waited for Mr. Kardooni, but this time he arrived with a crane. Two men pushed a solid wooden plank through the open windows of a Volkswagen car, attached a rope to either end, and the crane lifted the vehicle into the air. To our surprise, the roof did not bend. It swayed over the dhow and was lowered onto the deck. They placed wires on either end of the Land Rover's front bumper while they attached our tow rope to the back bumper and rested the plank across the roof rack. The ropes creaked as the vehicle swung and dangled at a precarious angle over the dhow, while the huge hull of a grain ship, the *Atlantic Horizon,* dwarfed both.

Once on the deck, three crew members stood on our roof as they removed the ropes. The sides of the dhow reached the middle of our wheels. The crew cast off. The dhow, which looked perilously small in comparison to the massive ships and tankers, drifted away over the glassy water to some unseen anchorage. Driving back from the docks, we followed grain trucks spilling their cargo. Women in threadbare baggy clothes swept up the grain from the road. I felt distressed to witness their desperation.

On our third night in Bander Abbas, we had used up our determination. As we ate supper, Gloria and I speculated if we were ever going to cross the Gulf. In the morning, we were still uncertain if we would leave that day, but when Mr. Kardooni arrived, we checked out of the hotel. On the dock, we said our farewells and thanked Mr. Kardooni. At noon, after our captain took us through customs, we scrambled onto a small boat with an engine. Enroute to the anchorage, we stopped at a police control. After warning us not to take photos of the Iranian Navy, the policeman paddled alongside us in a small dugout canoe. Just when we saw the dhow with our Land Rover in the distance, the policeman requested that our captain go back to the shore with our passports. After another forty-five-minute wait, he returned. We puttered over the choppy sea to our dhow, which bobbed amongst dozens of dhows swinging on their anchors on the afternoon breeze.

Once onboard, we acknowledged the crew with *"Salam alaikum."* May peace be upon you. I could have mistaken our crew for pirates. A young man who wore a white turban, a pink long-sleeved shirt, and a green dhoti, a strip of cloth wrapped around his waist, heaved up the anchor rope. His taut biceps pulled the bilge pump lever and left an oily film on the surface of the sea. Another couple of crew members pulled up a cloth made of old sacs around the short deck walls and lashed it to rickety wooden rods.

"That'll give us a little more protection if it gets rough," I said.

"I had scary visions of our vehicle toppling into the ocean depths and never seeing it again," Gloria said.

"I suppose that's why no one will insure a trip like this."

A couple of crew members came out of the cabin. They said something in Arabic as they waved their arms around and unrolled a Persian carpet on the deck space in front of our vehicle.

"Shukran," we said, gratefully nodding our heads.

"Wow, we're getting the royal treatment,"

"Thank God, we're on our way. I thought we'd never leave," I said.

"I expected to wait on the anchorage until the weather turned good, or at least until the morning," Gloria said, as we sat cross-legged on the carpet and spread out our handbags, journals, and books.

"I'm curious about how long the trip will take. One or two days?" I said.

"Who knows? What are the names of those islands? Let's look at the map," she said.

Gloria laid out our Bartholomew's sheet map of the Middle East. The captain and several of the crew walked over the flour sacs and joined us on the carpet. They chatted enthusiastically amongst themselves. Our captain removed his toothpick from his nicotinic teeth to point out our route, north of the Straits of Hormuz to Dubai.

They returned to their work. The smell of curry mingled with the sea air. Gloria and I dug through our bags for our cameras to capture the watery sun sinking into the Persian Gulf. To our astonishment, a crew member brought us each a plate of fresh fish, limes, and rice.

"*Shukran,*" we smiled in gratitude.

"I never expected to get fed too. This is delicious. Much better than our crackers and cheese," she said.

"These guys are amazing. I don't feel scared anymore. They respect us," I said.

"And the sea is glassy. I expected a raging storm," she said.

When night came, we lay in our sleeping bags and stretched out on the carpet. I stared in awe at the velvet sky speckled with a multitude of stars that stretched to infinity. As the dhow cruised over the calm waters towards Dubai, I thought of how men had sailed these waters for thousands of years. Totally engrossed I witnessed the age-old skills of these dedicated sailors and felt the universe hold me in an intoxicating embrace.

Gloria with our captain and crew

The crimson orb of the sun rose out of the eastern sea and cast pink light on the blonde arid coast of The United Arab Emirates. The dhow motored up the creek—the long arm of the sea that dissected the tall skyscrapers of Dubai. Large wooden dhows, golden in the morning light, lined the wharf. With no space on the dock, the captain maneuvered alongside another dhow. One of our crew threw a rope. It fell on what appeared to be cargo, but a man jumped up from underneath a sack and let out an angry stream of Arabic. This time, we did not have long to wait before our dapper captain, now in a lime green turban, conducted the efficient unloading operation.

"The trip was much shorter than I expected," I said.

"It was awesome. Let's hope customs are not as complicated as Iran," Gloria said.

Unloading in Dubai

We proceeded with ease through our second last border. By mid-morning, we were driving along the modern streets of Dubai.

"It's only a day's drive to Oman," I said happily.

"It's impossible to get a map to show us the route. They don't exist."

"Gloria, it's four weeks since we left London."

"It's been a grand adventure. I can't believe we'll see our husbands tomorrow," she said.

In dismay, I watched women walk, their black burkas swirling in the breeze with only their eyes visible, accompanied by men in white dish-dashes.

The following day, we drove for a couple of kilometres along a modern two-lane tarmac highway. As instructed, we turned right at a modern roundabout and bumped straight onto a corrugated road that took us into a desert landscape with no shade or vegetation.

Through black volcanic hills, we wound along a dirt road, unsure if we were headed in the right direction. Here in the middle of scorched mountains, with not a soul in sight to ask for directions and just before our final destination, we were lost. The potholed road became narrower; tufts of dried grass grew between the two tire treads on the gravel. We continued and followed our noses to a hut that looked like an old garden shed. We spotted a small, faded sign that said, "The border post - Khatmat al Maiaha," while our entry papers said, "Buraimi Al-Ain." What to do? "Let's just play stupid," Gloria said.

"It would never occur to me that it might be an advantage to pretend to be ignorant," I said.

In the hut, a few officials jabbered in Arabic and waved their arms as they huddled around the table, examining our papers. We were quiet when an official squeezed into our vehicle and guided us to the new border post only fifteen minutes away.

With feelings that flip-flopped between elation and sadness, we drove the last one hundred and fifty miles on a new tarmac road. At Gloria's house, John and Clive warmly hugged us. After congratulations and cups of tea, Clive—who couldn't wait to get his hands on his new toy—left me speechless with his suggestion: "Let's drive five hundred miles to the salt domes this weekend, just to test the Land Rover out!"

"We have just driven it six thousand miles," I said.

It proved to be an enormous honour and a privilege to explore Oman's spellbinding deserts, villages, and mountains before it entered the modern era. I loved the wide-open skies, the rock amphitheatres, and above all, the peaceful friendly Omani people.

Me, looking up the north face of Jebel Akdar – at ten thousand feet it is Oman's highest mountain.

Descending Jebel Akdar

CIRCLING THE EDGE

Mohamed our barefoot guide on the summit of Jebel Akdar -he guided us halfway up the mountain from his village. Then we showed him the route that some of our friends had explored through the cliff bands to the summit. He enjoyed seeing his homeland from this new perspective.

Desert hospitality - mother and daughter make us coffee.

Children in Al Hamra dressed up to celebrate Eid.

The Wali and his sons from Al Hamra

Clive and his parents enjoying coffee in the mountain hamlet of Hal-hal

CHAPTER 10

Deepest, Darkest England

"You must understand the whole of life, not just one little part of it. That is why you must read, that is why you must look at the skies, that is why you must sing and dance, and write poems and suffer, and understand, for all that is life."
~ J. Krishnamurti

November 1975

On an overcast day, in a junior secondary school in northeast England, as a science teacher, I stood in the laboratory, holding a fire extinguisher. The pinhole cameras I had constructed with boxes and greaseproof paper were in flames. With no thought of scientific observations, the young male pyromaniacs were gleeful. With my hard work in charred fragments, my jaw wobbled and my teeth clamped, but I knew that to cry in front of them would be my ultimate failure.

A few months earlier in Oman, to avoid a future as expatriate alcoholics, Clive decided to return to Durham University to do a Master of Science in Geophysics. At first, I resisted, but the promise of more travel won me over. For four months, we drove through Iran, Pakistan, Afghanistan, Turkey, and Europe.

Back in Britain, we settled into a one-bedroom council flat in a coal mining village. Esh Winning was not the cutesy English village I had imagined overseas. There were no pink roses and hollyhocks curled around pretty thatched cottages. This was a working-class estate with blocks of flats, peeling paint, dog poop, and litter scattered in the grass. It claimed to be the only village in Britain that had run the policeman out. In the early 1970s, when the coal mines closed, it had caused industrial unrest and resulted in unemployment that produced poverty, depression, and yawning apathy. This opened my eyes to people as unfamiliar as those I'd encountered on my travels.

One autumn day, with orange leaves swirling around us, we met our neighbours. After a life of working down the coal mines, the old man above us suffered from the "dust." His loud hacking coughs rumbled through the ceiling and interrupted our sleep.

"What are you doing, sonny?" he asked Clive, ignoring me.

"I'm studying for my master's degree at the university," Clive said.

"Could you no' be doing something better than that, laddie?" he asked.

"I leave my milk float full in the garage overnight," the milkman across the road informed us. "God help anyone that breaks in. They wouldn't get out alive. Come, I'll show you my gun."

"When we first arrived here, we had nothing," our social-studies-student neighbours Carl and Suzie told us. "Bits and pieces of furniture mysteriously appear on our doorstep. People are kind."

"How generous! What happened to your eye? It's bruised," I asked.

"Last weekend, we were invited to a party next door," Carl said. "My neighbour and his brother started to fight. I tried to intervene, but both brothers and their wives began to punch me. I couldn't believe it."

While Clive expanded his understanding of geophysics, I fought a losing battle as a science and math teacher. I expected my pupils to sit like angels, awed by my superior knowledge, and listen to the sound of my voice. No one at teacher-training college had addressed classroom management, or how to motivate kids, or how to encourage them to listen. Brainwashed by the unspoken British class system, I was ignorant about how to develop human potential.

My boss, a kind man with gold-rimmed glasses, ran the science department. Like a magician, he performed miracles with the teenage boys. Using his wizardry with welding equipment and tin cans, he taught them how to build model steam engines. He encouraged my efforts, but I was overwhelmed. Fire in the science lab was one thing, but my unruly math classes were misery. Thirty young teenagers wandered around the classroom, yelling and swearing. My reprimands had no impact, and my mathematical explanations were wasted. In a moment of frustration, I pinched one girl's arm. A few days later, the headmaster called me into his office.

"Elizabeth's mother came in and complained about the bruise on her daughter's arm."

"S-she refused to do her geometry and k-kept yelling across the room," I stuttered as I fought back tears. In the silence of the night, I imagined humiliating tongue-lashings by my Scottish forefathers: *"You should be ashamed of yourself! You'll never make a good teacher!"* After a couple of terms, shocked at my act of inflicting pain on a child, and with Clive's support, I resigned.

In the spring, as blackbirds sang and flitted in the apple blossoms, ignoring the litter and dog poop, Clive and I walked to the village pub, arriving at ten thirty p.m. for a quick pint. Several evenings, after the heavy wooden pub door closed at eleven, with the low light glinting off the brass horseshoes on the walls, Tony, the six-foot-tall, rotund publican, invited us to join the locals, and we drank into the small hours.

"If that customs and excise man comes here with his snooping ways, I'll finish him off and bury his body in six feet of concrete in the cellar," Tony told us. "He would never be found."

"If any woman dares to mess with my Tony, I'll scratch her eyes out," his wife added.

This led to my next job: barmaid. This was another secret I hid from my mother to protect myself from her statements about the evils of alcohol. The other barmaid's hair curled over her slender shoulders as she poured pints of beer while her husband sat at the other side of the bar drinking her earnings. He kept his jealous eyes alert, allegedly to protect her.

"He sleeps with a bread knife under his pillow," she told me fearfully. "I can hardly get up to go to the toilet at night without him thinking I'm trying to escape. He has held me at knifepoint more than once. What can I do?" I had nothing to offer. Domestic abuse was unmentionable.

During the day, on the moors, Clive and I strode out over the heather, our calf muscles stretched and strong, while he took gravity measurements for his research. After a couple of years in the desert, the fresh wind, the new leaves, the fragrance of the earth, and the constant birdsong enlivened us. In the evenings, desperate to shut out my conflict about my role as a woman and failure as a teacher, I typed Clive's thesis. A month hiking in Norway thrilled us both.

In the fall of 1976, Clive accepted a position at British Petroleum in London. Frozen with dread of unruly children, I attended an interview for a science teacher position.

"What makes you think you are qualified for this job?" I mumbled my answer, and their rejection was a relief.

When I found a job in a medical lab, I felt fortunate to find work that used my microbiology degree and the experience I had gained as a medical lab technician in Oman. On my first day, I strode out of the crowded underground, jostling with Londoners who crouched under their umbrellas, avoiding puddles. I stepped down the steps into the mildewed basement of the private doctor's office in Mayfair Place. This was nothing like Oman's up-to-date modern laboratory in which I had worked. The domestic fridge held plastic phials encrusted with dried blood. I imagined I'd be infected with a life-threatening disease. That step towards my brilliant career lasted a whole day and a half.

With the bright future I had envisioned for myself in ruins, I returned to job-hunting, filled in application forms, waited for interviews, walked past the houses of Parliament, and stared at the clock face of Big Ben as damp seeped into my bone marrow. In social situations, I happily bragged, "I have climbed the highest mountain in Arabia. I have been to India." Yet in the silence of the night, my inner demons conjured up ghoulish dreams revealing a gnawing unworthiness.

When I awoke, my left hip and back ached. What was the matter with me? Society had led me to believe that, as the wife of a well-dressed husband who left each morning for his office in the city, I would be satisfied. As a dutiful daughter of patriarchy, I performed my wifely duties, ironed shirts, did laundry, baked wholemeal bread, and cooked dinner. Both my sisters produced babies soon after their marriages. But despite my thwarted career, I was not ready for motherhood.

Feeling powerless, I withdrew like a turtle, hiding my soft vulnerable parts with an impenetrable shell. When Clive asked me what was wrong, I answered with my teeth clenched, "Nothing, I'm fine." I still believed that, if he loved me, he would know what I needed without any communication on my part. My emotional cauldron simmered for several days before erupting in venomous rage.

At my lowest ebb, in an attempt to challenge my poor self-esteem, I pasted a copy of Max Ehrman's inspirational poem, "Desiderata" on the wall. *"Be gentle with yourself. You are a child of the universe, no less than the trees and the stars: you have a right to be here."* Again, Mother's God was mute in my angst. Indeed, fearing her judgement, I could not talk to her. In time, I became aware that rejection was not the worst outcome. I had to take action on my own behalf.

I swallowed my intellectual arrogance and enrolled at a secretarial agency. On my first typing job at the post office, I painstakingly searched the Olivetti keyboard for the letters. The permanent young women completed page after page before I finished one. Every time I made a mistake, I had to start again. I blushed when the typist opposite me said, "Oh, that poor typewriter!"

I found a permanent position in a scientific employment agency, in an office whose nicotine-coated walls had not been painted in years. I pretended I was using my science degree, but this was a blind alley. I consumed mugs of coffee until my eyes twitched as if electrocuted. I made phone calls on behalf of others and celebrated when my boss placed someone. At lunchtime, inhaling exhaust fumes, I walked to St. Paul's Cathedral where I sat under its majestic dome as uplifting organ recitals soothed my troubled spirit.

I accepted a job as a research assistant performing clinical trials for a cardiac pacemaker company. For all intents and purposes, I was a shepherdess with a herd of seven sheep with cardiac pacemakers surgically inserted in their clavicles. I sought to bring some scientific rigour to the haphazard trials. My training led to an unexpected detour: a couple of visits to a London teaching hospital to observe open-heart surgery and the insertion of pacemakers. In the operating theatre, covered in a white coat, mask, and gloves, I observed the hierarchy of doctors. The youngest performed the first incision, the second burned through the flesh, the third cut open the ribs, and the fourth, a bushy-browed consultant, poked his pinkie finger through the tricuspid valve to release yellow gunk and proceeded to stitch up the patient hidden underneath layers of green cloths and tubes. To keep myself from fainting, I gazed in awe at the glistening aorta, the human ribs, and the majesty of the pumping heart.

Back in the pacemaker factory, my erudite, suit-clad male manager was reported making sexual passes to the youngest female technical assistant. To protect her, several of us ensured that she was never alone with him. There were no official lines of complaint. His abusive behaviour was swept under the carpet. When this man promoted me to my immediate supervisor's position, I asked for a pay rise. "You have a husband and can't expect to get the same pay as John. He has a wife and two kids to support," he audaciously replied.

After a year, the factory closed, my small herd of sheep were euthanized, and I became redundant. Another chapter in the life of my less than brilliant career came to a sticky end. British Petroleum offered Clive a posting to Denver in the United States, thrilling us both. In a few weeks, when this fell through, I found myself stuck with no job and no travel prospects.

Scrambling along An Tealach Ridge, Scotland.

Our mountaineering-weekend escapes to the Lake District, North Wales, and Scotland found me spread-eagled on precipitous rock faces, following Clive's courageous rock-climbing leads. Striding through the heather, breathing fresh mountain air, we both found solace and exhilaration in nature and each other. While these trips satisfied our hunger to wander in hills, back in London, our mutual dissatisfaction with urban living propelled us to seek alternative interests. Although we could not travel to eastern cultures, there were opportunities to learn about their complexities from English-speaking instructors. We enrolled in Buddhism and meditation classes. My life took a guarded turn inwards.

After work, we met in a basement classroom with fluorescent light, expecting a long-haired hippie. Instead, a middle-aged man in a grey business suit, smoking cigarettes, introduced us to Buddhism. He taught us about the eightfold pathway and how human suffering came from craving, ignorance, and attachment. As I sat in meditation, I observed spasms in my stomach. I thought I had outgrown my mother's religion, but believe it or not, I heard her voice in my mind: *"Work out your own salvation with fear and trembling."*

One evening, my instructor challenged me. "Can you truly focus on doing more than one thing at a time? Like eating and reading the newspaper?" Rather than argue or discuss, he sent me away to learn from my experience and discover for myself. "You don't need to accept anything until you know it to be true for you." His invitation was revolutionary.

I thought about the Buddhist belief in cyclic existence and reincarnation.

"Why is it easier for a man to reach enlightenment than a woman? Why, if I am well behaved in this life, might I be reincarnated as a man or a holy cow?" I questioned our teacher and did not receive a convincing answer. I asked myself, *Don't I, as a woman, despite my emotional turbulence, have value? Does my inferiority as a woman somehow contribute to my feelings of failure? What is it about a penis makes men superior?* No matter what religion I investigated—Islam, Christianity, or Buddhism—women were subservient to men.

In a meditation class, I sat cross-legged on a cushion, listening to the instructions of Sri Lankan monks dressed in orange robes:

"Count up to ten breaths. Breathe in, hold, breathe out one, breathe in, hold, breathe out two... Pay attention to the air going in and out past your nose hairs. If you lose count return to one..."

Within minutes, I lost count, and my wayward thoughts focused on everyday things: *What's for dinner? How are we going to pay the mortgage? My bum is sore.*

Wait a minute, I told myself, *back to my breath: breathe in, hold, breathe out, one.* Maybe I'd reach five counts before the monkey chatter diverted my attention: *My legs are going to sleep. My office job is boring. My stomach is fat. My head hurts. I can't wait to go to the mountains next weekend.* Like a dog holding on to its favourite bone, my mind was tenacious. However, when the monks instructed me to breathe into my headaches, to release the tension on the out-breath, to my amazement, I found the throbbing eased.

Next, we learned "Loving Kindness" meditation.

"Think of someone you love. Recognize the feelings that are evoked in your body. Extend those sensations of love to yourself." I did experience warmth in my upper chest, but I was more familiar with self-judgement than self-love.

"Next, take a few minutes to extend these feelings to someone you love." With ease, I radiated love toward Clive.

"Now, send feelings of light and love to someone you dislike or hate." This practice I found almost impossible. I thought love was hit or miss; either someone loved you or they didn't. While I had no idea if this practice had any measurable impact on others, afterwards, I felt calm. But some nights after the meditation, I woke from my old nightmare of a man with his hands around my neck.

I imagined these monks, from the palm-fringed beaches of Ceylon, were like Buddhist missionaries. Under their shaved heads, their beaming smiles and aura of contentment intrigued me. In contrast, with their woollen socks wrinkled around their ankles as they carried cans of antifreeze to their car, they did not fit my picture of pious monks. Their wise advice challenged me: "The trick is to take the stillness found in meditation or the forest back to Piccadilly Circus."

We both enrolled in an adult education class on Gestalt psychology. On the first night in a school classroom with blackboards and a periodic chart on the wall, thirty participants sat in a circle. The middle-aged lecturer walked in late and dishevelled. He wiped his forehead and red cheeks with a crumpled handkerchief as he sat down on a creaky chair and silently looked around the room. Most of us fidgeted on our chairs.

"How do you feel? What is going on for you?" he asked in his lilting Irish accent. As a diligent student, I sat poised with my pen and paper, prepared to make notes, which I expected to rote learn. "How do you feel?" he repeated, ignoring our notepads and pens. At that moment, the teacher-student expectation shifted one hundred and eighty degrees. He asked me to present information about myself. How did I know if I would be right or wrong? Nobody had ever asked me about my feelings. My mother thought anger was a dreadful flaw. In this stiff-upper-lip culture, crying was a sign of weakness and something to be ashamed of. Now my temples and head throbbed. What was I supposed to learn in this situation, with no lecture, no notes, and no books?

Over the weeks, some insights came to me. I became aware that, in Clive's presence, I hesitated to speak up. What if he didn't like what I said? I had been a child who was seen and not heard. No one encouraged me to speak up—not my family and not at school or university. In one class, to my discomfort, and aware of throbbing in my pelvic area, I questioned: *Nice girls aren't supposed to feel that way or talk about erotica. Am I becoming a brazen hussy?* While I enjoyed sex with Clive, I expected to be the passive recipient of his desire. Sex was not something I initiated. My mother or my sisters or girlfriends never spoke about their sexual desires. I thought that my mother, like biblical Mary, had an immaculate conception. In class, I remained silent.

On the last night of the course, I found the courage to ask, "How do I make decisions?" The simple answer stayed with me:

"Think about it as if you're deciding whether you want a cup of tea or a cup of coffee. Imagine you had one and how you would feel at the end of it."

Like good academics, Clive and I rushed to the bookstore to read about Fritz Perls, the creator of Gestalt therapy. This planted small seeds of a radical way of living: being in the moment, in touch with my feelings, and taking responsibility for myself.

Using my improved typing skills, I worked three days a week in an insurance office and spent two days exploring my new interest, history, which had been awakened by my travels. In the vast British Museum, I studied the rise and fall of ancient Empires. Intricate carvings on the Elgin marbles from the Parthenon in Athens, Egyptian mummies, hieroglyphics on the Rosetta Stone, and the laws of Hammurabi from Mesopotamia all confirmed the skilled craftsmanship of long-dead people.

One morning, puzzling about the demise of civilizations, I left the museum's entrance of Greek columns, climbed down the worn steps, and walked to the Theosophist Bookstore. The old door creaked, and the bell tinkled as I pushed it open. Smelling the musty books crammed onto the shelves, I crossed squeaking floorboards and delved into this Aladdin's cave of philosophy and world religions. My hunger to understand the meaning of my life overpowered my childhood dragons, which continued to bellow, *"You shalt have no other Gods before me."*

Quieting my inner voices, I left clutching a book by the modern philosopher Krishnamurti. In direct opposition to my mother's conviction that trust in Jesus would make me whole, I read, *"In oneself lies the whole world and if you know how to look and learn, the door is there and the key is in your hand. Nobody on earth can give you either the key or the door to open, except yourself."* While Gestalt and meditation had opened my inner door a chink, I puzzled over this statement.

A week later, back in the bookstore, I purchased *Tao Te Ching*, a book by the ancient Chinese philosopher Lao Tzu. His instruction bewildered me: *"If you can empty yourself of everything, you will have lasting peace... If you want to be filled, become empty."*

The Tao of Love and Sex – the Ancient Chinese way to Ecstasy, by Jolan Chang, demanded my attention with the engaging quote on its back cover: *"Sex may be joyful, but only loving can be a true joy."* Worried that my interest in sexual pleasure would be judged, I never dared to share this book with my sisters. I read that these ancient Chinese masters thought that love, food, exercise, and good sex promoted longevity. That they paid great attention to the sexual satisfaction of women astounded me. The Tao of Loving master, seventh-century physician Li T'ung Hsuan, endorsed the benefits of a *"thousand loving thrusts with his jade stick into her jade gate."* I had a willing partner in the practical exploration of this concept.

Jolan Chang's belief about women jumped off the page: *"In the Taoist scheme of things, man is a yang force, and he has all the attributes of maleness. He is more volatile, more active and quicker than a woman, who has the attributes of Yin, the female force. She is more placid, her movements calmer – but ultimately she is stronger."* I never felt stronger competing in a man's world—not out in the mountains nor in the workplace. But I wanted to.

A weeklong adult-education course, "In Search of Self," attracted me. In the enrollment queue, sixth in line, my feet twisted and turned on the worn tiled floor. *Will I? Won't I?* I tottered on edge as my fear of looking within threatened to overpower me, in case I found there an unredeemable flaw. As I moved to the counter, with my jaw locked and my hands clammy, I resolved to stay.

That enlightening week, I was introduced to the hexagrams of *I Ching*, which in Mother's world was the evil world of the occult. But rather than being punished, smitten down by the devil, the material and the people I met stimulated my innate inclination towards growth and provided the antidote to the toxicity of the poisoned apples.

One wet February day, the winds blew in our Edinburgh University friends Tommy and Fi, who had moved to New Zealand. They enthusiastically painted a vivid picture of their wonderful life.

"You can ski and sail on the same day," Tommy said. "The ski hills are only half an hour from the beach. Fi is involved in a successful environmental campaign. It's easier to be effective down there." They raved about kayak trips on untamed rivers and climbing glaciated mountains. After their departure, London's traffic, the crowded underground, and the endless drizzle challenged me more than ever.

Synchronicity intervened. The following week, Clive answered an advert in the paper for a geophysicist position in New Zealand. Silence ensued. In the meantime, BP offered Clive a two-year posting in Stavanger, Norway. We ordered a brand-new Renault 4 with a left-hand drive and the required specifications for Europe. While I craved travel, I was unsure what I would do without a working visa in Stavanger.

Weeks passed, and Clive did not hear back from New Zealand. He wrote a letter, stating he was no longer interested, and put it in his briefcase. The next day, he received a phone call from the New Zealand High Commission asking him for an interview. With nothing to lose, he attended the meeting, and then, to his amazement, they offered to fly him to New Zealand for a second interview. Without thinking twice, he told his manager he was taking a week's vacation in Scotland. After his interview in Wellington, and with a job offer in hand, he visited Tommy and Fi, who were now parents of a baby boy.

Clive returned jet-lagged and fell asleep at his office desk. Energized by the wonders of New Zealand, we had a real decision to make. We agonized for days. Which country did we choose? Pros: I could work in New Zealand, while I couldn't in Norway. Cons: New Zealand was far away while Norway was just a ferry crossing from Scotland. In the end, despite its position at the bottom of the earth, New Zealand won. A visit to the New Zealand High Commission for our visas led us to believe that those two islands in the Southern Oceans were paradise and that only a fortunate few were permitted into the country the locals called "God's own."

Before I headed to the other side of the planet, I reflected on the unfinished business we had talked about in Gestalt, in particular my difficult relationship with my mother. While her dogmatic beliefs irritated me, I worried about her living alone. Moreover, there had been the shadow of an older woman in my early life. Doctor Dorothy Seton had delivered me at home in Aberdeen. My mother, a midwife herself, admired this woman and had appointed her my godmother. Her christening gift, a silver mug engraved with "Wilma Grace," sat tarnished on my bookshelf. For some reason, I felt compelled to visit my godmother, whom I had not seen since my father died. As far as I knew, Mother rarely phoned her. Unusual for her time, she was a childless career woman, a pioneer. Did I unconsciously seek her approval for my travels?

I drove through Aberdeen's streets, which were lined with dull granite houses, and knocked on her door. The doctor, dressed in a Harris Tweed suit, welcomed me into her comfortable garden apartment. She served me tea in bone china along with a plate of dainty cakes. I shared some of my adventures, how I had taught in India and worked in the hospital laboratory in Oman. Her full-frontal attack winded me worse than if I had fallen off a cliff. "Your father was a God-fearing man. He deserved better than you."

"But...!" I spluttered in self-defence.

My eyes and heart stung with her cruel condemnation as I drove through my beloved Highlands to meet with my mother. The roadside trees bent precariously in the wind as the windscreen wipers droned.

I picked Mother up at the Aviemore railway station. "On the train, I prayed for good weather," she said as she greeted me. I pursed my lips and rolled my eyes. We drove west for half an hour through the rain-swept hills before the sun burst out. We had perfect weather for our five-day trip. That was almost unheard of in Scotland.

I did not tell her what the doctor had said to me. We chatted about her recent trip to Africa to visit my sister Ruth. She was deeply troubled about Ruth's eldest daughter, who had epilepsy.

"Dorothy's kids call me Raisin Granny. I take them packets of healthy raisins, not sweets." She laughed.

We pitched my tent on the sandy machair at Arisaig, blew up the airbeds, and settled in. The fresh air, the pink, yellow, and white flowers, and the golden sand framed the sea while shiny clouds rambled across the wide sky. The evening sun sank into the Atlantic Ocean. The rugged ridges of Skye and Rhum stood out against the fiery sky. The clarity of light and sweeping sea views gave Arisaig an otherworldly feel.

The following day, inhaling the sea air, we clambered onto the Inner Isles Ferry. The crew untied the mooring ropes, and we chugged out of Mallaig Harbour. In the warm sunshine, as if on a Mediterranean cruise, we bobbed over the Sound of Sleat towards the sinuous mountains of Rhum.

"The sea reminds me of my childhood in Belfast," she told me. "In the summers, I took my three sisters and brother to the beach where we swam and collected whelks. Back home, we boiled them and pulled out the bodies with a pin. What a treat."

"When were you born?" I asked.

"In 1911. I was a child during 'the troubles.' Men fought in the streets and smashed the shop windows. One evening, I remember my mother, her white knuckles pushing the pram with Harry and my sisters, rushing to get home before the curfew." She frowned and rubbed her hand through her hair.

"That must have been terrifying."

"My father wanted to be a doctor, but his father used all the family money to try and cure himself of a fatal disease," she continued. "So, my dad ended up working in the shipyards as a welder. We joked he built the Titanic. He and his crew were paid in the pub on Saturdays."

"Paid in the pub? That's dreadful. I wonder how much of their money got home." I shook my head, staring at the waves.

"My father lost his job during the depression. In those hard times, my mother said that, if she had known about Maria Stopes, she would never have had five children."

I wanted to talk about her birth control habits but couldn't bring myself to broach this forbidden topic. Then she continued as if on a roll.

"I left school at fourteen and worked as a tailoress. I was nineteen when I began my training in the Belfast Royal Infirmary. I worked seventy-hour weeks, cleaning up vomit, changing bedpans, and making beds with perfect envelope corners. The eagle-eyed sisters criticized the smallest imperfection. Then I went to England to work in a Sanatorium. It was there I contracted Tuberculosis."

"That was a killer. How did you survive?" I asked.

"The treatment was rest and fresh air. I focused on a healthy diet. I have a cold shower most days. As soon as I was well, I was accepted into the Glasgow infirmary to do my midwifery training. On the boat from Belfast to Scotland, I met two American women, and they told me about Jesus. They changed my life."

"Was it hard to leave all your family behind?" I asked.

"Yes, but it was a great opportunity. At the beginning of the war, I worked as a district nurse and midwife in the Scottish Borders. On snowy nights, I drove over the moors to deliver babies. I loved it. During the war, when I married your father, I gave up my career. One of my friends went to Florida and became a matron." With a faraway look in her eyes, she told me, "She writes to me every Christmas."

"Did you miss your career?"

"In those days, I didn't have a choice. Ruth was born the year after we married. She was premature. When she turned blue, I knew to hold her tight and keep her warm."

I had heard many of her stories before, but somehow on that ferry with the wind in our faces, I began to understand what a strong-minded woman she was.

In the long Scottish twilight, with the western sky awash with reds and Mother asleep in the tent, I pondered her life challenges. Aware that our New Zealand contract was for two years, I made an effort to enjoy the highlands with her.

The next day, on a boat trip to Loch Nevis, we sat together at the front, relishing the salt spray on our faces. On the way back to Edinburgh, we stopped and hiked through a rockfall to the towering cliffs of the Lost Valley in Glencoe. The intense green of summer seeped into our spirits, bringing peace and connection to our turbulent relationship. Then I drove my mother back to her lonely house, and returned to London to pack for our move.

One month later, Clive and I returned to Scotland to say goodbye to our families. With Mother, we walked in the woods.

"You'll come and visit us in New Zealand as soon as we are settled," I said lightly.

"It's so far away. I am not sure I can travel all that way on my own," she replied.

As I hugged her goodbye, not a woman to show her emotions, she stiffened in my arms. Reluctantly, Clive and I piled into our old Renault. She looked small and vulnerable as I waved goodbye. In that moment, I questioned my choice to go to the opposite side of the planet while I wiped my tears.

At Heathrow airport, I bought two identical cards with a poem that reminded me of India and my meditation classes. I mailed one to Mother and tucked the other in my journal as I headed for a stopover in California before starting a new chapter in New Zealand.

"*Look to this day*
For it is life
The very life of life
In its brief course lie all
The realities and truths of existence
The joy of growth
The splendour of action
The glory of power
For yesterday is but a memory
And tomorrow is only a vision
But today well lived
Makes every yesterday a memory of happiness
And every tomorrow a vision of hope
Look well therefore to this day."
~ Ancient Sanskrit Poem

CHAPTER 11

Aotearoa - Land of the Long White Cloud

"Following the light of the sun, we left the old world."
~ From the Journal of Christopher Columbus

September 1978

Balanced on the edge of our skis, on the narrow peak of Paretetaitonga, one of the snowy summits of the North Island volcano Ruhapeu, Clive and I stared at each another in dismay as our brand-new friends Rob and Tim, with a skillful flick of their skis, disappeared into the mist.

Their last words rang in our ears: "We're just kiwis. We're not very good skiers."

I positioned my unwilling skis into a snowplough, stuck my bum out, pushed my hands forward, and began my tortuous descent. After several falls, wiping snow out of my mouth, I joined the group on the edge of the crater.

"What took you so long?" Rob asked with a grin.

"This is our first-time ski touring. We're above nine thousand feet!" I said. "The last time we skied in Scotland, the sleet flew horizontally across the patches of snow and heather."

"That must be draughty in your kilt. Clive, what do you wear under yours?" Rob teased. My nostrils stung from the pungent hydrogen sulphide that hissed out of black fissures. My eyes focused on the inky geothermal lake in the summit crater, its steep sides covered in ash and surrounded by snow-covered peaks.

"This is a volcano. What'll we do if it explodes?" I asked. Nevertheless awed by the primal beauty, I soon forgot my insecurities and shaking limbs.

A few weeks before this, with a Wellington street map clutched in one hand and the steering wheel in the other, I drove around hairpin bends up Victoria Hill and surveyed my new city. White weatherboard houses with corrugated iron roofs climbed up the green hillsides and clung to the ridges surrounding the harbour. Fast-moving clouds made an ever-changing mosaic of greys on the white-speckled sea while the wind blew through my cropped hair like a hairdryer. Lured by the postcards of snowy mountains in my high school geography project, I had willingly followed Clive to New Zealand. Every morning, he disappeared to his downtown office while I mulled over my uncertain prospects.

In London, I had eagerly anticipated this move, but now, everything felt upside down. Many times, I walked north toward the sun, thinking it was south. I wandered into a department store with aging paint, grey floors, and poor lighting as if the clock had been turned back ten years. I asked the white-capped assistant at the deli section for "brie," looking forward to some gooey cheese. "Oh, the breeead counter is over there, dear!" she replied in her New Zealand accent.

Once again, I sought solace in a bookstore. I left clutching *The Feminine Mystique* by Betty Friedan. At the age of twenty-eight, was it time to start a family? I curled on the couch, listening to the windows crackle in the brutal winds, and the seagulls screech as I devoured each page. Friedan questioned traditional feminine roles—woman as a man's helpmate and mother of his children—and suggested there was more to a woman's life than the American dream of a suburban house and family. She proposed that the way to avoid this trap was through meaningful work that used a woman's full mental capacity. The possibility that I was capable of more than my boring secretarial job in London, more than a housewife, more than a sexual object, both scared and excited me. Betty Friedan's words reignited my desire for a profession, a career. Again, entrenched cultural expectations resurfaced. *Why bother? Your marriage should fulfil all your desires.* On my growing edge, these felt like a curse.

I responded to an advertisement for a high school chemistry teacher. It had been ten years since I'd studied Chemistry 101 at Edinburgh University. When, to my surprise, Erskine College, the Sacred Heart Catholic girls boarding school, offered me the job, memories of my unsuccessful teaching experience troubled me with dogged persistence.

I stood in front of sixteen young women, scribbling the chemical equations I had learned the night before on the board. Five minutes before the bell rang, Charmaine Coventry, her name embedded in my memory forever, asked, "What questions do you want us to do for homework?" I faltered, astonished that she was interested in chemistry. More than that, she had a desire to learn, to pass her state exams only a few weeks away. I staggered home exhausted and opened up the turgid textbooks to study the periodic table and atomic theory for the next day's lessons. I worked late until my eyelids refused to stay open. Then test tubes, electrons, formulae, equations, rude comments, and unruly pupils tortured my night dreams. In the first light of dawn, I washed my bleary eyes and headed to school.

Friday afternoon in the bar, I chatted to a new friend. It was not so much a chat as a general complaint of all that was wrong with teaching.

"They don't listen. They should pay attention. I work so hard to help them learn chemistry."

"Wilma, you need to teach for yourself," she said. "Not because you know what is best for them, not to save the world, but because you want to do it."

"Isn't that selfish?" I asked.

After the solid stone Scottish houses, the white wooden house with the tin roof we had rented for a few weeks until our furniture arrived from England was flimsy and musty. At night, the floorboards creaked, and stale cigarette smoke seeped from the threadbare carpets. When Clive travelled to the oil fields, and I was alone, I imagined the sickening odour came from dead bodies locked in the cupboards. After school, when it did not rain, I fled to the garden, overgrown with grass and fragrant onion weed. Under the magnolia tree's purple-tinged flowers, I inhaled the fresh earth and soothed my anxiety as I prepared my lessons.

I had been teaching for three months when a grey-haired nun knocked on my science lab door and told me I had a phone call. She led me to a mahogany booth in the bowels of the school.

"I am so sorry. I don't know how to say this." With that, Clive launched straight in. "I have terrible news. Your mother has been killed in a car crash."

"W-What?" I stammered in disbelief. My eyes stung, my mind blanked out, and my stomach cramped.

Now that the unimaginable had happened, stressed and grief-stricken, I boarded the Air New Zealand plane and headed back alone to Scotland, my mind in a dense fog, my heart caved in, and my shoulders slouched. On the twenty-four-hour journey, the plane tossed and pitched through tropical turbulence. I couldn't concentrate on my book. I tried my newly learned meditation techniques and focused on my breath: inhale and exhale. But nothing comforted me. I landed red-eyed in Edinburgh, my nose dripping and my pockets stuffed with damp tissues.

Mother's three sisters, her brother from Belfast, and Ruth, who had flown back from her young family in Zambia, greeted me with tears and warm hugs. Around the kitchen table, we drank tea and ate biscuits as we shared our shock and anecdotes about Mother.

"Last Wednesday, Mother and I walked with kids to the pond. She was quiet and took a while to interact with them," Dorothy told us, sobbing. "She obsessed about a recent murder in the newspaper. I think she was depressed. She left to catch the bus back to Edinburgh," she continued in a shaky voice. "When the bus did not come, she must have walked. You know how she loved to walk. Out in nature, she let go of her worries and the weight of the world." Dorothy paused, covering her face with a man-sized handkerchief, struggling to regain control of her voice. "Later that night, the police came to the door. I couldn't believe what they told me."

"How terrible for you," I said, blowing my nose.

"My guess is she walked along the bus route. In the twilight, she walked straight out onto a busy road. With her cataracts and tinnitus, she mustn't have seen or heard the car. The policeman said she would not have known what hit her and was killed instantly." We all rubbed our weeping eyes. "I had to go to the mortuary and identify her. You shouldn't go. Remember her as she was." We sobbed in each other's arms. In this unexpected turn in the spiral of life, there was nothing gentle in this visit from the angel of death. It was as if a violent terrorist had crashed the party.

The next day, under a dense sky, we drove to the austere Holyrood Abbey Church. Ruth, Dorothy, and I steadied ourselves as we walked down the aisle where we had all been married. At the front of the altar, flowers covered the oak coffin that held mother's crushed remains. I could not believe that it was only four months since she and I had hiked together. In celebration of my mother's life, we sang her favourite hymns. *"Praise my soul the king of heaven, to his feet thy tribute bring.*" My diaphragm tightened as the words stuck in my throat.

After the funeral, we gathered in her home, drank tea, and ate egg-salad sandwiches and fruitcake. My aunt wore a beige sweater under her black suit, and I caught a glimpse of her well-ironed petticoat.

"I believe when your time is up, your time is up," she said, balancing her china teacup and saucer in her hand.

"You think so?" I asked, letting out a sob.

"Do you think Mum saw the car light, like God calling her to heaven?" Ruth added.

"I have no idea," I replied. I wanted to say I didn't believe in heaven, hell, or the afterlife but knew this was not acceptable in this company.

"Strange things can happen after funerals. Take care," my uncle advised in his warm Irish brogue

Then in the cemetery overlooked by Mother's beloved Pentland Hills, enveloped by the fragrance of damp grass and under dripping umbrellas, we read the condolences from her friends. A rainbow of sweet-smelling flowers covered Mother's grave. Just at that moment, the rain stopped, and the sun broke through the forbidding clouds and bathed us in light.

The house emptied as Mother's sisters and brother returned to Belfast. Ruth and I stayed, rattling around our home. We did not hear Mother sing in her morning bath. Cans of evaporated milk for her coffee remained in the cupboard. There was no smell of her delicious treacle scones and no comforting hot-water bottles tucked under our duvets. As we sorted through her clothes, I imagined this was a bad dream and wished she would come through the back door, rosy-cheeked from a walk. In a feeble effort to fill the cavernous hole, I selected her beloved Chinese shirt to take back to New Zealand.

Over the next week, Ruth and I comforted each other,

wandering along Princes Street, dipping in and out of stores, trying on colourful dresses, shirts, and shoes as if we were teenagers. Dorothy, busy with her three young children, did not join us. On our last shopping trip before Ruth's departure, we climbed the stairs, lined with eighteenth-century pictures of Edinburgh, to the café on the first floor of the bookstore, a favourite haunt of hers. I drank coffee, but with the loss of my appetite, the shortbread was hard to swallow.

"Ruth, guess what? On my way back to New Zealand, I can stop in Hong Kong for a few days." I smiled.

"Wilma, on your own? That's way too dangerous. I do worry about you."

"What?" my voice rose. "I have travelled all over the Middle East. I'll be just fine."

"But you had Clive with you then."

"Don't worry; I can take care of myself," I crossed my arms and snapped, though I did recognize she was overprotective because she loved me.

True to my uncle's warning, the night before Ruth flew back to Africa, she was in the middle of a conversation when our brother-in-law hung up the phone. The conflict over my mother's estate had escalated. At first, we all agreed that Dorothy and her husband could move into my mother's house. With more thought, Ruth and I decided it would be fairer to sell the house and divide the money between the three of us, according to Mother's will. Yelling at each other was not our style. Our family handled conflict with the silent treatment. For years, our conversations were riddled with distrust.

Once again in London, with my head bowed, I shuffled onto a plane. I lost myself in the buzz of Hong Kong's crowded streets. Here, flat-cooked ducks hung in shop windows. Jade ornaments and whiffs of incense in the Buddhist temple captivated me. A ferry ride across the harbour, teeming with junks, tugboats, and freighters, took me away from the crowded skyscrapers to the forested island of Lantau and offered welcome moments of forgetfulness. The tropical warmth soaked into my bones while the vigorous energy of the Chinese people, who lived on crowded wooden junks and in high-rise buildings, breathed life into my sorrow and angst.

Back in New Zealand, it was the summer holidays. Clive and I now lived in an airy apartment with fine harbour views. After that first ski-touring trip, we regularly participated in weekend trips with the Wellington Section of the New Zealand Alpine Club. In an attempt to put my mother's death and family discord out of my mind, I busied myself packing for our first multi-day wilderness trip in the Southern Alps. The kiwis called it a "Christmas trip." I pushed my fleece jacket, waterproof parka, sleeping bag, crampons, first-aid kit, and camera into my backpack. I calculated daily food rations and fretted about how I would carry my heavy pack.

On the ferry crossing to the South Island, Clive and I hugged as we hung over the side. A school of about fifty dolphins played and jumped out of the water in perfect unison, their joy infectious.

We drove five hours to the west coast road end and camped. When I awoke to the melodic bird song of bellbirds and fantails, I knew I was not in Scotland. Mist enveloped the mountain summits and hung in wisps around the tall trees of the temperate rainforest. Ten minutes before the six men and women in our group finished packing, one of the party, Graham Mac, a lean man in his fifties, set off up the narrow track. His words hung in the damp air: "Oh, you young guys will catch up with me in no time." For three nonstop hours, we marched, brushing past dripping tree ferns and stumbling over river boulders before we found him, sitting by a stream eating crackers and salami.

After another three hours of sweat, sore shoulders, and taut calves, we arrived at the Welcome Flats hut nestled in a flower-filled meadow surrounded by rainforest. I groaned with relief as I dropped my pack, rolled my shoulders, claimed a bunk, and headed with Clive to soak in the natural hot pools.

Dilemma. What to wear? My bra and pants? Or should I slip in as Mother Nature had made me? I was too shy to ask anyone what was expected. How could I expose my naked body in front of the men? I did not want to arouse their "uncontrollable urges." I decided on just panties. Slowly, I immersed my body in the warm water and felt my tense muscles ease. I watched the steam evaporate as my eyes feasted on the mountains. This was bliss. With obvious pleasure, the uninhibited kiwis soaked in their birthday suits. No one displayed any "uncontrollable urges," except the sandflies that swarmed around our heads and devoured our exposed flesh, resulting in itchy red welts.

After a good night's sleep, we hiked through the moss-draped trees toward the jagged snowy summits. In time, we escaped the forest into the silent alpine grasses and bushes—hebes, dracophyllum, and coprosma. Our first New Zealand Christmas found us in the crystalline air, high in the Southern Alps, sleeping under the huge Douglas bivy rock with its million-dollar view. There was no sign of human habitation. The deep-forested valley with the irritating sandflies stretched out below. All night, the wekas—flightless birds, like small brown speckled hens—rustled around. In the absence of predators, we did not scare them. Graham hopped up and down to chase them away as they cheekily dragged his boots into the long grasses.

My mother's crushed body troubled my dreams. Then uneasy questions arose in my sleepless mind: *Will the crevasses swallow me? Will I die in an avalanche?* In the pre-dawn gloom, I tied my bootlaces and set off with the others to climb Mount Sefton. At 3,157 metres, this was my most physically demanding test to date.

On the glacier, as the sky tinged pink, I struggled to strap on my new crampons—metal attachments to mountaineering boots that provide traction on snow and ice. I puffed hard to keep up with the others. Fear gnawed in my abdomen, and even with my best efforts, they pulled away from me. I caught up as they unravelled and tied into the rope to cross the neve, the Alpine region where snowfall accumulated and the movement of the glaciers created crevasses, or "slots" as the kiwis called them. We weaved around the seracs—house-sized blocks of ice that could topple without warning. Beyond, there was a peak with a knife-edge ridge that led to a summit. Unused to the massive scale of these mountains, I pointed to this peak.

"Is that the top of Mount Sefton?" I asked.

Our friends laughed. "That is Mount Cook." I breathed with relief; the closer summit was our destination. With gritted teeth, I watched the kiwis climb up the steep convex ice slope un-roped. While envious of their skill and faith in those tiny ten-pointed crampons, I enjoyed the security of the rope.

On the summit, I revelled in the waves of mountains and glaciers that stretched to the north and south. I looked down the precipitous east side. Thousands of feet below, the houses and hotels of Mount Cook village looked like matchboxes, and the broad Tasman Valley widened onto the plains of Mackenzie country. I devoured my ration of salami and cheese, elated as I admired the magnificent jumble of snowy peaks that stretched to the glistening Tasman Sea.

"The avalanche danger increases as the sun warms the snow. We need to leave," Graham warned us. We retraced our steps and moved as fast as possible away from the jagged seracs and back to the safety of the bivy rock. There, enveloped in earth musk, intense after the snows, we picked up our sleeping bags and headed back to the hut. As I lurched after the group across the big boulders in the stream, I slipped and gashed my shin. Blood dripped down my leg. The thought of the hot pools and a bed propelled my exhausted body down the mountain.

On the fourth day, we walked back along the narrow trail, the tree ferns brushing my face and arms. I was determined to keep up with Graham Mac. Just as I thought I'd never reach the road, we heard an enthusiastic, "Yahoo!" At the trailhead, our friend Rob had driven from Christchurch after spending Christmas with his family. He welcomed us with fresh tomatoes and white bread. This provided a brief respite before we headed up a different valley for another six days.

Mountaineering in the Southern Alps

Although these trips challenged us, when we returned to the city, the elixir we drank in the wilderness with our new friends energized us. I did think that competing with the men at their own game would bring me the success and fulfillment I craved.

To continue our Buddhist explorations, and in hope of making friends, we signed up for a weekend meditation retreat held in a community hall in the country. As Clive and I arranged our sleeping bags in a spartan bunkroom, a young man came and removed his backpack from a top bunk, stuttering, "A-a-a-a-a woman in the r-r-r-r-room will interrupt my m-m-m-meditation."

"What have we let ourselves in for this time?" I asked Clive, my eyes wide.

In the hall, there was an altar with flowers and candles. The tendrils of smoke from the sandalwood incense curled around the large brass Buddha. I sat cross-legged on a meditation cushion, focused on the air as it rushed past my nose hairs into my lungs. Before long, the focus of my meditation changed from my breath to my back and my legs, which screamed in discomfort. By Sunday afternoon in the dark hall, my gaze refused to stay on the altar, my open eyes drawn to the window and the enticing sunshine.

"Have you been to the river?" I asked my new friend. "Do you think we can swim there?"

"I didn't bring my swimming stuff," she said. "We can go in our underwear."

Collecting our towels, several of us left the silent meditators, and inhaling lungfuls of clean air, we ran joyously over the gravel. We swung on a rope and plunged into the brown pool of warm water and frolicked like dolphins. Above, cumulus clouds graced the sky while the emerald leaves of the forest shone in the sunlight. My heart quivered with pleasure and affirmed my fascination of the outdoors.

In the months following my mother's accident, I obsessed about her at night. While I missed her loving Irish voice on the phone, her death released me from the strangling grip of her values and opened the door to the entangled chaos of my emotions.

Although she survived my father by eighteen years, she never came to peace with her loss. Her sister had told me, "Your mother always lived more in heaven than on earth." Her oak coffin held her physical remains along with her contradictions, her stuffed bra, her nervous hand rubbing, and her love for me. Holding my head in my hand, I wrote in my journal. *I feel lost. I wish a gust of wind, screaming down the chimney, would miraculously return her to me. At a press of a button, this world might be destroyed by a nuclear holocaust. Should I live in the moment and "be here now?" How do I come to terms with death? Will I burn in hell or will all be revealed in the ultimate reality?* One glorious sunny day, preoccupied with these issues as I ran with thirty-year-old Clive, I popped the taboo question: "Have you come to terms with your mortality?" He let out a small yell as he tripped over the curb. I never did hear his answer.

That autumn, I read an advert in the local paper for a residential Gestalt weekend group for couples, *"for people who are functioning well and want to communicate even better."* While Clive was on a business trip to Indonesia, I signed us up. The next Friday evening, Clive and I joined ten men and women sitting on cushions in a circle. I chewed my lips as I teetered on my unknown edge. After introductions, Sophie the therapist invited someone to take the hot seat while the rest of us observed.

"It's three months since the bastard left. I feel alone in bed. I don't know what to do with myself. He betrayed me, running off with my best friend. How could he do that?" the young woman lamented. Then she pounded the pillows with a baseball bat with a force that scared me.

When she calmed down, she caught me off guard and addressed me personally. "I'm jealous you have a warm man in your bed every night." I had taken Clive for granted, believing we had married for life *to look after each other in sickness and in health, until death us do part.*

Another woman confessed she was depressed. After the therapists' detective-like questioning, in floods of tears, she disclosed that her mother had taken her own life when she was a young teen, and somehow, she felt responsible for her mother's suicide. I had no idea that the roots of my emotions might be found in my childhood experiences.

I wanted to escape into nature. At one point, I had a massive nosebleed, and I dabbed my dripping nose with a bundle of tissues.

"Be aware. Maybe this is what happens to you when something's coming up," Sophie said.

"What do you mean?" I queried.

"When couples get together, each person comes with a pile of unconscious 'shit' that they each have to sort through to grow," she explained.

On Sunday morning, I recognized that if I did not speak up, I would leave the weekend disappointed in myself. I plucked up courage and took the hot seat.

"I don't know where to start. Since coming to New Zealand, something doesn't feel right in our marriage. It is as if a heavy rock weighs on my belly," I muttered.

"Why don't you go round this group of men and women and say the first thing that pops into your head?" Sophie instructed me.

"I am attracted to you," I blurted out to a man. *Was I mad? A raving nymphomaniac?* My face on fire, I was disgusted at what came out of my own mouth, yet powerless to stop. I had no time to think of Clive's feelings. Heat blazed through my body from the tips of my toes to the ends of my hair. Somehow from there, Sophie's skilled questions took me to the root of the matter. Years of confusion around my sexuality, combined with a build-up of resentments toward my mother and her wrathful God. It was my turn to release my fury with the baseball bat into the cushions.

When my rage was spent, Sophie gently suggested, "Imagine your mother on the cushion in front of you. What do you need to say to her?"

"Mum, I can't believe you died so suddenly. I miss you." I wiped my eyes. "You judged me harshly. I will never be good enough. I am always trying to prove myself to you." I hesitated. Sophie encouraged me to continue. I thought hard. "I am truly grateful you gave birth to me. Your life must have been so difficult after my father died. I am sad you will not visit us in New Zealand."

Sophie's final question was, "What do you need now?" Because I'd exposed sexual desires and anger, I feared Clive's rejection. The fact that my anger was directed at Mother and God, and not at Clive, reassured me. With all my being, I chose the comfort of Clive's welcoming arms.

Later, I read Nancy Friday's ground-breaking book *My Mother Myself*, which explored the complex relationship between mothers and daughters. How did I reconcile the plucky young nurse who'd left Belfast with the Bible pushing teetotaller who disapproved of my religious and sexual choices? I wanted freedom from my mother's voice in my head.

This cracked open my mask. I embarked on a stop-start conscious adventure from my head to my heart. Like my move from England to New Zealand, nothing was familiar. I wanted to tape my exterior veneer back together. There was no way back. Little by little, as I made adjustments, I un-muzzled my inner child and an unfamiliar vitality seeped into my bones. Clive, rather than being alienated by my newfound individuality, supported and loved me as I climbed mountains and pursued a career.

Most holiday weekends, we headed to the South Island. One weekend, we drove through the night and arrived at the road end of the Cobb Valley at five a.m. After a short sleep, we headed up the valley in the rain with the intention to camp. Once again, I was the only woman. We reached Fenella hut damp and weary. Rob placed his sleeping bag on a bunk, joking, "Just in case we decide to stay!"

"It is only one o'clock. It's too early to stop," Clive muttered. My ankle ached, and I dreaded camping in the rain. I wanted to stay in this warm dry hut but feared speaking up and risking being teased for my feminine weakness. The hut had been built as a memorial to Fenella Druce, who was one of four people killed when the Three Johns Hut in Mt. Cook National Park was blown off its site in 1977. Her family lovingly maintained it. The outhouse had an artistic stained-glass window and a stone washbasin. As it turned out, I wasn't the only one seduced by home comforts. We stayed.

We woke refreshed to a clear and sunny day. The bush was damp and earthy. We hiked over a high ridge and down to Lonely Lake Hut. My stomach grumbled, and my mind protested. *It's so far to the camp spot. I still have to go over that mountain, past the lake, and up the next ridge.* To keep up with our fit friends, Clive and I carried the minimum amount of food. At the hut, we rifled around the kitchen and pounced on a stock of army biscuits and honey to augment our meagre lunch of crispbread and cheese.

With a full belly, I began with a spring in my step as we walked through the gnarled beech trees, which reminded me of an enchanted forest in *Lord of the Rings*. There were no trails. After hours of bushwhacking up and down mountains, I stopped high on a crest.

"I'm shattered. I can't walk another step," I announced to Clive as I dropped my pack.

"If you're too tired, then don't come on these trips," Clive snapped. Before I could think of a suitable reply, the others caught up with us. I was not alone in my fatigue; our friends took one look at the knife-edge ridge ahead, and we unanimously decided this was a suitable camping spot. To my relief, the peak could wait until morning.

From this airy camp, on top of the world with waves of mountains all around and not another person for miles, I ate my dehydrated meal with gusto. Packet cheesecake, prepared as carefully as a cordon blue dessert, melted on my tongue, and I savoured every sweet bite. We sat around the campfire.

"The best part of these trips is when we stop. That's the only reason I come." Then I decided to tease the kiwis. "I think it would be better if they drowned NZ up to the treeline. Then we could just walk along the tops without bush-bashing." Later, as I struggled in the cold wind to go to the toilet, one of the guys said, "I know why not many women come on these trips."

In the tranquillity, we admired the alpenglow that was followed by a myriad of pinpricks surrounding the Southern Cross and upside-down Orion. The mountains and the warm camaraderie of friends were a euphoric combination.

Back at home from the mountains, Clive and I talked long and hard about his challenge to me up on the ridge. I worked through my need to blame him. I decided that, even although these trips were arduous, I treasured them and did not want to miss out. This introduced me to physical training. I bought a pass to a gym, began running, and biked three times a week to school.

In December 1980, at the end of Clive's two-year contract, we were overjoyed to visit Bali, Nepal, and Zambia on the way back to Scotland. In Nepal, we flew to Lukla, trekked to Namche Bazaar fascinated with mani stones, slabs of stone inscribed with prayers, rainbow prayer flags fluttering in the breeze, and the friendly Sherpa people. We ascended slowly to acclimatize. At the Tengboche monastery, at a height of 3,870 metres, we were the only trekkers, and the monks showed us ancient manuscripts and Buddhist Tanka's. We left the main Everest base camp trail and turned up the valley to the hamlet of Goyko, dominated by the awe-inspiring Cho-Oyo. We stayed in a simple teahouse managed by a cheerful Sherpani who also took care of the yaks.

Sherpani milking her yak

It was well below freezing when the two of us adventured over Chola Pass, at 5,330 metres, using our recently acquired glacier skills. We spent the night in a derelict shepherd's hut. Back on the Everest base-camp trail, several times with a pounding headache I lay on the grass sucking the thin air. The next day, we ascended, one breath, one footstep, at a time to Kala Pattar above the base camp and gazed at the formidable face of Mount Everest. Reluctantly, we turned around. I did not want to leave, as mountain after mountain took my breath away, as did the smiling faces of Sherpas and their children.

Chola Pass, Nepal

Clive and I on Kala Pattar under the formidable Mount Everest

I flew to Zambia to visit Ruth and her two beautiful daughters. We renewed our warm relationship and visited the breathtaking Zambezi Falls.

In Scotland, we spent a happy Christmas with Clive's family, a day of gifts, a walk on the beach, and a stomach filled with turkey and at least four different desserts. I visited Dorothy and enjoyed her boisterous young family. Warm memories of previous New Years in the hills enticed us to the West Coast for New Year festivities with Clive's brother and his climbing buddies. The rain lashed the heather hillsides and darkness descended by mid-afternoon.

I had told my New Zealand friends I was going home, but I was at war with myself. What did it mean to go home now that Mother was no longer there and the family house had been sold? On street corners, red-kilted pipers played plaintive tunes as my eyes filled with tears. As I sipped coffee in the renovated cafe in a vaulted gothic cellar under St John's church, I admired the elegantly curved turrets and revisited my grief. The gravestones, encrusted with centuries of smoke, and ivy-covered beech trees spoke to me of continuity, survival in the face of change, and resilience despite loss.

CHAPTER 12
Full Tilt

"A mind that is stretched to a new idea never returns to its original dimension."
~ From the works of Oliver Wendell Holmes, Sr.

Wellington, New Zealand 1981

Back from our overseas adventures, Clive resigned from his job at the government oil company. To accommodate our expanding roots, he built an office on the ground floor of our house and established himself as a geophysical consultant. I timed my morning departure by the ferry that sailed across the harbour to the South Island. The rush of air invigorated me as I jumped on my bike, teetering down our hillside path to the road to school.

With two years' experience teaching chemistry and physics, I had not pinched any students, and they performed well in their state exams. As the sixth-year, grade-twelve, form teacher, I gained a measure of confidence. Nevertheless, now and again, the students ran rings around me. Julianne's shrill voice talking about her weekend exploits interrupted my laboured explanation.

"Quiet, please. Shh!" I pleaded, feeling like a steam engine. "Now where was I? Yes. Pressure is measured in kilopascals. One atmosphere equals…"

Julianne whispered to Cassie. Victoria dropped her book. Sarah's hand went up.

"I don't understand."

"I'm trying to explain but…"

Julianne dragged her chair along the floor. *Why can't she sit and listen?* The defiant look in her eyes aggravated me. I looked away and tried to continue but the three of them chatted.

"Pay attention!" I yelled.

"It's your fault I failed my science exam," Victoria announced with a sneer. The class burst into laughter.

"Turn to page fifty. Do questions one to five. Finish them for homework," I instructed, choking back tears. A girl in the back row mouthed over the racket that she could not hear. I wrote the instructions on the blackboard, then escaped into the prep room, which was lined with bottles of chemicals, to compose myself.

I cycled home. In our hillside garden, I dug my bare hands into the damp earth, pulled weeds, and planted magenta cineraria and yellow primula. Unlike my pupils, these plants did not talk back to me, neither did I have to provide complex academic instructions to encourage their growth. The cool breezes from the southern ocean played on my skin, as I listened to the silence between the bird songs and filled my lungs with the fragrant aroma of honeysuckle.

At a chemistry-teachers conference, a man with a kindly smile and receding salt and pepper hair introduced himself. Jack Shallcrass remarked on my Scottish accent and told me he had visited Edinburgh for an education conference. Jack invited me to visit him in his university office. Light streamed in through the large windows, illuminating shelves overflowing with books on humanism, psychology, and educational theory. One of our conversations went a bit like this:

"I left home at seventeen and have never been back in a church except for weddings and funerals," he told me, shaking his head.

"At my confirmation, I tried to concentrate on the mysteries of the crucifixion, the love of God, and the power of prayer but nothing happened. No joy, no magic, and no revelation"

"As a teenager, I was baptized and experienced total disappointment," I replied.

Jack's empathetic ear provided a safe place for me to explore my teaching struggles. He was like an oasis in my life, a much-needed watering hole.

"Wilma, I have been teaching for fifty years. I know I can't change the system. I have learned to work within it." He pulled a couple of books from his crowded shelves. "Here, you might find these helpful." I left clutching, *Why Children Fail* by American educator John Holt and *The Unbowed Head* by R.F. Mackenzie.

That night, I read the statement from the back cover of Holt's book: "Children fail due to humiliation and confusion." This reminded me of my high school French teacher. I recalled how my face burned as she shamed me in front of the class because I could not articulate the word "cuisine" to her satisfaction. It took me three attempts to pass O-level French. In my abdomen, I felt the sting of her sarcasm.

I met Jack for coffee. "I read the Scottish headmaster Mackenzie's book." I said eagerly. "I loved how he treasured the outdoors and wanted to pass on his delight to his pupils. He believed that intimate contact with nature and the mountains taught a child self-reliance and self-responsibility."

"He was a radical, ahead of his time," Jack said. "He wanted to move Scottish education away from its Presbyterian roots and replace it with a child-centred system. He believed teaching needed to be an exploration in a caring environment. He wanted to ban corporal punishment and replace exams with continuous assessment. His opponents condemned him as too permissive. They used the old argument that academics were all that mattered, and that his pupil's O-level results were poor."

"At university, I crammed scientific facts into my head the night before the exam, regurgitated them onto the exam papers, then promptly forgot them," I said, my brow furrowed. "It's as if pupils are robots. It's frustrating. At least the university entrance level uses continuous assessment."

"Have you read *Summerhill* by A. S. Neil? He's a progressive educator."

"Doesn't he believe that externally imposed discipline prevents young people from developing internal self-discipline?" I replied, my brow furrowed.

"His school encouraged the pupils to decide for themselves when and what they will learn. They had a voice in how to run the school. They develop self-determination and self-motivation."

"I can't imagine a school with no bells, no periods, no exams," I replied, folding my arms. "He believed that to be anti-sex was to be anti-life. My mother would have called him the devil's advocate."

"Do you know 'devil' and 'lived' have the reversed spelling?" Jack laughed. "By the way, I have recommended you to the Chemistry Curriculum Development Committee."

After a few meetings of this group in a smoky room full of red-faced grey-haired men puffing on pipes, I overcame my innate timidity. "I think that we need to add the chemistry of cosmetics to the grade-ten syllabus."

"That wouldn't prepare the students for university," replied a crusty bushy-browed man as he cast his disapproving eye over me.

"Only a few of my students will go on to study chemistry at university," I said. "Chemistry is everywhere in our world. My young women need to be educated consumers. To understand what chemicals are in the products they buy." My argument failed to convince them.

Since my legs cramped up in meditation, I decided to try yoga. I began with caution, worried I might be brainwashed into relinquishing my free will or kidnapped into a cult. Wednesdays at five p.m., Clive and I found ourselves focusing on our inhales and exhales while stretching into downward dog, warrior pose, and forward bends. I slowly became aware that my education, which valued cognitive function, had turned me into a talking head, cut off at my throat. I was mostly ignorant of the intricate workings of my body. Even though I taught human biology, it took me much patience to locate my pectorals, transverse abdominals, abductors, and hip flexors.

After an hour of twisting into a pretzel, I lay on my foam mat ready for relaxation. I listened to the instructor's soothing voice and followed his directions, "You don't need to think about anything else except this present moment." My hyperactive mind often diverted itself to planning lessons or weekend activities. As soon as I noticed, I returned my focus to my breath. Letting go swept through me like a wave, and for a few blessed moments, I dropped my qualms of what others thought of me, my teaching abilities, or how I measured up with the men in the mountains. As I practised, my sleep improved, and I gained more poise both in the classroom and the mountains. Like the Sanskrit poem "Look to this day for it is life" that I brought from London, I had inklings that *to be here now* meant to ride the currents of life with less resistance and struggle.

At Erskine College, our staff was eager to participate in our first-ever professional development day presented by a woman whom I called the American psychological nun. This was a pivotal stepping stone in my life. Unlike the nuns in our school, who wore black and white habits, she dressed in a suit and floral shirt. Early in the day, this enthusiastic woman asked us to discuss in pairs: "What are you passionate about as a teacher?" No one at teacher training college had broached this subject; logic and cognitive thinking were more reliable than passion. Following my heart had never been encouraged.

"This is difficult for me." I sighed as I searched my brain for inspiration. "I am not enthusiastic about sulphuric acid, Newton's laws, or the periodic table. When I do experiments in the fume cupboard, I dread inhaling poisonous gases." I chewed over the question and decided, "I do like to teach my students to think for themselves."

She introduced our staff to personality types and learning styles. I discovered that, while my predominant personality type liked to search for knowledge with questions, most learners preferred to be presented with clear facts and figures. This initiated a new beginning as I explored different ways to build relationships with my pupils and facilitate learning. I learned that teens were not to be feared, as the newspapers sometimes suggested, but needed support and understanding. While teachers influenced their behaviour, the groundwork of self-esteem was laid in their families. Much later, I met one of my graduated students who commented to her friend, "Wilma was the only human teacher in the school."

Motivated by these insights, I enrolled in an evening class on "values clarification." I wanted to understand my beliefs and values, then use them as signposts to make better decisions. In the last class, I drew a shield to display my values and a motto. The words *"I create my destiny"* dropped onto the page from nowhere. For a woman raised in the victimhood of Calvinism, *I create my destiny* was so extreme that I hesitated reading it out loud. Since Mother's death, sometimes I felt like a leaf swirling in the winds of overwhelming forces. Nevertheless, I had grown far beyond the life prescribed for me. I did not feel like a rudderless yacht at the mercy of life's storms, but rather a woman who had her hand on the tiller of her own life—at least some days. Flirting with destiny taught me my desires were not immoral but were actually arrows, like invitations to dare, pointing to a more fulfilling life.

With our energetic group of friends, Clive and I lived at full tilt. Most weekends found us tramping or biking or windsurfing.

"So why were you late this morning? What did you get up to this weekend?" asked Sue the physical education teacher as she flipped her waist-length hair and flashed her freckled dimples.

"I was tramping with Rob and Clive in the Richmond Range in the South Island. We camped out on Saturday night. On Sunday, we thought we had plenty of time, so we enjoyed lunch on the summit. The guys trundled rocks over the cliff, then listened to them crash far below into the deserted bush." Sue looked at me as if I was mad. While I loved the mountains, she loved to party.

"On the descent, we lost our way and bushwhacked down a creek bed. We jumped and scrambled down fallen tree trunks and waterfalls. At one place, Clive threw his pack down a waterfall, and it disappeared in a back eddy for several minutes before surfacing. It was dark when we hiked out of the forest. We missed the last ferry and spent the night in Blenheim airport, the four of us stretched out on the seats in our wet sleeping bags. In the morning, commuters in their business suits and high heels tiptoed around puddles of water, avoiding the wet seats."

"Wilma, you are the only teacher that looks more exhausted on Monday than you did on Friday." Sue shook her head and laughed.

As a professional couple, with access to birth control, Clive and I were at the forefront of exploring our relationship in ways not possible for previous generations. While we enjoyed recreational activities together, conflicts arose over housework and grocery shopping. My father had cultivated an extensive vegetable garden, but I never saw him help in the kitchen. That was my mother's territory.

Our mountaineering friends Noel, a skilled carpenter, and Mary, a land evaluator, were renovating their old house. When they threw a racy 1930s party, all dressed up, we twisted and rocked to the music into the early morning.

Life at school eased and I had more time for friendship. With the growth of feminism and shifting roles, I wondered how their relationships worked. One lunchtime in the Mount Cook Cafe, Noel and I sat across from each other. Out of the windows, I watched rushing clouds and yellow gorse climb up the hillside. Between mouthfuls of quiche, above the noisy coffee machine, we chatted about our mountain exploits and reminisced about our recent week's sailing trip. "I loved the day we walked on that island up through the forest to the hermit's cabin, hollering to you down on the silver beach. It was magic," I said.

"To think it was because Rob broke his leg skiing that he organized the sailing trip."

"Did I ever tell you when Clive and I saw him in the hospital? He was asleep, so we left. When he woke up, the old man in the next bed told him a couple of young punks had come to visit." We laughed, with Noel's smile framed by his blond hair and John Lennon glasses.

"I have half an hour before class. Have you time to walk along the rocks?" I asked. The wind swept the spray off the towering surf as it whistled over Cook Straight from Mount Tapuaenuku, the highest peak in the northeast of the South Island. Clive and I had recently enjoyed climbing it. Between gusts, we talked. "I have been thinking about my relationship with Clive in the mountains. On our last trip across the Olivine ice plateau with Margaret and Rob, we descended from the glacier down a precipitous gully in a thunderstorm. Clive and Rob set up the belays and the ropes. I was happy to follow their directions. Margaret was uneasy with their lead. I like to be part of making decisions, but Clive is a more experienced climber than I am. I respect his mountain know-how."

"We both make decisions," Noel tilted his head.

"Last weekend in her vegetable patch," I replied, "when I told Mary about the bike trip I just did with Linda and Margaret up the west coast of the South Island, she told me that life was too short to cycle. She surprised me. Cycling with women is a new way of belonging to ourselves. I love it."

"Mary's stretched for time right now. She's studying for her land-evaluator exams. A couple of weeks ago, we tried to climb Mount Hicks near Mount Cook. A storm came in, so we retreated. We are going again as soon as the weather looks settled," Noel said.

We walked back over the slippery rocks, inhaling the smell of seaweed. I hugged Noel and jumped into my car. "I can't be late for grade eight. I hope they don't massacre me. Take care on the mountain."

CHAPTER 13

Against the Wind

"What does not kill you makes you stronger."
~ Friedrich Nietzsche

September 1981

It was my third New Zealand winter, and everything that morning went according to plan. In brilliant sunlight, five of us flew in a tiny ski plane from Mount Cook Village, over the Main Divide, to Pioneer Hut on the west side. We landed on the Fox Glacier. I was captivated by the amphitheatre of magnificent peaks—Lendenfelt, Douglas Peak, and Mount Tasman—glistening in the sun. A few months before, in the May holidays, autumn in New Zealand, I had stared up at these peaks when I biked with Linda and Margaret along the West Coast. As I sucked air up the hills and coasted down through the forest, alive with bird song, I had longed to be up those inaccessible mountains. Now that dream turned into reality.

After day two of the ski-mountaineering trip, I wrote in my journal. *This morning, under clear blue skies, we had crossed pristine glaciers and picked our way through the icefall to Katie's Col. Awestruck, we ate our lunch under the formidable face of Mount*

Tasman. The weather changed. On our return, we battled the brutal nor-west wind. The hut vanished. The spindrift stung my face. My eyes filled with snow. Tony's skis, a few metres in front, disappeared into the whiteout. I prayed he saw the crevasses. I concentrated all my energy into sliding one ski in front of the other. I did not let Tony's skis out of my sight, not for one second.

Two days later, when the weather cleared, our group headed over the Main Divide. This tested my endurance and ski skills. Under the spine of the Southern Alps, we skinned up the glacier. Tony's friend, a wiry man, and his equally fit girlfriend set a gruelling pace. I was paranoid I'd get left behind. My pack contained the minimum essentials to survive a night out at nine thousand feet. As I pushed my skis, my body, and my pack up to Graham Saddle, we passed four young men with beads of sweat on their foreheads.

"We are going over Graham Saddle and down the Tasman Glacier," one of them announced.

"We are camping up on the Divide and hope to ski up Mount De La Beche," Tony said.

"Oh, we are not as fit as you," one young man said. Instantly, I had a revelation. Here was living proof that I was fitter than many men. What a mistake to compare myself to the fittest. I would never measure up with some, but I was strong and fit. Not a weak female after all.

Above Graham Saddle, we roped up and wove our way through broken cascades of tumbling ice. While in awe, I trusted a serac would not fall on my head. Silently, I asked the weather gods to be kind and to decline from sending a vicious storm. That evening, we pitched our tent on a snow shelf high above the world. The sun sank into the Tasman Sea. Nature's light show cast a pink then golden glow on the peaks, a lavish reward for my hard work. To my amazement, Tony's friend pulled out a three-quarter full, heavy glass bottle of Grand Mariner and offered it around.

The icefall.

Camping on the Great Divide

The following day, Tony and his friend headed to the summit of Mt. Del la Beche and narrowly missed falling into a crevasse. The rest of us traversed around the mountain and down the Tasman Glacier. On the Ball Hut Road, we met New Zealand's first female mountain guide who pointed to the faint trail clinging to the side of the massive mountain and asked, "Are those your tracks?" Smiling to myself, I thought, *I have come a long way since my first ski-touring trip three years ago.*

A few weeks later, the phone rang. It was Rob. "I can't believe it. Graham Mac died in an avalanche on Whakapapa Ski Hill."

"Oh my god, what happened?" I asked, my hand clutching my throat and my voice shaking.

"On the last run, he skied down a thirty-foot gulley, and the wet snow avalanched. The rescue team dug him out in fifteen minutes. He was face down. They couldn't resuscitate him." My shoulders stiffened, and my legs shook.

At the reception after Graham's funeral, I mingled among the large crowd, many from the Alpine Club, and reminisced with my friend about my first Christmas trip up Mount Sefton when I'd met Graham. We laughed about how we had raced up the valley, trying to catch up with him. His son talked to me about Graham's many daring first ascents up NZ's remote mountains. This new loss triggered my unsettled grief at my mother's violent death, and my version of the lyrics of Simon & Garfunkel played in my head: *Come on darkness my old friend; come and talk to me again.*

My old pal wanderlust accompanied this unwelcome visitation of death. I joined Clive on a week's business trip to Sydney, Australia. The sunshine, and the diverse Kings Cross nightlife, which included a visit to "Les Girls," the gorgeous all-male revue, burned away more fragments of my narrow-mindedness.

On Clive's day off, we hired a catamaran at Balmoral Beach. We hummed along. Clive always pushed his limits and looked at the water beyond the Spit Bridge.

"I wonder what's through there?" Clive asked.

"Look," I cautioned him, pointing to a turbulent current. "See the white caps. The tide is rushing out."

"No worries," he said, and with his single-minded determination, sailed under the shadow of the bridge as cars drove over our heads. Then the current caught the hull and swept us out of control into the bridge pier. I screeched as the mast stuck on the bridge. There were some ugly moments before the racing tide freed us and we floated back in the gentle waters of the bay. My voice shaking, I snapped at Clive.

While Clive attended his meetings, I learned to windsurf in the warm waters. As I skimmed over the waves, I found myself imagining what it would be like to live in Sydney.

Back in Wellington one evening, Rob knocked on our door. "Noel and Mary have died on Mount Hicks in Mount Cook Park," he told us.

"W-What?" I stammered as if punched in my gut.

"They were climbing the east face. It appeared they had reached the summit and were on the descent when a North West storm overtook them. It took several days for the storm to pass before the mountain rescue helicopter searched for them. One of the rescuers thought he saw Noel's arm waving. When they found them, his sleeve was blowing in the wind and his crampon was broken. They both froze to death." My body warmth drained away.

The next day, Clive left to work a short contract in Australia. Southerly storms rolled in, and rain pounded our windows. A small earthquake shook my home. I wrote in my journal. *As the wind howls, the house creaks and groans. Are these accidents a result of fate? Is it farfetched to think that I create my destiny? What do I want mine to be? I want to feel life pulsing through my veins, Clive's warm arms around me. Yet I feel desolate and alone. I want someone to reassure me that everything is going to be okay.*

When Clive returned, we chewed over our friends' deaths. "I can't believe we'll never see Noel and Mary again," I said, wiping my tears.

"I can't understand why they didn't stop," Clive said.

"This was their second attempt at this route. They were so determined."

"Hypothermia and freezing to death must be horrific," Clive said. "It's weird. We saw them just a couple of weeks ago at the movie, *Picnic at Hanging Rock*. Those schoolgirls went climbing around the rocks and never returned. It's unnerving. The mountains are cruel taskmasters."

"They were so full of life," I said. "What happens after death? I don't believe in hell as my parents did."

"I think death is the end. There's nothing afterwards," Clive said.

"What about reincarnation?" I said. "Will they return in another body? I know that my parents have died. I can't get my head around my mortality."

Later, a mutual friend told me that Mary had thought death was the ultimate challenge. To me, these deaths were catastrophic. A waste of two people full of potential. Later that month, on a tramping trip, a nightmare forced me awake. I felt a claw at my throat and heard Noel scream in terror. A couple of weeks later, Rob, Clive, Sue, and I used the tickets that Noel had purchased to see the Australian band "The Icehouse." In a peculiar twist of fate, the stage looked like an ice cave, and the lyrics chilled me to the bone. *"It's always cold inside the icehouse."*

After Noel and Mary's deaths, I developed an aversion to the mountains. One Saturday morning, in search of a less treacherous recreation, I ventured down to the Royal Port Nicholson Yacht Club. Lean men, dressed in yellow oilskins were busy coiling ropes, unrolling sails, and tying halyards. Hesitantly, I approached a woman in a striped shirt. "I can sail." I said, "Do you know if anyone needs crew?"

"You could try *Omega*. They often need help," she replied, pointing to a green yacht with white letters on the bow. They welcomed me on board. I clipped the headsail onto the front stay.

Out on the harbour, the wind verged on gale force. Beating into the wind, the boat keeled over and the hull pounded over the sea, the deck awash with frothing surf as salt spray stung my face. The weather-beaten skipper with grey hair peeking out from his sailor's hat called out, "Gybe ho!" We, the crew, worked the winches and pulled in the sheets fast. *Omega* raced downwind with the fleet of dancing yachts, their colourful spinnakers billowing in the northwest wind.

After the race, in the clubhouse, beer and talk flowed. As the noise levels rose, I pricked up my ears and heard that several boats were committed to crossing Cook Strait on the Easter weekend.

"Do you want to crew?" Richard, a friendly skipper, asked me.

"Can I bring my husband, Clive?" I asked.

"Sure," Richard said.

"I have always wanted to sail across the Cook Strait," I beamed.

Easter Friday arrived, a sunny day with cirrus clouds in the azure sky. The crackling radio predicted southerly winds in the Cook Strait with a weather front coming about six in the evening. Richard was thirty-six, thin, tanned, and unshaven with tousled hair. Like a modern-day gypsy, he lived on his boat. Using tide tables and winds, we calculated our departure time to reach the notorious rip at low tide and to be across before the front came. Early afternoon, Richard fired up the engine; we threw off the bowlines and reversed into the channel. Fascinated, Clive and I watched the marina with its forest of masts recede into the distance. *Winsome* chugged up Evans Bay, out past Pencarrow Head and moaning Minnie, the steel buoy that audibly warned sailors of the jagged reefs. In Cook Strait, the passenger ferry to the South Island passed us. It looked huge and stable, while our thirty-nine-foot ferroconcrete yacht felt diminutive and exposed. Anticipation tinged with unease grumbled in my stomach.

Out in the open ocean with the sails up, I looked with alarm at the increasing size of the waves. I talked to Matthew, Richard's seven-year-old son, who stood in the stern.

"These waves are huge," I said.

"They aren't as big as the ones *Geramco* had," he replied.

"Who's *Geramco*?" I asked.

"*Geramco* was one of the boats in the Round the World Whitbread Yacht Race," he answered.

"Hmm," I said, surprised at his confidence.

Winsome pounded over the waves on a broad reach. Ahead, it looked like bedlam. The waves came from both directions and met with a massive crash. This was the infamous rip. I stood, my hand clenched onto the backstay, in my stomach, a demon, was wide-awake and growled in alarm as the boat pivoted and rammed through the chaos. When we left the rip behind, the waves settled into a regular rhythm, and Richard set course for Karori Rock, a lighthouse that marked the edge of serrated reefs on the South Island.

Ominous clouds with winds over twenty-five knots replaced the clear sky of the morning. It began to rain. Matthew, feeling sick, headed down below to the cozy aft cabin. I calculated we had two hours to go. Cook Strait, the only break along a thousand miles of land, with its powerful currents, tested me far more than I expected.

"Look! Dolphins!" Richard shouted. I watched a school of about thirty dolphins play, and for many euphoric moments, I forgot the dread in my belly.

Just as I became comfortable with the waves and felt excited, Clive began to move forward. There was an urgent cry from our skipper. "Clive, hold on." Richard's voice disappeared in the crash of water while the force of the wave knocked him to his knees, the cockpit awash, the sheets swept overboard. Down below, the splash of water woke up Matthew, who vomited.

Dark squalls of rain obscured the South Island. Walls of sea with foaming crests surged around us. Richard broke the crowded silence. "There's the ferry!" It was a faint white blob in the gray dusk. In his element, his eyes danced as if electrified, "That's Tory Channel, where we're headed. Look, we're surfing down the wave."

With the wind behind us, the boom trailed in the water as *Winsome* charged through the rough seas. Anxious to reach the safety of inland waters, my adventurous spirit had evaporated. Even as the lights of Tory Channel flashed their welcoming glow and drew closer, the final forty-five minutes dragged on. The white foam of the waves booming on the black cliffs inched closer until I could almost reach over and touch them. When Richard turned the engine on, the chug, chug, chug cheered me. The smell of diesel mixed with salt water filled the air. Catapulted out of the raging storm, like a stopper popping out of a champagne bottle, we were sucked into the gap between the cliffs. With the land on both sides, the dark glistening water became flat, although the gale swirled in all directions. The crew raced into action, lowering the sails, though not fast enough for our skipper who shouted obscenities from the cockpit as the mainsail thrashed in the wind.

The pool of light from our searchlight swept over the inky water. We hunted for the flag marking the entrance to Deep Bay. When we found the orange buoy attached to the mooring, Clive and I hauled up the rope and tucked it onto the bollard at the bow. The constriction around my throat released, but my teeth chattered as we tucked the sails away and tied up the sheets. I clambered down the hatch to welcome warm domesticity. We soothed ourselves with hot soup, chops, salad, potatoes and liberal quantities of whiskey and green ginger wine.

That night, tucked up in my sleeping bag, the rain pounded on the deck, the wind screamed in the rigging, and the water gurgled in the sink. In the brief periods of calm, I lay wide awake, anticipating the next maelstrom. I pulled my pillow over my head to dull the noise, but it was an interminable night. Near dawn, one of the halyards hammered on the mast. I ventured up on deck to tighten it. The chaos of white caps and spray made me think that Dante's inferno was not of fire but water. I rushed back to the warmth of my sleeping bag.

Soon after, Richard stretched like a cat, exposing his hairy belly, then looked out of the hatch at the tempest and quickly retreated. In the middle of making tea, I heard a grinding noise from the hull. "What's that?" he shouted in alarm. He ran to the hatch. "We're aground." Richard rushed to the engine; he threw towels, oilskins, and boots onto the floor, pulled the cord, and pushed the throttle. The engine jumped to life. Pumped with adrenaline, Clive and I raced onto the spray-soaked deck, alarmed to see the seaweed-covered rocks a few feet from the boat. Using all our strength, we heaved the jammed mooring rope off and threw it over the side. *Winsome* slowly headed away from danger. In the ferocious winds, she had dragged the concrete mooring.

We motored to Picton, the town at the head of Charlotte Sound. The cold wind whipped the spray off the surface of the water into tornadoes about a hundred feet high. The raw power of the gale riveted me. I vacillated between being out on the deck and staying in the warm engine cabin where the dinghy lashed to the foredeck obscured my view.

Sunday dawned full of promise, cotton wool clouds danced over the sky. After morning tea, with the sails up, we headed to Queen Charlotte Sound. As the day progressed, the breeze freshened. *Winsome* skimmed over the water. The sun shimmered on the turquoise sea. Sunlight bathed the hills, while ahead, some dark clouds looked menacing. Clive and I dangled our legs over the side, enjoying our good fortune and sailing at its best. We sailed past the Bay of Many Coves at a speedy seven knots. Gannets, petrels, and terns shared the sky with our white sails. "Weird winds around here; they change directions in a second," our skipper commented. At one with the sea and the wind, Richard focused on trimming the sails.

The landscape in the Sounds looked exploited, the native forest burned down long ago and the scarred hillsides grassed over to provide fodder for some of New Zealand's sixty million sheep. We passed a few geometrical plantations of Pinus Radiata and

Monterey Pine, originally from California and valued for their fast growth rate.

Our destination appeared: Ships Cove. Richard called gybe ho and the boat moved smoothly onto a broad reach. Passing the helm to Clive, he turned on the engine. This was followed by swearing, tinkering, and silence. The engine refused to start. To avoid ramming the boat on the land, we went about and headed back out to the sea.

"We'll have to sail on to the jetty," Richard told us. "Take down the mainsail. We'll sail in on the jib. Clive, when I call, you lower the jib. Wilma, you jump on the jetty." Silently *Winsome* charged landward. The jetty was too far away for me to jump. Richard leaped onto the rocks to stop his boat. Clive clambered onto the jetty.

My period and all the nervous tension exhausted me. Happy to be on solid ground, I soaked in peace as I walked through the lush bush where epiphytes and tree ferns gleamed in the sun. In 1770, Captain Cook had spent time here replenishing his ships with food, water, and wood. I could barely imagine the unbelievable courage of those sailors.

On my return, the sight of the starting motor strewn on the jetty, like thousands of pieces of confetti, shocked me. Richard's face was smeared with engine grease, which added to his dishevelled appearance. Twenty-four hours later, the motor had been reassembled, replaced, removed, and replaced several times. Disappointment, deep sighs, and stress filled the air. Nobody said much. I found it difficult to control the pressure and enjoy the beauty of this place. Clive and I needed to get back to Wellington for work. I tried to talk to myself. *If you get yourself into these things, you must have patience when things don't work as planned.* At one thirty a.m., the engine sputtered into life but only at half speed.

In the morning, the weather forecast predicted more gale-force winds. Always up for an adventure and reluctant to admit failure, we decided to sail back to Wellington. For a while, I thought, *I love this, so exciting.* After a few hours, we identified a beach on the North Island where we often went hiking. With a sense of relief, I went below to fetch our sandwiches. *Winsome* went about and headed back into the middle of turbulent Cook Straight, and my respite was short-lived. The prevailing northwest gale was on the nose, coming from the exact direction we were heading. We still had to go through the rip, and on top of that, the engine only worked at half speed. It never occurred to me that we could turn about, and with the wind behind us, reach the safety of the Sounds where we had come from. I had time to contemplate a watery end.

Richard and I sailing across Cook Straight

With only three of us on board, I sat at the back of the cockpit, my arms tightly crossed, head bowed, and our lifelines clipped into the rigging. Even with six layers of clothes, I shivered. *If I ever get off this boat alive, I'll never...* My thoughts were interrupted as I cowered from yet another wall of icy Cook Strait water that seemed intent on eliminating me from the planet. Water dripped off Richard's face as he concentrated on steering his boat through the mayhem. Clive stood behind me. His only comment, as a wave towered up to the spreaders, was, "Oh shit! Oh shit, that's a big one!" I couldn't believe that I had thought sailing to be a safer sport than mountaineering.

Ten hours after leaving Ship's Cove, we reached Wellington Harbour. Never before had the city lights appeared so welcome. I hugged my cup of hot chocolate. My teeth clattered as my body shook all over. Once home, I soaked in a hot bubble bath. With my eyes closed, I breathed to the bottom of my lungs and thanked my lucky stars that I was alive to go to school the next morning.

Did I keep my promise never to go sailing again? A few weekends later, as southerly rain spattered on the windows, the insistent ring of the telephone interrupted Bette Midler's earthy voice on the record player singing "The Rose."

"It's Richard. How are you doing? I'm in Picton, and we're sailing to Wellington tomorrow. I have fixed the engine and the weather forecast looks good. Will you come?"

"I don't think so. I have to work on my physics classes. Clive is away on business..." I hesitated, knowing that I never liked to miss out on an opportunity.

"Michaela and Rob are here. The southerly wind will be behind us."

Bette Midler's voice oozed *"It's the dream afraid of waking..."* I swallowed my indecision and rushed to catch the afternoon ferry.

That evening when I joined *Winsome* and crew, I made the mistake of drinking too much. Sunday morning, the sun shone on an ocean that looked manageable. But the heaving ocean did not mix with my hangover. I hung over the side, seasick. By the time we had almost reached the safety of Wellington Harbour, it was pitch dark. Then we saw the huge form of the ferry bearing down on us. PANIC! This time, our navigation lights did not work, and again, the engine refused to start. After much cursing and swearing, it burst into life, and we veered away from our collision course.

But I did not give up on sailing. With stubborn determination, I braved my fear. My third and final crossing was in a light northwest wind. Richard, Clive, and I left from Wellington, sailed gently over the Strait; the huge spinnaker pulled us along like a bird skimming over the ocean. When dolphins swam on the bow, I valued my persistence, Richard's skills, and my deepening appreciation of the ocean.

On my next holiday, Clive and I, along with my biking buddies, Linda and Margaret and their partners, flew to Fiji with our bikes stashed in the hold. In the morning, the cock crowed, and church bells called us to early morning mass, interrupting my bizarre dreams. Rain pattered on the roof. The water ran down the drainpipes. The tropical frogs croaked. I inhaled the delicious fragrance of frangipani flowers. A cool wind blew through the Kapok trees as their sparse foliage dripped. The leaves of a huge mango tree glittered in the rain. Humidity pervaded the atmosphere, and even my body felt soggy.

A group of locals came in for breakfast. They were shaken after a wild sea crossing from another island. Their skipper laughed as if it was a joke, but I identified with their fear.

The rain stopped, and we set out to cycle to Lovoni. Tropical emerald undergrowth fringed the road. Coconut palms swayed high above the breadfruit and cassava trees. Mist veiled hills dotted with small, whitewashed houses surrounded by flowers. Like a welcoming committee, the children and adults greeted us with a shout of "Bulla!" On the gravel road, my road bike with its narrow rims was like a bucking horse with a mind of its own. On arrival at a remote beach, we swam in the sapphire ocean. A young boy with a machete climbed up the palm behind us and knocked down some coconuts. He generously cut open a fresh coconut for each of us. This was paradise.

The next morning at the Old Cabin Inn, we chatted to our cheery hotelier.

"We're going snorkelling. We're worried about the sharks."

"No need to fear the sharks here. You'll be fine," he reassured us.

Out on the reef, the fish of all colours hung as if in suspended animation. When we scared them, they darted into the shelter of the coral where moray eels concealed themselves in the crevices. I swam beside Clive. "These are fantastic, but I want to see a big one!" he said. Cold, I swam back to the boat. Linda pointed to Clive, who was standing on the reef up to his waist in water shouting, "Shark!"

On the Geiki snowfield in the Southern Alps

"Oh, don't worry. I am sure he's only pretending," I said, squirming into my dry clothes.

When Clive returned, he told me, "After you left this, huge dark form came towards me on the deep side of the reef. Just as it was upon me, the six-foot shark turned away!"

Back in the hotel, the front page of the *Fijian Times* had a picture of a man covered from head to foot in bandages after a vicious shark attack. Clive confronted the manager.

"I thought you said not to worry about the sharks. Look!"

"Well, here in Fiji, we think that the sharks only attack certain people, like the ones who have been up to no good and stealing from the church collection," he replied without missing a beat. Unsure of our karma, we didn't test our luck with the sharks again.

Less than thirty-six hours after we left Fiji, Rob, Doreen, Clive, and I stood on our skis on the Geiki Snowfield on the Frans Josef Glacier in the Southern Alps. Standing beside our mountainous packs, we licked the ice creams Rob had bought just before our small ski plane took off. We looked dreamily at the plane, returning to the relative civilization of the west coast of the South Island. Without a doubt, if life was *"the pursuit of wow,"* I had certainly found it.

CHAPTER 14

Ragged Edges

"I do my thing and you do your thing.
I am not in this world to live up to your expectations,
And you are not in this world to live up to mine.
You are you, and I am I, and if by chance
we find each other, it's beautiful.
If not, it can't be helped."
~ Frederick Perls, Gestalt Therapy Verbatim

1982

The days shortened, clouds raced like demons, and the trees moved as if possessed. A few weeks into my fourth year of competently teaching science, I had not organized my next holiday and found it difficult to settle. With Clive away on long business trips, I missed his loving touch and comforting arms. I sought consolation more readily at hand: coffee, chocolate cake, and wine with friends recalling our past trips and planning future ventures. The following mornings with throbbing temples and a short temper, I biked to school.

One night, as the southerly winds rocked my house, I picked up the phone and dialled the therapist's number. Before it rang, I dropped it back onto the cradle. In the kitchen, I gobbled cookies. *What good can shrinks do? They will mess me up. I am not mentally ill.* But my interior world, like a truculent toddler, was not content to remain unknown to me and demanded exploration. Crumbs fell off my chin as I phoned again. A male voice informed me, "A group starts next week. There's one place available."

So, I returned to the basement where I had participated in the couples weekend after my mother's death. David, the tall, bearded therapist, set out the ground rules and asked us our purpose for being there. An author talked about his writer's block; Susan, an attractive woman with short hair, talked about her wish to heal after leaving an abusive relationship. Confused, I told the group I was trying to decide whether or not to have children as, at thirty-three, time was running out. That evening, I uncovered a more unnerving issue. An insistent fire raged in my vagina, spread into my abdomen, and burned up my restraint. With the development of reliable birth control, it felt like musical chairs among my friends. When the music stopped everyone changed partners.

Hesitantly, I shared my curiosity about sexual experimentation. "When I took my marriage vows in Scotland, I pledged to stay together *through sickness and in health until death us do part*. I don't break my promises," I said. "Now some of my friends are having affairs. Before I was married, my mother wept for two days after she discovered my diaphragm on my bed. I never discussed sexuality with my mother or my sisters. Nice girls were not subject to sexual cravings. Nice girls said *no*."

"You must have someone in mind?" the therapist asked. I felt myself blush from my belly button to the crown of my head.

"Heavens no!" I lied.

I discovered the group did not share my terrors about infidelity. I ignored the imagined wrath of the patriarchs and my dead mother. With Clive away on business, that weekend at a party I found the object of my desire, our unmarried biking and mountaineering friend. He had sandy hair, blue eyes, a six-pack, and a tight cyclist's butt. Emboldened by wine, we embraced. With the moist burning sensation in my genitals irresistible, we found ourselves in bed and hungrily explored our bodies. With my lust satiated, the aftertaste of guilt stuck in my throat as my wedding ring dug into my finger.

The next Sunday, back to normal on a cycle tour, I chased my ski-touring friend Tony up a hill through the bright green fields in the Wairapa. He startled one of New Zealand's sixty million sheep, and in a flash, it jumped between our bikes. With no time to swerve, I hit it with full force in the ribs, flew over the handlebars, and landed smack on my jaw. Who knows what damage I did to the sheep? It was nowhere to be seen. The front wheel of my bike never went around again.

Cartoon by one of my pupils

A few days later, Clive returned from Indonesia. We nuzzled into each other, my arm flung over his tanned torso. I softened to his familiar feathery touch and welcomed a sea of pleasure. In the morning, we untangled our limbs. But I was in shark-infested waters. On our patio, as we sipped coffee, I stared at the ground, my teeth digging into my lips.

"I slept with Johnny. I am sorry. I didn't want to hurt you," I confessed as my temples throbbed and my stomach cramped.

"What? How could you? Him of all people!" Clive's face contorted as he kicked the table.

"I was at a party... I had a bit much to drink, and one thing led to another." I rubbed my eyes and held my hot cheeks in my hands.

Late for school, I snaked down the hill on my bike. My front mudguard scraped on the wheel. In motion, I kicked the wheel. For the second time in two weeks, I found myself groaning on the road. Pain pierced my cheek, thumb, and hips. Tears streamed, and my body ached all over as I picked myself up, shook off the gravel, and limped with my fractured bike to my doctor's office, only minutes up the road. I called the school secretary, "I'm not going to make it in today. I just went over the handlebars of my bike."

That week, I showed up at group therapy with my left arm in a white plaster cast and my thumb protruding at an awkward ninety-degree angle. First in the hot seat, I told my bike stories adding that, "I didn't want to hurt anyone."

"Your jaw and arm look so sore," David said. "Grab that child's bike over in the corner and sit on it. How does it feel?"

"I'm scared to go cycling again. I've had two accidents in two weeks." I sobbed.

"Are you punishing yourself? How were you disciplined as a child?"

"Mother and Father hit me with a hard slipper," I said through my clenched teeth.

"Ouch, that sounds painful," he said.

"I didn't know any better." I wobbled on the bike.

"Where do you feel sadness in your body?" he continued

"I swallow it. It sticks in my throat and chokes me." After more reflection, I continued.

"When I cycle, I don't need to compete with my fast friends. I must pay attention."

Later, David stood up with his hands on his lower back and announced. "I have hurt my back. It's a message that I need to take care of myself."

"How can you take care of your back? Isn't that the doctor's job?" I questioned. The notion that my accidents and body aches were trying to get my attention was revolutionary. Many times, over those eight weeks, my mindset was challenged.

"Don't rush things. When you're set to make a move forward, it happens with ease," David said. "I have just stopped smoking. I knew it'd happen when I was ready and able to meet my needs in more healthy ways." These self-care concepts were alien to me. It was as if I had landed on a different planet.

After my mother's death, and my friends' deaths on the mountain, I refused to accept his statement that "accidents don't happen." I resisted taking personal responsibility that far.

"My wife and children are important to me," David told me. "My kids provide me with so much stimulation. They're always trying to persuade me to do fun things like tennis and skiing." The others in the group reinforced the love of their children.

"Having children is the most creative thing I've ever done," said Susan, the mother of two boys. I looked at her, baffled. I worked on my resistance to motherhood.

"I don't want to be like my mother," I eventually said. Like a skilled archaeologist, David's questions had dug deep, through the layers of my subconscious beliefs.

"My mother thought life ended after children," I heard myself say.

"I can see how you might not want to have children if you believe that," David said. After a few minutes to allow this to sink in, he asked, "Imagine five years from now, and you have some children. What is the best it could be? What is the worst?"

He suggested I try cuddling a cushion as if it were a baby. I lost interest in the inert cushion when he made the next statement: "Personal change comes from therapy, travel, and relationships." While my opinion of therapy was still in question, I did know that travel, friendship, and mountaineering inspired me more than anything. This prompted me to talk about my listlessness and discontent in the classroom.

"What would you be planning if you were responsible for your happiness?" David asked.

Although I had stated in my values course that *"I create my destiny,"* it was only in fleeting moments of optimism that a chink of light seduced me into believing that more was possible. However, the answer to David's question was easy: more travel—in fact, a whole year of travel. Was this even possible? Here was an opportunity to discover if I created my destiny or not. Wayne Dwyer's book *The Sky is the Limit* provided more motivation.

In the basement where the group met, there was a sauna. After one session, I was astonished that both sexes went in naked. I stripped down, wrapped myself in a towel, and curled my shoulders and arms over my breasts.

"What are you hiding?" David asked.

"My boobs are too droopy," I replied, my face burning.

"Your body is beautiful," he said. Only Clive had told me that.

What is he after? I thought suspiciously. Ever so gradually, I ditched my shame and grew more comfortable with my own body.

One evening, as my eyes smarted as I cycled up the hill to the group, grieving the untimely deaths of my mother, Graham, Noel, and Mary, the brilliant rays of the sun erupted behind the towering cumulus clouds and lit up the harbour. I remembered the burst of sun that shone down at Mother's grave. This reminded me that, when the light shone on my Indian ring, it revealed a six-pointed star. With this in mind, I released my sorrow and mental attachment to these tragic deaths and opened to the mystery of the radiant force, which nourished the life my mother had generously given me.

On a wet windy day, I stared at a torn sepia photo, patched with sellotape, of my mother sitting on a bench built around a tree trunk, holding the hands of a man with slick-backed hair. Their heads touched. She wore a coat with an elegant fur collar, and his tie on his white shirt was askew. On the back of the photo, in spindly writing, was *"Billy Whiteside, Carron Tower, Co Antrim."*

I imagine this was the young man she had told me about, the one she had walked with on the Cave Hill dressed in her Sunday best. In the 1930s, it was not polite to speak of bodily functions of any kind. Desperate, she had sneaked into a toilet, done her business, then rushed out. To her horror, when she looked down, instead of her umbrella, she clutched the toilet brush.

Now I wanted to know about her relationship with Billy. Did her heart beat so fast that she stopped thinking? Did she like his touch and then feel guilty? Or did the admonishment of her father about loose women scare her into repressing her longings? Her beau looks confident of her affections. Her sisters always affirmed she had an eye for the boys. Did her desire to be a midwife win over her attraction for Billy? I imagined her career move away from Belfast's brutality to Scotland was her way of pursuing her ambition.

At home, Clive and I jostled around one another, had bitter arguments, and slammed doors. We sank low, and for days at a time, we barely spoke. I had no sympathetic family to run home to and his was on the other side of the world. After many angry dialogues about separation, we established that neither of us wanted to leave our home, plus we loved going on trips together.

We decided we'd live together and came to a sketchy agreement to risk an open marriage. As the daring one in my family, I had figured out how to be a bad girl.

On one level, I thought an open marriage would be fun and exciting. While we both experimented with other partners and tasted momentary pleasures, my experiences did not live up to my expectations. The pendulum swing from repressive sexual extremes to free-fall with no rules quickly turned into quicksand and wreaked havoc. Romantic rivalries unearthed dark subterranean jealousies that tore me apart. I learned that, for me, an open marriage was unsustainable. I did not want to share Clive, the man I loved. More than that, I appreciated his unconditional acceptance, loyalty, and sense of humour.

As the school year wound down, the mountains that we both cherished called loud and clear. Accompanied by Rob and his friend Ed, we set off on a mountaineering trip to the Butler River in the West coast of the South Island, Rob in his pink parka, his brown eyes twinkling as he stooped to haul his pack onto his city slicker shoulders. His frequent jesting, calling out, "Are you a mouse or a man?" lightened our efforts.

After a day and a half of bushwhacking through the forest, dripping clouds obscured the summits. We stopped at a precarious two-wire bridge fifteen feet above a raging torrent that felt like a reflection of our relationship struggles. Clive walked across in perfect balance and gallantly returned for my pack. I watched Rob wobble and feared he would fall into the river. Once across, he quipped, "Go back, you'll all be drowned." Then with my arms extended, shivering and dizzy, I held on to the top wire and slid my boots along the bottom wire. On the other side, I stretched my foot onto the rock and welcomed Clive's outstretched, strong hands.

We laboured up piles of moraine and strode over crevasse-strewn glaciers to a high pass over to the Butler valley. Rob laughed, "If at first, you don't succeed… give up." Hungry on the descent, we looked forward to our food drop. That night, we consumed tinned treacle pudding and custard as we sat around our campfire. After our long day, we listened to Ed's enthusiastic stories about skiing around Banff in the distant Rocky Mountains. Being far from the city, the serenity of the night sky, the mountainscapes, and Clive... all made my heart sing.

Mountaineering in the Southern Alps

We hiked over another pass to stay the night in a small hunter's hut. My unrest bristled at posters of women in sexually suggestive poses. Perhaps, to the hunter, women were only of value as sexual objects? Something was missing for me as a woman in this male world. We hiked back to civilization between the silky beech trees.

"Clive and I award you with the title of 'honorary male,'" Rob said. Hadn't this been my goal all along? Now his teasing stung. I marched through the bush, my mind in a whirl of accusations and uncertainty. After all, I wasn't a man. I was a woman with complex emotions and needs that were not wrong, or flawed, but pointed me in a new direction.

Once more, I found myself at a crossroads. I had explored my life out to its ragged edges, honed my skills on the mountain and in the classroom, and uncovered my shadowy underbelly. Given Clive's and my difficulties, we needed a fresh challenge. Our mutual friend wanderlust hammered on our door. From the opposite end of the planet, a trip to Europe fired our imaginations. We'd ski, bike, hike, and visit our families.

Early in 1983, we packed our belongings into the cupboard that Noel built, rented out our home, and almost windsurfed our way to the airport. I clutched Clive, with the words from Bette Midler's song "The Rose," ringing in my ear: *"love it is a flower and you it's only seed."* I left New Zealand with an oversized rucksack filled with some resentments tucked between warm layers of evocative memories of teaching, mountains, sailing, and friendships.

CHAPTER 15

U-turn on the Edge

"Stand on the precipice of uncharted territory."
~ Alan Cohen

Clive and I biked across France over several Alpine passes.

1983

As Clive and I visited family, skied, and biked in Europe, doing what we did best, we renewed our relationship. One morning in Corsica, walking through the scrubby bush by the silver sands, a black snake slithered over my bare thigh. My chest tensed as if punched with a cricket ball. Unsteady, I walked to the village where I sipped a cappuccino to recover my composure. I watched a curly-haired toddler with her podgy arms wrapped around a big cat as she bundled it across the patio. The clarity of my next desire blinded me.

Back in Scotland, I visited my sister's families, and the vitality and laughter of my four nieces and nephew, chasing each other over the meadow, confirmed my longing. Clive left to work in Australia. I travelled alone for a couple of months in Kenya and China. On a third-class train to Kunming, as a solitary western woman, squashed on the hard bench between two Chinese men, I watched a man with gentle eyes pull his coat tenderly over his young daughter as she slept. His love confirmed my wish as the words, *"It's now or never"* reverberated through my mind. With no doubt as to whom I wanted to father my child, I found myself on a plane to Sydney. Tanned, slim, muscular, and a treat to my eyes, Clive met me at the airport.

We returned to New Zealand for a Christmas mountaineering trip. Rob, Margaret, Clive, and I stood beside our enormous backpacks. The receding hum of the aircraft and the smell of engine fuel were replaced by the damp musk of the bush, the melody of the river, and the song of the bellbirds. "No going back now!" Rob said, stating the obvious. Bent double, we groaned as we raised our packs, then headed up the trackless Hollyford Valley towards the mountains. In the temperate rainforest, I mustered all my perseverance to pull my body over tree roots and walk around rocks as big as small houses. We scrambled up the gravel moraine to the glacier and set up camp. Keas, inquisitive parrot-like birds, eyed our food. After a few days, I settled into the wilderness.

"Imagine if the so-called civilized world blew itself up," Clive said, munching salami.

"The cold war's terrifying. It would only take one deranged person to push that button, and it'll be the end of the world," Margaret replied.

"The air could be filled with radioactive fallout, and we'd never know," Rob added.

"Supposedly the trade winds will keep it up north. We should be okay in the Southern Hemisphere," Clive said.

"Hope you're right," I said.

"I can't imagine bringing a child into this crazy world," Margaret said. "Better a life of adventure than kids, eh, Wilma?" Ignoring her reminder of our informal pact not to have children, I strapped on my crampons. I did not tell her I had changed my mind. That afternoon, we roped up as we wove between enormous crevasses on the ice plateau. As the majestic mountain views unfolded, my stomach growled with increasing ferocity.

"It must be time for a snack," I announced.

"Wilma, you've already eaten all our rations for today. You'll have to wait for supper. It's lovely dehydrated chili again," Clive said.

"I'm starving," I said. I dug deep, waiting until we set up camp for dinner.

The day before we flew back to Sydney, I followed Rob and Clive on a rough trail fringed with lilies to climb Mount Rolleston, whose precipitous glaciers towered over us. I lagged behind, mystified as to why I could not keep up with them. On the summit, with peaks in all directions, a flutter of excitement raced in my heart. "I think you might be about to become a father," I whispered in Clive's ear. He stared at the view in silence that I recognized as his hesitancy to change our bold lifestyle. Then with a warm hug, together, we entered a doorway to the unknown terrain of pregnancy, through which there was no return.

Back in Sydney, unlike the time I had moped alone in our London apartment or the hesitation I'd experienced when I moved to New Zealand, I recognized that, to thrive in a city where I knew no one, I needed to work. At my first interview at a private all-girls school, the school marm looked askance at my elegant pink-toed sandals and bare legs. "We wear stockings on all but the hottest of days!" she warned me with a click of her tongue. As the temperature was at least 90 degrees Fahrenheit, I speculated that she must be heat deranged.

At my second interview in another private school, sweat ran down my forehead as I arrived late. With the male principal, vice-principal, and head science teacher, I discussed my teaching experience. "I am two months pregnant," I blurted out. In my ignorance, I pictured that my belly would become huge and stay that way for seven months. I did not know that my bump wouldn't show until I was about five months pregnant. Either the pro-British principal honoured my honesty or he was desperate for a teacher.

The following Monday, at the morning assembly, I stood in the back row on the stage with the other teachers and sang, "God Save the Queen." Taken aback at this display of colonialism, I caught one teacher's raised eyebrow as we both stifled a giggle. I learned that her name was Pat, and she taught art.

On Fridays, Clive and I met with my colleagues in one of Sydney's many restaurants, jabbing chopsticks into a steaming bowl of Pad Thai as I chatted with Pat.

"Do you have children?" I asked.

"Yes," she said. "I got pregnant when I was nineteen. I immigrated to Perth from England when they were little. I have three teenagers."

"Wow. I'm nervous about becoming a mother," I said, chewing my lips.

"You know, Wilma, having children is why all these suburbs are here." I raised my puzzled brow. "I went to art school and trained to be a teacher when my kids were little," she told me. I looked at her in awe, wondering how she managed all her responsibilities.

"I am determined not to let being pregnant slow me down," I said. "I am going hiking in the Blue Mountains on the long weekend. I swim most days after school. It helps my backache. I'll feed my baby for a few months and then return to teaching."

"Woah… take it easy," she replied.

"Pat, I need a gynecologist. Last year, I visited one. After he gouged my cervix with forceps, he told me the ties had fallen off my ten-year-old IUD," I confided.

"Oh, God, that sounds painful," she said.

"He said the IUD had to be removed under general anesthetic. Then as I lay naked from the waist down, trying to pull my T-shirt over my pubic hair, and with searing pains racking my abdomen, he asked me if I planned to have children. When I told him I hadn't made up my mind, he said, 'Only idiots don't have children. It's your duty to have children. It's so selfish not to have children.'"

"What a nerve," Pat said. "It's absolutely a woman's own choice to have a baby. A professional needs to help you make an informed decision, not bully you. A friend of mine liked Doctor Sutherland. He encourages natural child-birth."

Later that month, I peeped into the doctor's garden where flowers and butterflies danced the tango while breezes filled with frangipani fragrance blew into his office. He covered the routine questions. "What kind of birth do you want?" he asked.

"My sisters gave birth in the early seventies. My sister Dorothy told me she did not like being induced," I replied, shuffling in my seat. "My sister Ruth gave birth to her first child in Africa. Later, when her daughter was diagnosed with epilepsy, she discovered that she had been too long in the first stage of labour, which caused brain damage. I don't want that. I suppose I want it to be as pleasant as possible." I mumbled my ludicrous request thinking, *Isn't birth supposed to be painful?*

"I do home births, or I use the Birthing Center in The Royal Hospital for Women in Paddington. The rooms are like motel rooms rather than hospital rooms and staffed with midwives. In case of problems, the delivery rooms with all modern technology are down the corridor," he explained. He recommended I read *Active Birth* by Janet Balaskas.

In Scotland, both Clive and I had been born at home. Over the next few months, *Active Birth* became my bible. I endeavoured to keep medical involvement to a minimum and to prepare myself for a natural birth.

When my nose oozed green mucus, I delved into alternatives to mainstream medicine. I made an appointment with an herbalist who asked weird questions about my life. "How is your libido?" I didn't know what to say but realized that, after my repressive upbringing, it was a testament to biology that I had any libido at all.

"Do you have a healthy creative life?"

"I teach science. That's not artistic. I don't paint or do crafts. I journal, but I don't think it's creative," I said, hiding my confusion about what creativity had to do with my cold. Then she shone her light onto my irises.

"It looks like there is something here inherited from your mother." I looked at her, drawing a blank. She continued. "Your irises show that your body is too acidic, and you need to eat more alkaline foods like vegetables and fruits. Cut back on red meat, coffee, and no alcohol. You are in the second trimester. I recommend the herbs: nettles, lemon balm, and chamomile. Raspberry leaf tea will help tone your uterus and ease your labour." I took tottering steps to follow her dietary guidelines. I stocked up on her herbs, but they cluttered the kitchen shelves until I threw them in the garbage, while the raspberry leaf tea made me throw up.

Far from our friends, family, and mountains, Clive and I felt rootless and disconnected. We circled our growing foothold in this new country. In the flat, traffic-congested city, we woke to the unfamiliar caw of the currawongs and the same pale blue sky every day. As the day proceeded, the air thickened with hazy pollution. At dusk, the flight paths of black fruit bats heralded the night. To grow roots, we joined the Middle Harbour Yacht Club and North

Sydney Bushwalkers Club, where we learned how to treat snake bites and made friends on fun trips. But in my apartment, I had visible emotional anchors displayed, not of Scotland but photos of us on a glaciated mountain in New Zealand with my white lips, like those of a clown, plastered in zinc oxide to protect them from the high-altitude sun.

One weekend, with beads of perspiration on my forehead, smelling eucalyptus and listening to the waves thunder up the beach, we walked through the Kuringai National Park at the edge of the city. "I wonder what Rob and our Kiwi friends are up to this weekend," I said.

"Probably biking, or tramping in the Tararuas, or windsurfing," Clive said wistfully.

"I don't suppose I could keep up with them now. I miss them. Couldn't we go back to Wellington? We have two houses there and great friends," I said.

"We've been through this," Clive said. "There is no work for me in New Zealand," Clive said. With my chest deflated, I kicked the sand and breathed in the sea air to calm myself.

"With all our family in Scotland and our friends in New Zealand, I am lonely," I said, tears stinging my eyes. "It is a big responsibility to bring a child into this world. I need your help. I don't need either of us to have affairs."

"I will support you." He put his arm around me, and I snuggled in.

However, my next request met resistance: "Will you come to the birth?"

In Scotland, in the seventies, neither of my brothers-in-law had been present at the birth of their babies.

"I don't know that I want to be there," he said.

"I don't think I want to be there either," I replied.

While I had gained confidence as a teacher and mountaineer, in the early hours of the morning, when sleep eluded me, my insecurities taunted me. I worried about labour, my ability to be a mother, my relationship with Clive, losing my body shape, and my loss of independence. An insensitive comment by a male stranger at a bar had triggered my irrational fears causing me much anguish: "Older women have babies with squint eyes." Added to the turbulence of adjusting to an unfamiliar country, there were a few days when it was all I could do not to disappear into a sinkhole of vulnerability. I reassured myself that, if our relationship didn't work out, I had a house in New Zealand and could teach to support my baby and myself.

On my many better days, I marvelled at the miracle of the baby growing inside my body without any need for me to think about it. *Oh, today we will grow a leg or an eye.* I surrendered to this miraculous process that was beyond my control. I discounted the gentle flutter of the first kick as too subtle to be sure it was my baby. Then on a camping trip in the Snowy Mountains, the kicking against my muscles was unmistakable. I placed Clive's warm hands on my extended abdomen to share my wonder. As my pregnancy continued, the worrywart in me didn't think my baby moved enough. But after recording a frenzy of activity, the prenatal nurse reassured me, "You have a whole football team in there!"

When I was seven months pregnant, we escaped the city to the Blue Mountains. That morning, remembering how fit I had been a few months earlier, I told Clive, "These are only tourist tracks in small mountains. I'll manage them no problem."

Overjoyed to be out of the city, we left the plateau and hiked through the tinder-dry eucalyptus forest and down the track that was interrupted by precipitous sandstone cliffs.

"Look, Clive," I said, marvelling at exquisite scarlet flowers that fit into my cupped hand.

"That's a waratah," he replied. Further on, we stared at a large, camouflaged lizard with dark scales, grey strips, and cream splotches. "It must be a goanna. They were a food source for the aborigines." Eating avocado sandwiches by the river, only a few feet away, we spotted a coiled up black and white python as fat as my arm. "Don't worry. It's not poisonous," Clive reassured me.

On the return track, I listened to the waterfall, the cockatoos, lorikeets, and crimson rosellas as if we were in an enchanted forest. But I had underestimated these "easy" tracks with their wooden ladders up the vertical walls, and the intense cramps in my abdomen alarmed me. As I slowed my pace and breathed deep between each step, the Braxton Hicks contractions eased. The next day, I wanted to hike the Blackheath Grand Canyon trail, but Clive refused. I guessed he didn't want to be a midwife out in the bush.

I stopped teaching two weeks before my due date. Still living at full tilt, I showed up at the yacht club with my turquoise sweatshirt covering my belly, looking forward to the afternoon social race. My genial skipper, a fireman, was used to handling emergencies but looked askance at my pregnant body. "Okay, I'll take you this week but not next week!"

My due date came and went with no contractions. Two weeks overdue, I was impatient. I'd read in *Active Birth* that to avoid needing to be induced or a caesarian, sex and walking might bring on labour. Despite my awkward size, slow kisses and soft caresses invited pleasure but no contractions. I walked eleven kilometres around Kuringai National Park but no contractions.

Then a florist handed me a purple orchid. "Giving birth makes women high. My wife has four children," he said. I looked at him mystified. No one had ever conveyed such excitement about birthing. The thought that it might make me euphoric was inconceivable. I contemplated his statement as I walked, or rather waddled, over Sydney Harbor Bridge to the Botanic Gardens. Back in our apartment, at eleven thirty p.m., standing in the bathroom, clear water trickled down my legs. By midnight, my contractions were six minutes apart.

CHAPTER 16

The Crux

"The moment a child is born, the mother is also born. She never existed before. The woman existed, but the mother, never. A mother is something absolutely new."
~ Osho Rasneesh

September 1984

As if going on holiday, I grabbed my pre-packed bag, tape player, and my orchid and breathed my way through my nerves to the car. In the Birthing Centre, I settled into the simple room with no technology.

"I want you to rock your baby down. Baby will be born by seven a.m.," the midwife said. I panicked. *Oh my god! I am not ready to be a mother!*

This was no holiday. I doubled over my abdomen, as tight as a drum, as wave upon wave of contractions sucked all the breath out of me as though someone was battering me with a mallet. Although I had read all the books, attended classes, and watched the required movies, I had no idea how to do this birthing thing. I showered, walked, and attempted to breathe through the penetrating pain.

"How about a bath?" the midwife suggested. As I relaxed in the warm water, a murky mustard colour spread.

"That's meconium. Your baby has pooped and is under stress. You need to go to the labour ward," she said. My expectations for a natural birth were thwarted. My disappointment was swamped by an agonizing cramp that started in my back and radiated across my diaphragm. I sat in a wheelchair as Clive and the midwife pushed me along the corridor. In the ward, three men—a male midwife, the doctor, and my husband—guided me. *What can these guys know about birthing? They have never done it.* I took comfort in that two of them were highly trained professionals.

The doctor examined my cervix. "You are fully dilated. You can push now," he said. After I pushed for at least an hour, the doctor re-examined me.

"Somehow, you are only seven centimetres dilated." I felt discouraged. Clive massaged my shoulders while mumbling that my muscles were too strong. Even with the monitor attached to my baby's head, I paced, squatted, and tried an upright birthing chair that looked like it came from a torture chamber.

Hours passed as I thought, *this is so much harder than I expected. I had no idea how tough and gutsy women are.* Clive tenderly applied hot packs to my aching back, and the physiotherapist massaged my feet. "It's your day. We're here to support you," she encouraged. "You two are working well together. Many couples are not like this."

After fourteen hours of labour, I wanted to give up. The doctor sat down beside me.

"Your baby is under stress. Its head is not coming down. We need to get it out," he said.

I nodded.

"You have three options," he continued. "We can put a suction cup attached to a vacuum pump on the head and use forceps to stop your baby from moving back up the birth canal. You can have nitrous oxide for the pain. The other alternatives are an epidural or a caesarian section."

"Let's go with the first choice. It is the least invasive," I replied decisively. Wanting the pain to stop, I lay like a beached whale with my legs in the feared stirrups and sucked hard on the laughing gas.

"Go easy there!" the doctor said. I pushed through the burning sensation in my groin and dug my nails into Clive's palms. The doctor placed the suction cup on my baby's head. With another couple of torturous pushes, and with the assistance of forceps, his head emerged. The doctor cut the cord, which was wrapped twice around his neck, allowing his body to emerge.

My sublime reward: a tiny boy with a mop of dark hair and a pixie face lay on my stomach. I caressed his vernix-covered body, relaxed after his fourteen-and-a-half-hour entry into the world. His brown eyes, bright and alert, did not have a squint. A wave of love surfed over me as I saw that he was more perfect than I ever imagined. I knew he would be a knockout with the ladies. The nurse whisked him off to have the meconium pumped out of his lungs, which decreased the risk of pneumonia. My labour continued as I pushed out the placenta.

"See, this placenta is calcified," the midwife said, pointing to some chalky brown tissue attached to the crimson liver-like organ.

"Oh," I said, feeling as if I had done something wrong. I remembered, two months before, the contractions on my hikes in the Blue Mountains… or maybe it was because I was two weeks overdue. I was too tired to ask. The doctor expertly stitched my tear. Remembering that mothers and babies died in childbirth, I was grateful to have the advantages of skilled care for the health of my baby and myself.

I showered before Clive and I bathed our newborn. I felt clumsy. I didn't know how to hold him and worried I'd break his neck.

"Look how long his hair is," I said.

"I think he likes the warm water trickling over his skin," Clive said.

"Our baby is so handsome," I said, my heart softened, as a warm affection spread across my chest.

Out in the waiting room, bemused, I watched an old Jewish mama dressed in black, accompanied by her skull-capped, bearded son, waiting for his wife to give birth. With enviable composure, Clive walked around talking to his own son who was held firmly in his arms. "He thinks it's a little doll," the Jewish mama said, looking at Clive.

Elated with the marvel of birth, I thought I would have twenty babies. It did not take long for the steep learning curve of caring for him began to sink in. For most of my life, I'd thought babies and small children were annoying and best avoided. How did I look after a baby?

Even after attending prenatal classes, I did not know that my milk would not come in straight away. I expected breastfeeding to be pleasurable, but in the first few days, my cracked nipples were a new form of distress. The doctor prescribed Bepanthen cream and exposure to the sun. Between feeds, I sat with several new mums in the privacy of the hospital courtyard, sharing our birthing experiences as we soaked the sun's healing rays into our raw nipples. In a few days, I turned into a veritable milk machine; milk jetted in all directions and left embarrassing wet circles on my blouse.

After three days in the hospital room designed for Mother and baby, I looked forward to going home, as I now thought of our garden apartment. The jasmine covering the fence wafted its fragrance through the open windows. Clive picked up our son, held his head, with his feet on his chest, and toured him around the two-bedroom apartment, introducing him to each room. With the circuit complete, Clive placed him gently in his wooden cradle and rocked him to sleep.

"I am going sailing this afternoon," he said. "Remember how we said the baby was not going to change our lives? We need to start as we intend to continue." I fought back my tears, hungering for the companionship of my faraway sisters and friends.

The following day, Clive lovingly tied our baby close to his heartbeat with a sling, a recent innovation in the west. We walked past jacaranda trees to our local park, listening to the raucous kookaburras. Eucalyptus trees were rooted on sandstone outcrops surrounded by the sea. Holding hands, we admired our son. But on the way home, my face taut, I waddled up the road clutching my throbbing abdomen, harbouring my disbelief at the rawness of my ache.

Mountaineering had never been this tough.

After a few days, Clive returned to work. Alone in this big city with no family or friends, I needed to reach out in order to avoid my dark hole. The doctor's office had advertised a mums' support group in my neighbourhood. With much effort, I managed to get my baby into the car. I knocked at the door of a house overlooking the harbour.

"Hi, I am Rowie. That's my son." She pointed to a toddler throwing a ball across the room as she introduced me to a woman with a cute boy hanging around her legs. "This is Jane and Julius."

"How was his birth?" Jane asked

"It took fourteen hours," I said.

"Julius, what do you want? No, don't hit." Jane interrupted.

"Ooh, your diaper stinks. Come here and I'll change it," Rowie said to her toddler.

"Look at all your son's hair and long eyelashes. What a little possum!" Jane said, introducing me to the affectionate term Aussies called their "bubbies."

"Yesterday we took him to the beach, and he smiled," I boasted.

"I hope you'll come back to our group next week," Jane said with a big smile.

Driving home, I thought that nothing in my previous life had prepared me for the friendly chaos of that morning. This made my wildest science classes look like a haven of peace, and I asked myself, *Is this group going to be my worst nightmare or my saviour?* In time, these vibrant, compassionate women became my lifeline.

That evening in the kitchen, between walking Chris to comfort his colic, Clive and I talked. "I always thought I'd call my baby William after my father. It is so long since he died though that I don't think it fits. Your dad's name, Theodore, is old-fashioned." I said.

"How about Bruce?" Clive suggested.

"That's like Scottish Jimmy; it's Aussie slang for a man."

"John?"

"I taught a badly behaved boy called John," I said.

"We need to file his birth certificate," Clive said.

"I want his middle name to be Russell after my family."

"How about Christopher?" Clive said.

"The patron saint of travelling? Neither of us believes in patron saints!"

"Maybe there is something in all that stuff. It is a beautiful name," Clive said.

On good days, I danced around the carpet, immersed in the moment, looking with awe at Christopher's tiny form cradled in my arms as I sang with Stevie Wonder on the radio, "*I just called to say I love you.*" But weeks of sleepless nights, demanding days changing diapers that smelled of rancid milk, incessant feeding, and burping, when nothing I did soothed Christopher, tested me in ways that I had never experienced in the mountains. Remembering how adamant my mother was about breastfeeding, I dialled the twenty-four-hour helpline to The Nursing Mothers Association of Australia.

"My baby has suckled all day, and screams every time I put him down," I complained.

"How old is he now?" she asked.

"Six weeks. I expected that he would be on a regular four-hour feeding schedule by now."

"Babies go through a growth spurt at that age."

"A friend told me that, if I pick him up every time he cries, I'll create a rod for my own back," I said.

"No, no. As they grow bigger, they need more milk. They build it up by frequent breastfeeding. It is a supply and demand system. Babies need touch."

"But if I feed him on demand, won't he get fat and spoiled?"

"Babies on breast milk don't get fat. There is a support group that meets in your neighbourhood park on Wednesday mornings. With the help of a facilitator, mothers connect and support each other." This became a treasured event on my calendar.

At a Nursing Mothers talk called "Is there self-esteem after motherhood?" I sat in the comfort of a mother's circle and learned about a concept called IALAC, short for "I am loveable and capable." The facilitator recommended we repeat this phrase to ourselves often. I recalled that, in Scotland, many mothers looked downtrodden and did not have a high opinion of their role. Even after my world travels, mountaineering, and what I had learned in therapy about taking care of myself, to tell myself that I was loveable and capable as a mother initially felt akin to blasphemy.

While I followed my mother's conviction that breast was best, I struggled with her belief that babies must sleep in their own rooms and not be picked up. The expectation that babies should sleep through the night caused me to seek professional advice. When my childless male doctor's advice, "Be strong; leave him to cry" failed, I sought out a child psychologist, who hooked me in by saying, "We have some great ideas for children that don't sleep through the night." I found myself drinking tea with the moms in her parenting class.

"I recommend Dr. Green's book *Toddler Taming*," she said. "You have to let them cry one night and then each successive night they cry less and less. You need to do this for a week, and then they will never do it again."

That night, I followed her advice and let my baby cry. When he woke up in the morning with a shitty diaper and a cold, I felt guilt-ridden. I asked myself: *What belief is my child forming if I leave him to scream at the top of his lungs? That nobody is here for me?*

Then at Rowie's group, I watched Jane breastfeed her toddler. "What am I doing wrong?" I asked. "Chris doesn't sleep through the night. Is he trying to manipulate me?"

"For a long time, Julius slept beside us. That made it easier to comfort him. Listen to your intuition," she said. "Wilma, you know what is best for your baby." Sometimes, I woke up at night and thought, *My baby, hasn't woken up yet.* When in a few minutes, I heard him cry, I would reflect: *That's strange. It's as if we are connected.* I found a book called *Nighttime Parenting*, by William Sears. His advice resonated with me: *"Answer your baby's cries… build up trust… get in touch with your baby."*

I battled with my inner perfectionist, who mocked me about getting mothering wrong. In addition, when my libido vanished, I questioned if I was normal. After all, the popular culture used female sexuality to market everything from dishwashing liquid to cars and reinforced that my worth as a woman was linked to my sexuality. It was more acceptable to display my cleavage than to breastfeed my baby in public. As if it was shameful or offensive, I covered my feeding baby behind a blanket. Then my warrior instinct surfaced, and proud of my body, I fed him in public.

Since my baby didn't talk in sentences, I became a detective to work out what he wanted. I learned that when I attended to Chris's requirements for comfort by rocking, nursing, or cuddling him to sleep, we both felt good.

I found a wise guide in Scottish Maggie Currie, the director of the Occasional Day Care Center. At five feet, she oozed love from every pore of her being. She hugged us older new mothers, and with her Glaswegian accent, called our children precious. She didn't let babies cry themselves to sleep. She rocked them in strollers out among the crowd where they were seen and would not feel abandoned. I learned that, for the first eighteen months, babies didn't feel separate from their mothers. Her encouragement was a priceless gift. Every time our children got sick or hurt themselves, she would say, in her strong brogue, as a way of acknowledging our distress, "Kids take ten years off your life."

As a modern career woman, I planned to stay home for a few months, and then like my peers, return to the workplace. Somehow or other, I suffered from maternal amnesia… or was it passionate love? It may have been different if I'd had a supportive community in Sydney. But when it came time to decide to return to teaching, I could not cut the umbilical cord and leave Christopher with a babysitter. After years of feminism, I surprised myself. I joined the endangered species list and became a stay-at-home mother with no intrinsic financial value.

For the first time in my adult life, I couldn't go to the mountains where I found peace. Living in the city, we needed a way to connect to nature. When Chris was six weeks old, Clive, with his irrepressible sense of adventure, suggested we buy a yacht. With no desire to end our lives in the watery deep, I requested a solid seaworthy yacht. We became the proud owners of a twenty-eight-foot Compass, with three-quarters of a ton of lead in the keel. Its aboriginal name, *Murungar,* meant 'The Wanderer.' Like a caravan on water, it came complete with duvet covers and pillows decorated with the Australian flag.

Clive dreamed of sailing *Murungar* to Norfolk Island, a three-day trip, or selling everything to sail around the world. Mothering and inland waters provided more than enough challenge for Christopher and me. The thought of a toddler on a yacht with no washing machine was abhorrent. In my new role, I needed all modern conveniences. Then there was the issue of my weather window: with wind less than eight knots, sailing bored me, and above eighteen knots, I was frightened. As a landlubber with a baby, sailing around the world was not for me.

Mama and Christopher at the helm of Murungar

CHAPTER 17

The Holy Sport of Mothering

"Adventure isn't just hanging on a rope on the side of a mountain. Adventure is an attitude that we must apply to the day to day obstacles of life – facing new challenges, seizing new opportunities testing our resources against the unknown, and in the process finding our unique potential."
~ J. Amatt, Straight to the top and beyond

1985

A creative mix of childrearing options, blended families, and same-sex couples had sprung from disintegrating nuclear families. Some of our divorced friends shared different time arrangements with their kids, but neither of us wanted that. Clive often travelled on business while I experienced solo parenting. I appreciated his generous economic and emotional support, and his enduring love. We made a conscious commitment to create a family together. The path that had been embedded in my psyche as my mother's daughter was a choice with which I have no regrets. I felt "clucky," the Aussie word for wanting another baby. I thought,

If I am staying home, I can look after two babies.

At Rowie's group, with toddlers clawing at our ankles, we discussed alternative theories on how to increase the possibility of having a girl.

"Get to know your menstrual cycle," said Jane, pregnant with her second. "Keep records of when you ovulate. Your cervix produces thick mucus around ovulation."

"If you want a girl, make love a few days before ovulation," Rowie added. "The X sperms are stronger and outlast the Y sperms. They are more likely to fertilize the egg when it is released."

Following this advice, I became pregnant, and morning sickness and exhaustion plagued me.

Around twelve weeks pregnant, I looked in disbelief at the blood on my panties. I phoned the doctor.

"I'm bleeding. What should I do?" I asked my voice breaking.

"Pay attention and let me know if it gets worse," he counselled.

"Can I go sailing on Middle Harbor tonight? I'll be a passenger. I won't be doing much."

"Take it easy and enjoy your evening," he said.

Christopher came with us. With his engaging smile, he won attention from both the young male and female crewmembers. Their caring concern helped make up for my lack of family.

That night, I awoke to find my pajamas soaked in blood. For several hours, I sat on the toilet with my hands on my head. *This can't be happening to me.* Tears flowed. I handled this with my dogged capability combined with acute disappointment. I stared in disbelief at a blood clot I thought was the fetus. At six a.m., I woke Clive who drove me to the hospital. Dizzy, I leaned on his arm as I walked to the ward. After a "D and C"—dilation and curettage—to clean out my uterus, I lay in bed. "One in four pregnancies ends in a miscarriage," my doctor gently told me. "Ninety-five percent of aborted fetuses are found to be abnormal. It is nature's way of getting rid of deformities. Give your body a few months rest, and you'll have no problem getting pregnant again."

Fragile, I hobbled back to our apartment, grateful for the warm support from my women's groups. My deep respect for women's courage and endurance expanded. Our forthcoming trip to New Zealand motivated me to recover.

I flew ahead with Christopher. At Wellington airport, the officials thoughtfully invited us to the head of the customs queue. A kind gentleman carried my hand baggage, heavy with two bottles—not of milk but Australian champagne.

When Clive arrived, we drove to the northwest of the South Island with my biking buddy Linda and her husband. On the four-hour drive, their two-year-old demanded we play Christmas carols—"Oh come all ye faithful" and "Silent night"—nonstop. We met two more families, one with two girls and the other with a baby. We named this trip Baby Rama. Our destination was Fenella Hut. A helicopter flew in a load of diapers and food. We walked twelve kilometres, carrying our babies in backpacks. After urban Sydney, I soaked in the peace of the alpine wilderness where the mist swirled around the moss, trees, and ridges. I breathed in the vast vistas and star-studded night skies, filling my mountain-starved soul. We tramped around the valley, which was filled with birdsong, and the kids played in cold lakes. I treasure the photograph of Christopher bathing in a white enamel basin.

The next week, I watched enviously as Clive and friends disappeared into the Southern Alps for a challenging backpacking trip.

Christopher and I stayed with my friend Fi from Edinburgh, whose boys were six and eight.

January 1986
Back in Sydney, it was fun to create another baby. A party and a backless black dress were all that it took. When I found myself devouring toast and marmalade, the only sweet substance in my cupboard, I knew I was pregnant.

As a thirty-seven-year-old mother, at fifteen weeks pregnant, I had an amniocentesis—a test to check for genetic abnormalities. The white-coated technician inserted a long four-inch needle into the amniotic sac to remove some fluid. Afterward, I sauntered through the hospital grounds, enjoying the blue jacarandas and harbour views enroute to visit my gynecologist. When fierce cramps spread throughout my abdomen, I doubled up and staggered into my doctor's office. The receptionist rushed me to bed and called the doctor. I curled into a fetal position, terrified I was losing my baby. In a few hours, the pains subsided. Shaken, I drove home. In two weeks, when the results showed I was pregnant with a normal healthy girl, my heart melted with floods of gratitude. Clive and I joyfully embraced, then phoned family and friends around the world to share our happy news.

To build my sailing confidence, I attended a six-evening weekly Day Skipper Course. It contained both classroom and practical elements that tested my navigational skills. The day after the final exam, a severe pain pierced my left groin. I felt as if I was ninety. Back in hospital, my doctor diagnosed appendicitis that might require surgery. Fortunately, after a good sleep, I felt better. I resolved to honour the needs of my pregnant body.

At five-months pregnant, I flew with twenty-two-month-old Christopher to Scotland. I wrote in my journal: *It's very emotional renewing old friendships and getting in touch with the land, the smell of heather and the language. Above all, my welcoming family.*

HOME—so familiar, part of my roots, my being—still there and always will be but so far away.

Back in Sydney, to prepare for this birth, I found Julia Sunden, a physiotherapist who taught a pregnancy exercise and relaxation class followed by a discussion group. In the smart North Sydney gym, filled with Lycra-clad men and women, we squatted with our protruding bellies hiding our toes. She timed us and equated the ache in our thighs with "It's only a muscle working." Then she instructed, "Your body and minds are connected. It is important to use your minds. Firmly internalize positive thoughts on birth. Give your mind an easy mantra, think, OPEN, OPEN, OPEN. Imagine the birth canal opening and visualize the baby moving through the birth canal."

"Any slight fear you have of the process will slow everything down," she continued. "You will not dilate easily." She talked us through a guided relaxation. After breathing tension out of our muscles and breathing in relaxation, she asked us to imagine our growing baby surrounded with warm pink love.

After working out, we gathered in a group, and Julia asked what resources we had to help us cope with the pain. Various answers came: pant, internal stamina, and sound. She encouraged us to journal about our previous births. A backlog of emotion about Christopher's birth spilled over my pages, feelings of failure at not giving birth naturally. I recognized the harsh judgments of my inner perfectionist. Writing helped me release my false expectations and move forward with gratitude for my healthy boy.

In this group setting, we circled the common thread that, while we had gained a baby, we had lost much of our independence. This massive change opened me to stormy emotions: sadness, anger, deep love, and joy. This welcome support provided a safe space and a foundation upon which to build my skills as a mother.

On a warm Sydney morning, four days before my due date, I clutched my squirming two-year-old on my hip as he squeezed on my pregnant belly.

"We're going to play with Julius," I told him as I clipped him into his car seat. I stepped into the driver's seat and screamed.

"What's wrong, Mummy," he asked.

"A huge spider just jumped out and crawled over my bare leg. It scared me."

"Can I see it?"

"No. It's disappeared under the seat," I said, shaking, I took a deep breath, clicked my seat belt, and drove off. We arrived at my friends' bungalow, which was surrounded by yellow acacia trees. Christopher joined the children in the paddling pool. Around the kitchen table, I drank tea with my friends.

"I don't know what's wrong with Julius. He woke up three times last night." Jane said.

"Maybe his back teeth are coming through," I offered.

"Did he have a tummy ache?" Rowie asked.

"I am exhausted. I swear he hasn't slept through the night once," Jane continued.

As I went to the toilet, a trickle of water ran down my legs. My face turned scarlet as I returned to the kitchen. "Oh God! My waters have broken," I announced. "A spider frightened me this morning. Maybe it triggered my labour."

"Do you have contractions?" Jane asked.

"No, I feel okay. I'll drive home," I said.

"Are you sure? I'll phone Clive for you." Jane offered.

I hugged her, then strapped Christopher into his car seat. Clive returned from work and took Christopher to the babysitter. After his fourteen-hour labour, I was not in a hurry to go to the hospital. When the contractions began around four thirty p.m., remembering the instructions from my prenatal class, I knelt on the back seat of the car. "Oh no, it's rush hour," Clive said. On the Sydney Harbour Bridge, the traffic slowed to a crawl. Pain swept through my body, and I wanted to yell at the pedestrians, *"Do you know how excruciating it is for women to have babies?!"* Clive looked at me groaning and panting in the back seat. "I wish this traffic would hurry up." When we arrived at the hospital, I waddled up to the registration desk where I doubled up with another horrendous contraction.

In the Birthing Centre, the midwife inspected my progress. "You're eight centimetres dilated. With a few more contractions, you'll be fully dilated. Breathe deep."

The powerful contractions came in quick succession with no time in between. With beads of sweat on my forehead, and praying for the agony to stop, I screamed out again and again.

"Can I have an epidural? This is awful," I pleaded.

"No, you're too far on. You are fully dilated. Keep going. It won't be long now," my midwife said.

I knelt at the side of the bed and repeated Julia's tips, "Open… it is only a muscle working."

"Push," the midwife said. "I can see the head."

"Where's the doctor?" I asked.

"He won't be here on time. Clive, kneel and catch your baby."

I pushed with all my effort. Clive had his arm around me as the midwife placed my dark-haired daughter covered in vernix on my stomach. Even though this was my second baby, nothing had prepared me for this miraculous moment. Again, my heart opened, and tingling love spread through my whole body.

The doctor arrived, delivered a healthy placenta, and stitched up my tear. This time, Clive and I confidently bathed our new baby. Utterly relaxed, she stretched out and dropped off sleep on the change table.

That night as Clive drove home back over the Harbor Bridge, he was frightened by the same spider that had initiated my labour. At the time, neither of us realized the connection between the spider and the thirty-first of October. We had a Halloween baby.

For months, we had known our baby's gender, but we still

struggled to decide between two names, Shona or Rona, both popular names and names of Scottish islands. At one point, Clive suggested Sarah Lee, not knowing it was the name of a brand of cakes. Together, we finally agreed on Shona, meaning 'my beloved wished-for child' and Marie, a Scottish variant of Mary in honour of her divine spirit, which I now believed to be present in every living creature.

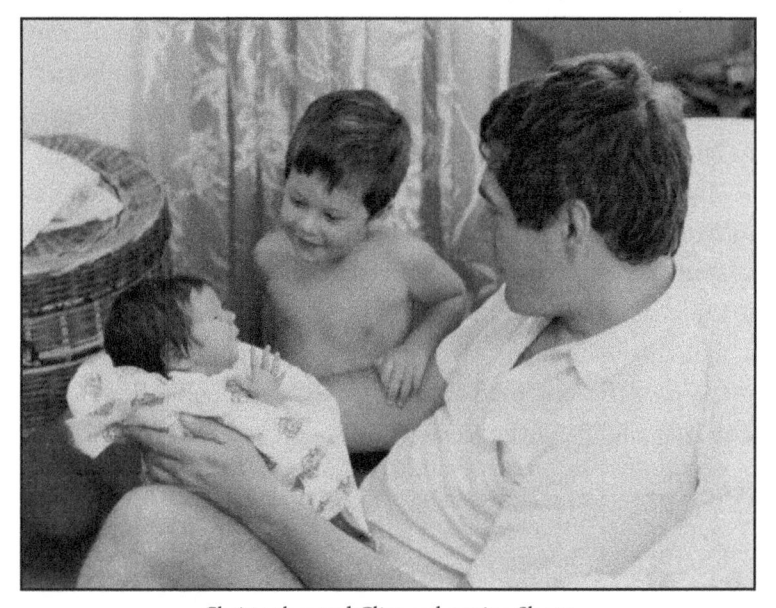

Christopher and Clive welcoming Shona

Six weeks later, I sat on the couch smelling breast milk. Shona gurgled on my taut breast. Fiery ache from mastitis radiated from my nipple. Two-year-old Christopher sat on the floor at my feet, building a multi-coloured tower with his Duplo.

"I'm hungry. I wanna cookie," he whined.

"Christopher, I need you to wait for a few minutes until Shona has finished feeding."

"No!" he shrieked, as he hurled blocks across the room to clatter on the wall.

A sharp pain seared through my breast down my arm. I wanted to smack him. Hard. "Christopher, stop that." Clutching a block, he looked at me, his face red and his lips tight.

"Come here. I will read you *Thomas the Tank Engine*," I pleaded, puzzling over how my cute toddler had turned into Attila the Hun.

In her baby chair, Shona played with the parrot dangling in front of her. I prepared dinner, my breasts throbbing. I turned my back for a few moments, gripping the potato peeler. Potato peels flew around the sink as I reflected on the advice in the *Nursing Mothers* newsletter that even amid our daily chaos we can learn to be and give love in the moment. Christopher pulled at my legs as he announced gleefully, "Mummy, I have peed on the baby."

That night, I gazed at my children cuddling their teddies, tucked under their crocheted blankets, and their kissable faces soft in sleep. My heart that had belonged to wild places melted. I began to understand that mothering was not a quick sprint but more like a high-risk endurance sport. Then, sipping peppermint tea, as if to prepare for the long road ahead, I picked up a book called *How to deal with your acting up teenager* by Robert and Jean Bayard.

Christopher and Shona at the helm

CIRCLING THE EDGE

Our family enjoying the Australian bush

CHAPTER 18

Tussles and Defiance

*"Love doesn't just sit there, like a stone;
it has to be made, like bread;
remade all the time, made new."*
~ Ursula K. Le Guin, The Lathe of Heaven

1987

Chris, clutching his plastic trolley, hurtled around the cracked concrete tennis court, scattering eucalyptus bark and leaves. My friend called him the kamikaze kid. My T-shirt stuck to my back as I folded towels, shirts, shorts, and diapers. I announced lunchtime and asked Chris to pick up his toys. With a look of defiance that said, *"You can't make me,"* he kicked over my basket of clean laundry. I looked at the mess of clothes on the dirt. Deep in the abyss, I yelled at him as I thought, *How dare he? All the time I spent folding it.* Remembering my mother's guiding principle, "to spare the rod is to spoil the child," I raised my sweaty hand to spank him. It wavered in mid-air as I recalled my distress when my parents smacked my sister or me. There had to be another way.

During nap time, I picked a book from my pile, *Happy Children* by Rudolf Driekus and Vicki Soltz. Tears smudged my eyes as the phrase *"a misbehaving child is a discouraged child"* jumped off the page and hit me on the skull as forcibly as a wooden plank. How could my child be discouraged after all the care Clive and I had given him? Breastfeeding for eleven months, cuddles, healthy foods with no sugar, beach visits, and reading to him most days. Being a mother was a steep learning curve that challenged me to re-evaluate my upbringing, understand myself, and learn new skills.

I enrolled in an eight-week Conflict Resolution night class at our local community centre. A few weeks into the course, feeling inadequate as a mother but overcoming my fear of rejection, I plucked up the courage to ask about my child's bad behaviour.

"He is disobedient. He doesn't listen to me. He needs to do as he is told."

"What do you think was going on underneath his behaviour?" the instructor asked.

"He was just trying to upset me?" I suggested.

"How do you take care of yourself?" she continued.

"No matter how much time I give my kids, it is never enough. There is no time or money to attend to my needs," I said.

"Think about what you both need."

"That's hard. I had mastitis and was exhausted. My daughter is teething. Chris wakes up with nightmares."

"As a parent, you need to learn to take care of yourself as much as your kids."

"But isn't it selfish to spend time on me?" I asked.

"You do more for them spending some time on your emotional intelligence than being devoted to serving them," she said.

Many mornings, in a rush to leave for kindergarten, Christopher refused to put on his clothes. We yelled at each other, and it was all I could do not to spank him. I felt helpless until I remembered the "managing emotions" stuff I had learned. I wanted to get to him. Somehow, we found ourselves in the bedroom. I picked up a pillow.

Wham! "Ha, you missed!" he said. I threw another. "That didn't hurt," he laughed. We continued to pelt each other with pillows. Our anger was eventually spent and together we lay on the bed giggling.

One afternoon, Chris chattered on about "bloody" this and "bloody" that. Calmly, I practised my new assertiveness skills. "Christopher, when I hear those words, I feel irritated. Please don't use them." As instructed, I repeated this three times with no result. The next morning, when he continued, I felt a wrench in my gut. "I don't want to hear those words," I repeated, my jaw tight. "Oh, Mummy, I am sorry. I didn't know you didn't like those words," he replied to my astonishment.

Later at the beach after an ice-cream treat, Chris asked me for another ice cream. I replied, "No, I am sorry, it is out of the question." Then I remembered the instructor's words: *When you say no, make it clean, with no excuses for your opponent to latch on to. You will only have to say it three times, and they will give up.* After his second request, I repeated myself. Then after my third reply, "No, I am sorry it is out of the question," Christopher stomped his foot, spraying sand everywhere, and said loudly, "But Mummy, it's in the question." I laughed.

Buoyed by my success, I followed this with another class: "Self Hypnosis and Stress Management." I anticipated it would help me tap into my creative writing. Instead, I discovered tension filled my body. I learned a five-minute practice to do twice a day. This involved progressively relaxing my muscles from my feet to the little muscles around my eyes. I used my mind's eye to vividly imagine descending steps into a beautiful garden and invoking all my senses: touch, sight, hearing, taste, and smell. Then I recited, *Each day I am becoming more calm and relaxed; as I become more relaxed, I feel better about myself. I can cope with anybody, anything, and any situation. My future is bright, joyous, and secure.*

I practised this with my scrambled brain, which I named "maternal amnesia." As I persevered, my mood and patience improved. One day after lunch, I placed eleven-month-old Shona in her cot with tall metal sides. Next door, I sat on my chair with my feet up and droned to myself, *Each day I am becoming more calm and relaxed…* Then I heard a heart-stopping thud. I opened the door to find Shona had climbed out of her cot and lay screaming on the floor.

I did return to teaching. At the end of the day, when I returned home with the thought that I might kill someone, I knew it was time for a change. Strongly motivated to find better relationship strategies, I jumped at the opportunity to train as a facilitator with the Conflict Resolution Network of Australia.

My next-door neighbour, who had three children, shared my desire for personal growth. After one deep discussion about mediation and reiki, she said, "life is about surrender."

"That won't work for me," I replied. I have eaten those words many times.

About this time, we all accompanied Clive, who was working for a Canadian oil company, to Canada for a three-week holiday and fell in love with the Rocky Mountains.

We visit Canada from Australia and hike up to the Larch Valley.

Back home in Sydney, we spent a weekend with a gardener, who was the kind of woman who took the time to show our young children how to hug trees and feel their rough barks against their soft faces. After a day of re-envisioning our garden, we planned to remove exotic plants and replace them with Australian Natives. I expected the garden to be replanted there and then. Much to my frustration, she left a dozen potted plants in our yard and a long list of garden tasks were added to my overloaded schedule. Clive chopped down three oleander bushes and tied the poisonous branches up in bundles for the garbage. The twenty-year-old plants were deep-rooted in the ground. With the children asleep for their afternoon nap, I picked up an axe and crowbar and pounded on the entrenched stumps.

I made little progress until I remembered what I had learned in my recent courses about expressing my emotions. I tapped into my subconscious. Under the pretense that all was well, I uncovered cynicism, stoicism, and denial. I powered the axe with my triggers:

Clive forgot to phone to say he would be late for supper. Hack.

My children did not help to tidy up their toys. Hack.

That company cancelled my Conflict Resolution Workshop. Hack

Recent irritations and feelings of self-doubt charged down the ruts of my mind like a horse out of control. Then distant memories I had long forgotten surfaced.

In Kashmir, Mother did not think it appropriate that I, a married woman, should go trekking with David. Hack, hack, hack.

My mother did not allow me to travel abroad with Clive before I was married. Hack, hack, hack.

Chips of root and soil flew around the silver bark of the eucalyptus; humus musk filled the air, dirt-caked into my fingernails, and the stubbornness my mother thought a major character flaw held its own. Calmness spread through my body.

The next day, I came into the kitchen to find my kids painting my clean floor with the yogurt. I yelled at them until I saw tears run down their muddy cheeks. I retreated then to the bathroom to read my latest inspirational book, *The Course in Miracles*. "To attack your brother is to attack yourself" jumped off the page. I breathed deeply, dried my tears, washed my face, and returned to the scene, then cleaned up and made us all a snack. Oh, so slowly, I recognized the hurt my anger caused and worked to become grounded and centered.

On another occasion, after I left them at the Child Care Centre, I walked across the busy road to the bookstore. My eyes roamed the crowded shelves. A book with a rainbow heart on the white cover named *You can heal your life* by Louise L. Hay jumped off the shelf, demanding to be purchased. Although I didn't know why my life needed healing, her philosophy commanded my attention: *"We are one hundred percent responsible for all our experiences. We must be willing to learn to love ourselves and the bottom line for everyone is that we think we are not good enough."* As I have said, it was alien to give love to myself first. I was unpractised at it. Slowly I became aware of my thinking and replaced my negative thoughts with the mantra, *"Love is letting go of fear."* I worked to create my desired life.

Weekend sailing with our intrepid children.

On Friday evenings, although the mountains were out of reach, we used our sailing skills to introduce our children to nature. A forty-five-minute drive from our inner-city apartment, the protected arm of Pittwater Inlet felt like a thousand miles from Sydney and its four million people. As the sun slipped behind the Kuringai hills, inhaling the strong smell of seaweed, Clive and I loaded diapers, towels, and food down below, then set sail to our favourite anchorage. The yacht keeled over, her taut sails reaching towards the Southern Cross as the Milky Way meandered over the Australian night sky. I clutched the tiller, exhilarated as I admired the trail of phosphorescence twinkling on the wave crests. The white foam hissed on the bow, lulling Christopher and Shona to sleep. In the morning, as the first rays lit up the eucalyptus leaves, we helped our children clamber into the dinghy, then rowed to the golden beach. There in the wilderness, goannas, blue-tongued lizards, and wallabies roamed, and the kookaburras laughed as my naked children played in the water, rocked on the swinging branch of a tree, dug, and ate sand—gutter immunization I called it. In less than three years, my "life before children" had receded into a distant memory.

CHAPTER 19

Lust for Adventure

"There is something I notice about desire, that it opens the eyes and strikes us blind at the same time."
~ Jane Smiley

1989

In Sydney, my crampons rusted in the humid basement. As a busy mother, I had no time to pine after wild places far from the rumble of city traffic. I suppressed my vivid memories of the silent snows, the crunch of glacier ice, and the magnetic pulse of mountain summits.

Five-year-old Chris picked up the phone. "Daddy wants to speak to you."

"Do you want to go and live in Canada?" Clive asked. "The company has offered me a transfer to Calgary."

"I don't know. It's so cold there. I love this house. We've only been in it over a year," I mumbled, juggling the pots on the stove as three-year-old Shona clung to my leg.

Many times over the next few weeks, Clive and I walked along the sandy pathways of Sydney's coastal parks through hairpin banksia, pink begonia bushes, and flannel flowers. Above the growl of the surf, we discussed the pros and cons of an international move with our young family.

"How can we even think of moving? We've only just settled in. The kids love the pool," I said.

"Honestly, I'm not sure about the future of the office here," Clive replied. "A move would be good for my career. I know it would be hard, but we've always seized opportunities. The company will cover all the moving charges. It'll be easier than last time."

"What do you mean last time? I was excited to move to India, then to Oman. But remember how I struggled at first in New Zealand?"

"I thought you loved New Zealand," Clive said. "When we moved here, you kept talking about how much you missed your Kiwi friends and the mountains."

"I do love New Zealand," I replied. "Again, when I moved here, I was pregnant. I didn't know anyone. Now I've made great friends. I've just started facilitating Conflict Resolution workshops. Plus, Chris is about to start school down the road. Remember, that was one of the reasons we bought this house."

"I still have a job here. We don't need to go," Clive said. "You know how stretched we are money-wise. The mortgage rate has gone from twelve percent to eighteen percent. This might be a chance to get ahead financially."

"I know that," I said. "Our house is beautiful. I can't begin to think about selling it,"

"We could rent it out," he suggested.

"Maybe we're stuck in our ways," I said. "As a teen, I poured over magical photos in the *Beautiful British Columbia* magazines. I adored the Rockies when we visited Canada last year. We could ski with the kids."

"It is only an eight-hour flight to Scotland from Calgary. Chris and Shona could get to know Scotland, their cousins, aunts, uncles, and grandparents," Clive said, encouraging me.

"I'd love to be closer to my sisters and their families." I sighed.

"The weather sounds awful," Clive mused. "Today, it was minus twenty degrees Celsius in Calgary and plus twenty here. We must be crazy even to think about moving."

"Imagine! Calgary has only half a million people compared to four million here. You will move from one office to another. I'll have to start my life all over."

"I don't know what we should do. Still, if we work hard, we can make sure that when we arrive in Calgary, we'll catch the ball in the air and fly with it." Clive gave me one of his wide smiles.

January 1990, a huge moving container rolled up to the house. Chris, Shona, and I choked up as their beloved toys and our entire household of belongings were packed inside. I explained that our possessions were going on a ship to Calgary while we would travel in an aeroplane.

A few weeks later, as if the weather mirrored my feelings, we left Sydney, which I had grown to love, in torrential rain. We landed in a blizzard and drove cautiously on the icy roads. We spent one chaotic week in Calgary. Along with skates, long underwear, snow boots, hats, and gloves, we bought a house. We skied at Canada Olympic Park. Struggling with the clothes, the ski gear, and jet lag, the reality of skiing with two young kids was not quite like the crystal-clear vision I had imagined months ago of my happy family on a ski hill.

Cheerfully, we boarded a plane and flew to Scotland with a memorable stop in Heathrow, where on TV, I watched Nelson Mandela being released and talking to a huge crowd in South Africa. This major political breakthrough gave me hope for humanity.

My sister Ruth and her family welcomed us to her manse in the Borders. We spent several days outside in the snow with her teenage daughters who took our Aussie children sledding and cross-country skiing. After her delicious homemade meals, we sat around her fire, playing games and singing at the piano. Another day, my sister Dorothy's two daughters introduced their young cousins to Pickles, their sturdy Shetland pony, and patiently led them around the paddock.

For three weeks of short winter days, we lived in my welcoming parents-in-law's apartment, which was filled with antique plates and teapots. While I loved catching up with everyone who offered us warm hospitality, I was ready to return to my life in Sydney, not to a new life in Canada.

The plane landed in Calgary in thick fog, at minus twenty degrees, the roads and the sidewalks piled with snow. What an enormous change from Australia's surf-fringed beaches to this desolate landscape. On good days, we claimed we had exiled ourselves to the frozen tundra. How different could the two places be? Australia had nine months of hot humidity with winter temperatures of ten degrees centigrade. In Calgary, we joked there were nine months of winter and three months of poor sledding. I did speak English, although not Canadian. My words were often misunderstood when I talked about curtains not drapes, pavements not sidewalks, and toilets not washrooms.

Ten snowy days later, back in the airport, we waved Clive goodbye. He was off on the first of his frequent international business trips as he fulfilled his role as international exploration manager.

The kids caught chickenpox. Cold and disorientated, I bundled them up and drove downtown on an errand. When we returned to where we'd parked the car, it had vanished—towed to the pound. Two days later, I hit an all-time low when I left Chris at his elementary school. That night the phone rang. "I am Mrs. Brown, the kindergarten teacher. Your son kicked me today. We don't do that here." Devastated, I swallowed my tears.

Although I had spent time in mountains all over the world, nothing had prepared me for the ferocity of winter weather. The first night, the wind howled, and snowflakes shrieked past my windows horizontally. I thought to myself, *If the roof blows off, we'll all die.* I lay in the dark, fruitlessly speculating on what would happen if some disaster prevented the delivery of food on trucks, trains, and planes. The tenacity of Canadians who never let the treacherous weather interfere with their lives astounded me. For me, once again, it was a time of many adjustments.

After living in our new house for a month, I experienced deep discomfort. What was the matter with me? I recognized that, for the last six years in Australia, my windows had been open wide all year round. Here in Calgary, they were closed tight to keep out the extreme cold.

Once again, I had let go of the riverbank of life—all that was familiar. I was now in the current and drowning. Every once in a while, I managed to raise my head above the swirling waters and gulp some air before submerging in the chaotic flow. While I adored our escape weekends to the mountains, I did not care for the sprawling city.

Skiing at Sunshine Village

I made an appointment with a counsellor. "I've moved here from the southern hemisphere. My life feels upside down. I thought, if I followed my dream, I'd be happy and life would be easy, but I am sick, freezing, and sinking. I left my friends behind and have no one to talk to," I told her.

"We humans don't like change. It can be scary," she said. "All of your life is your career. You are the kingpin of your family." For the first time in months, I relaxed a little. I took comfort in her words. "Rather than sort out your whole life at once, 'chunk it.' First, organize the house, settle children into their routine, then do a little mountain climbing, and eventually, you'll get back to your work. Do it one piece at a time."

One day, I drove to a park. The leafless trees anchored in the frozen ground were stark against the ice-blue sky. To my eyes, this was a wasteland. Tears froze on my cheeks. There was no going back. I told myself, *You're here, for better or for worse. You know from previous experiences that, if you continue to find it hateful, it will be hateful.* I asked myself, W*hat can you begin to like?* I looked out of the car window into the vast Alberta skyscape. I could begin to love the bulbous clouds, clean air, and the distant mountains alight in the sunshine. I could begin to love the soft curve of Nose Hills's blond hillside. I certainly appreciated the school system that negotiated with young children.

That first spring, when the ice finally melted, I knelt and kissed the delicate purple crocuses that rose like angels from the hard ground. Yet the birthing pains of creating a new life in this unfamiliar territory continued. I returned to the counsellor.

"You look so sad," she said. Her words shocked me. I had no idea someone could read my emotions from my face. I felt exposed and raw. Late one evening, when Clive was in some far-off place looking for oil, I tucked the kids in bed. I lit a candle, and following the counsellor's suggestion, I began to scribble in my journal.

I wrote about missing the warmth of the Australian sun, the eucalypts, the yellow wattles, the crashing ocean on Manly Beach, sailing with balmy sea breezes, my close friends, the kindergarten my kids had attended, the Conflict Resolution Network where I had found support, and stimulation for my career. I wrote about the move from New Zealand to Australia, how I'd missed the wonderful friendships I had made striding over airy ridges in the Southern Alps. Three tear-stained pages later, the trauma of Mother's death spilled onto the page. It was as if my pen extracted sorrow from the hidden crevices of my consciousness. I came back to the present. That northern-spring night in Calgary, my children safe in bed, I released the dam of my buried grief.

In the long June evenings, the children asleep, and I went into my treeless garden and hacked at the solid river clay with a crowbar and excavated boulders. I dug deep holes in the earth and planted four lodgepole pines, a silver birch, and a mountain rowan. The familiarity of the northern air rekindled pleasant memories of my Scottish homeland. Assisted by the alchemy of the cool dusk around my face, with Canadian dirt embedded under my fingernails, I began to root myself in Alberta.

For our summer holiday, with our van packed full of camping gear and bikes, we set out to explore our new country. We marvelled as we drove through the majestic, glaciated mountains of Kootenay National Park to Invermere. We continued, restlessly, until we found ourselves camping in Kokanee Creek Provincial Park outside of Nelson. Surrounded by the peaceful presence of the tall cedar trees, I watched the children happily dig in the sand and swim in the warm lake. I knew I could make a life for us in this vast land.

1992

With a friend, I hiked up Mount Temple, at 3,550 metres the highest mountain in Banff National Park. In our haste, we wandered off the track and scrambled up a cliff band. My hands and feet clutched hold after hold. The September spindrift stung my cheeks as my climbing boot wobbled on a narrow rock ledge, and my hands slid on clear ice. My abdomen taut, my throat dry, I dared not look at the scree thirty feet below. Breathing deep into my belly, my stress poured into the rock. Then on my out-breath, like a miracle, the rock grasped me. I trembled in space until my partner lowered a sling, which I grabbed and tip-toed over the ice to safety.

With my legs like jelly and my thoughts churning, I arrived on the airy summit to appreciate the mind-blowing waves of peaks and glaciers that stretched as far as I could see in all directions.

On the summit of Mount Temple

CIRCLING THE EDGE

On the steep descent, I paid attention to each step. To my astonishment, at Sentinel Pass, Clive, Chris, and Shona sat on the rocks eating sandwiches and gummy bears. I hugged them tightly. My friend raced ahead, while I joyfully danced down the wide path, appreciating my athletic children framed in orange larch trees. That night with Chris and Shona tucked up asleep under their duvets, I drew an Insight Card. In disbelief, I read: "*As an eagle soars on currents of air invisible to the eye, so I am supported in hundreds of ways both seen and unseen.*"

CHAPTER 20

Sisters

*"Come away human child to the water and the wild,
for the world is full of weeping more than you understand."*
~ W. B. Yeats

The spring of 1999 found my family flowering in our adopted country. That February, twelve-year-old Shona represented Canada at Topolino, Italy, in an international ski race. While we wanted her to have fun, she surprised us with a bronze medal. Chris at fourteen was fourth overall at the Canadian Ski Championships. In April, they both qualified to race at the International Whistler Cup Event. I picked up the phone to share my excitement with my sister Ruth. When there was no answer, I called my sister Dorothy.

"Hi! It is good to talk to you. How are you?" I said.

"We are all well."

"I just tried to call Ruth to wish her a happy birthday."

"She is sick. There is something wrong with her kidney. She's lost thirty pounds," Dorothy said, her voice breaking.

"What? I can't believe it." I said, as my whole body stiffened.

"She gets the results of her kidney biopsy next week."

"Last time I talked to Ruth, she had been to the doctor with backache. He thought she was malingering and trying to get out of teaching. He gave her iron tablets," I said, shaking.

Although I hoped for the best, on my drive to the Whistler Cup, my thoughts spun around this catastrophic news as I remembered how Ruth had cared for me in my teenage years, our trips together in Mull, and that when I visited Scotland, she'd provided a home for us. A week later, her kidney and lung cancer was confirmed. Three weeks later, I phoned Dorothy again and her husband answered. "Dorothy's in hospital," he said. "She was rushed in, haemorrhaging."

"What?" I stifled a scream as he continued.

"They operated immediately. It was colon cancer. They have removed it all. She'll be in for a while."

"I am coming over in a couple of weeks," I said, feeling as if someone had punched me in the diaphragm.

Before I flew to Scotland, I spent the weekend in Banff, skiing with my family. I walked with Clive to Vermillion Lakes. Twenty feet up a fir tree, bobbing up and down, a screech owl chatted to us for twenty minutes—the only one I have ever seen. I was drawn to indigenous spirituality, in particular the idea that everything is interconnected. Invisible forces or spirits affect our lives and the visible world. I read from the Medicine Cards: *"Owls are the messenger between the worlds, representing wisdom, shapeshifting, and reincarnation. Owls announce the transformation of the soul's journey."* At this gut-wrenching time, I found solace in the belief that a person's soul is like an eternal spark of energy that chooses to inhabit a body to learn life lessons, and that once absorbed, the soul transitioned out of this physical plane as pure energy. I was in a quandary between wanting to be with my sisters and to be in Canada with my teenagers and husband.

I flew to Scotland and helped care for Ruth. I prepared hot water bottles for her bed and warmed her nightgown in front of the fire as Mother had done for us. Her once slender, strong body had aged, her feet and ankles were double their normal size, and her face full from steroids, but her smile was still beautiful. I coaxed her to eat. I read to her. I drove her two hours to the hospital for treatments they never performed. None of the health professionals could say the word "death" and instead talked about the quality of life.

Several times I visited Dorothy, who was recovering from her long operation and her own brush with death. "The doctors said they removed all the cancer. Now I have to build back my strength," she told me. Once I heard all the details, like old times, we chatted proudly about our children. Slowly she recovered.

One night, I dreamt that Ruth and I were floating over a tranquil warm ocean. She sat in our family's comfortable armchair, while I held on tight with my arms outstretched. Then reluctantly, as my arms weakened, I could no longer hold her. Calmly, I let go, and the gap between us increased as I watched her drift gently into the distance.

Later, writing in my journal, the words became smudged with tears as wet tissues piled up on the table. I remembered that, with my mother's sudden death, I'd never had an opportunity to say goodbye. I knew I had to return to Canada in a few days, but while I had come a long way in recognizing my emotions, I did not have the confidence to speak to Ruth about my need for closure. I selected a card for her with the quote:

"If I stepped out of my body, I would break into blossoms."

~ Issa.

In it, I wrote, *I need to write of our human journey together, the joys, sorrows, frustrations, anger, and love. We have walked together now and again. We have reached out across the gulf of our differences, judgments, and hurts. And now in your human vulnerability, our hands touch, our arms wrap around each other, maybe for the last time. I feel tears in my eyes. I feel love in my heart. This is to know we have lived and loved. To know while our bodies' part, our spirits, souls, divinity connect across the ether, and beyond, reminding us of the great unfathomable mystery that is life, faith, and God. Love is eternal. Love is forever.*

"How did you learn to express so much feeling?" she said, choked up. We held each other tight. "Go back to your family," she whispered. "Don't come to the funeral if there is one."

Back in Calgary, a week later, in a church hall with light shining through the stained-glass windows, I walked a labyrinth, which was my current spiritual practice. My body was overwrought with sadness and torment; step by step, I dragged my feet along the convoluted track to the centre, breathing out my anguish. In the centre rosette, I meditated until, in my mind's eye, I saw Ruth and her family surrounded by angels and light. With each return step, I became more grounded and calm. I phoned her and had a long comforting conversation. One week later, Ruth died at her local hospital.

That summer, on our family holiday, we visited the Grand Canyon. Seeking solace, I wrote:

Grief at her passing
Dissolved into rain torrents
And descended into chasm's depth.

A couple of years later, Dorothy's daughter phoned. "My mother is in the hospital. She has a blood clot in her leg and pancreatic cancer." Once again confronted with a terminal illness, I sought support from my friend. We walked through the trees in the Weaselhead, a Calgary wild area.

"Life is so unfair. My sister Ruth was only fifty-seven. Dorothy is only fifty-four. It is so painful to watch people I love suffer so much."

"It's heart-breaking for you, Wilma," my friend said, with her arm around me.

"Why do people have to hurt like this? What do I do? Drop

everything and go to Scotland?"

Under the wide Alberta sky, we sat on a bench by the quiet river. To my amazement, a flock of chickadees twittered around me but not my friend. That night I read, *"If you witness a chickadee when listening to advice or sharing from your heart, know the truth was spoken and you can trust your actions."* This comforted me as I once again boarded a plane to Scotland. A couple of months later, Dorothy was buried under a huge beech tree in the cemetery at the bottom of her garden.

It was a hard winter that year. Snow came before the golden leaves had fallen from the trees. Low temperatures froze the river into thick layers of ice that remained well into spring. I felt as if I was carrying lead weights on my feet; my shoulders drooped, and my brow was constantly furled. All the hard-earned self-care gifts that had once brought me joy had lost their effect. Nothing felt the same. My bloodstream felt ice-cold like the river. My sisters were too young to die. One day, surrounded by fog, I walked by the freezing river and spotted a solitary tundra swan, jogging my memory of my last walk with Ruth and her eloquent poem:

"Swan heard before seen
wind-bellows-beating white wings
above the Myer loch.
Pointed sunset sky,
up and around you flew
till above the grey night gatherings
you became golden in the after-glow
and on, up till the set sun flashed
heaven light from your mirror breast.
You wheeled, were out of sight
leaving us a contemplative glory,
quiet in which we walk."
~ Ruth Slorach, 1997

Many months later, in an Art Therapy Grief Workshop, I sat in a circle of men and women with a grey Irish wolfhound, the trained therapy dog, asleep in the centre. Meditation music wafted from the CD player as we sat in stillness. The art assignment percolated through the chaotic layers of my mind. Within minutes, as I faced my blank page, my shoulder blades tightened as I doubted my artistic ability. But I picked up a black marker and drew a large heart. Then I painstakingly pasted sharp pieces of black metallic paper onto the page, representing the shard-like daggers that pierced my heart. I remembered that, right after my mother's funeral, the sun had burst like a star through a chink in the charcoal storm clouds. In the spaces, I pasted colourful blossoms and wrote *"A heart broken open contains the whole world."*

We finished the workshop creating a "Precious Living Box"—a box to symbolically contain what I cherished. My box sparkled with sparkling rainbow spirals representing the inner world of my chakras. I decorated it with family and mountain photographs. As I shone the light on my grief, a reflection of my love, I learned to embrace each day and live a full life.

Whiskey Jack - Indigenous spirituality believes that everything is interconnected.

CHAPTER 21
Wasps and Yoga

"Each tree grows in two directions at once, into the darkness and out to the light, with as many branches and roots as it needs to embody its wild desires."
~ John O'Donohue, Anam Cara

2003

On the pine-clad headland jutting into the rippling waters of Kootenay Lake, the April wind rustled around the white temple that was dedicated to the light in all religions. Sandalwood incense wafted through the air. With my shoulders hunched, my tired eyes stared at the brass statues of the Hindu and Tibetan Goddesses—Saraswati, Tara and Sky Dancer—radiant with movement, sexual energy, and joy. They did not sit like Buddhas with their eyes closed but were eager participants in life. I yearned for this aliveness... to be vibrant and present in every moment.

Burned out from my driven lifestyle in Calgary, I was like a refugee. At first, far from the demands of family, facilitating Conflict Resolution and Parenting Workshops, the peaceful orchards and the warm breezes felt like heaven. When I sat cross-legged in meditation, I expected to float on a cloud in ecstasy. But as I worked with yoga postures, chants, and self-reflection, stormy anger and anxieties surfaced. My inner saboteur, the part of my psyche that complied with my repression, lay low like a prowler ready to attack. *What am I doing here? I want to run away.*

In a circle of sixteen women and men, I sat cross-legged, staring at the forest beyond the floor-to-ceiling windows.

A grey-haired female swami in a violet turtleneck explained: "India has 108 names for the Divine Mother who represents all aspects of the mysterious source of life. Diverse metaphors and symbols have been created by many cultures. Each holds a kernel of the truth that the answer to our human vulnerability is found within. They are a way of involving our minds in the spiritual quest." Pointing to different statues, she continued. "Krishna's flute represents our inner calling. Green Tara is the mother of compassion; her upright hand dispels fear while the other hand grants bounty. Here is White Tara who represents the highest intellect of the Buddha. She has seven eyes, two on her hands, two on her feet, one on her forehead, and two real eyes. She is clairvoyant and an aspect of Kali who wears a garland of skulls and devours her own creation. Kali is all creating and all-consuming."

I recollected that, in India, these goddesses had been totally alien to me. Bejewelled necklaces and garlands fell over their naked breasts and narrow waists. They never had bad hair days. Comfortable in their bodies, they confidently displayed their sexuality without guilt or shame. Saraswati played music, loved to dance, and composed poetry. Inspiring all forms of creativity, she did not demand perfection. She encouraged my fledgling poetry, whispering, *"Experiment, play, and enjoy."*

In sharp contrast, my nagging critic reinforced my dark suspicions and conflicting desires. *Pleasure is not to be trusted. If a woman likes sex, men will think her easy prey.* Without stopping for a breath, my relentless bully continued. *If you follow a creative path, you'll end up a homeless bag lady. You need to please others and find a real job.* Irrational beliefs that I thought I had dealt with a long time ago. But no. My past cycled back into my awareness for re-examination.

On the other hand, these healthy goddesses intrigued me more than the brutal symbols of Christ nailed on a cross, his hands and feet dripping blood. Or the disturbing images I saw in Ecuador of the Virgin Mary, her sad face downcast as her heart leaked blood.

Although over the years, I had swapped the angry God of my ancestors with more user-friendly terms like higher power or universe, these words sometimes stuck in my throat, leaving me dejected as if nothing—particularly my latest exploration into writing—was good enough.

"A mantra is a sound, a syllable, or a group of words that is capable of creating transformation, like an internal makeover," the swami explained. I found chanting the Sanskrit mantras *"Om tara tutare"* and *"Om namaha shivaya"* awkward. My twitching legs and yapping mind struggled. Determined at least to try, as I practised, I found comfort in their gentle rhythms.

Every evening in the temple, we met in a community called Satsang that was dedicated to devotion and prayer. Most people bowed to the simple altar of red roses, and photographs of Swami Radha and Sivananda who had inspired the ashram. I was mistrustful of releasing my problems to the Divine. *Does 'give it over' mean God will run my life? Will I become passive and give up?*

One ceremony resonated with me. I cupped the light from the candles in my hands, poured it over my head, touched my eyes, nose, mouth, ears, and murmured, *"May all my sense perceptions be purified by the light."* I looked at the familiar star on my Indian ring. When a swami offered me a tray of sweet treats, with sacred intent, I popped one into my mouth. Sucking slowly, I recalled the many sweetnesses in my life: my family, skiing, mountains. and facilitating parenting workshops.

I left the temple as the sun set over the lake and painted the sky crimson. Inhaling the fragrance from the cedar trees, I walked across the orchards, and my eyes feasted on pink magnolia buds snuggled in the lime spring leaves. The birds and crickets sang with striking clarity as the wind whispered through the deeply rooted larch, cedar, and fir trees whose branches soared into the heavens. That night, tucked under my warm duvet in preparation for the workshop on dreams, I asked for a juicy one that would map out my next steps and help me find well-being.

In the small hours of the morning, I turned over, looked out of the picture window to the stars sparkling between the shadowy cedars, and recorded a snippet of a dream in my journal. *I ask Swami Radha, "Should I take your class?" She turned towards me and answered, "Find out for yourself."*

Unsatisfied, I judged this as simplistic. I wanted something dramatic, easy steps to success, not something I had to figure out. I tossed around in a disturbed sleep and woke in the morning with a dream fragment about snakes.

I walked through the morning mist that was swirling around the cedars to my Asana practice. I pulled my fleece jacket tight as I relished the crisp air. Once in class, rubbing my eyes, I stretched into sun salutations, warrior, and camel pose. In cow-face pose, my legs crossed awkwardly over one another, my left buttock screamed while my ankle bone dug into the floor. I chewed on my turmoil. *This is excruciating.* When the class ended, lured by the aroma of coffee, I rushed to breakfast, collected a plate of granola, blueberries, and yoghurt, and found a seat on the veranda. Observing the no-talking rule at meals, appreciating my coffee, I ate in silence, enjoying the tranquillity and the majestic mountain view.

Refreshed, I returned to the circle. The swami asked us to write out our conscious issues. I scribbled over my page. *How do I express who I am, my spirituality, in the world? I have an ambitious to-do list: facilitate workshops on Conflict Resolution, Parent Education, and Stress Management, write articles, a book, and market it all. Post-script: What I want is to meditate, garden, hike, and ski.* We chanted for five minutes. I resigned myself to work with a week-old dream that I did not like. *Wasps buzz around my two children; distressed I turn to Clive, "You should have removed these. They might sting the kids." Over and over, I brush off the white-and-yellow-striped insects, which like mutants have dysfunctional wings. They refuse to move. On my right hand, three are half-buried. Agitated, I watch as three more wasps burrow under my skin. I can do nothing to stop them. I wake up nauseated.*

The Swami instructed, "Dreams are about claiming your own experience. All parts represent your consciousness. Any person is a reflection of you. Each of you has a unique symbolic language. You are the only person who can interpret your dream."

We repeated the Divine light mantra: *"I am created by Divine light. I am surrounded, sustained, and protected by the light."* This resonated with my soul, I experienced an innate calm. Then in my journal, I answered the question, *What did the wasp dream mean to me?* As my thoughts unfolded on my page, I accepted that I blamed Clive for not doing things my way. My resentments damaged us both. I recognized the irritations burrowing under my skin as worries about money, my "shoulds," and erroneous expectations of my career, which triggered my deep-seated inferiority. While I wanted to improve my life, I hesitated to cross the cusp from old ways to flow… to replace swimming upstream with freely responding to the currents of my life.

I welcomed lunch with delicious carrot-ginger soup and salad from the garden. I sat in the sun on the balcony overlooking the lake, silently surrounded by my fellow yogis. I recognized my exhaustion. I let go of judging myself as lazy and put on my headphones. Nestled on a bed of moss and cradled in the arms of the warm breeze, the calming notes of Mozart fortified me for the afternoon's questions.

What did wasps represent to me? Stinging and danger. Wasps never bothered me much until my son proved to be allergic to them. Then a sentence jumped onto my page that sent chills down my spine. WASPS represented the **W**hite **A**nglo **S**axon **P**rotestant values of my Scottish and Irish ancestors, who judged pleasure, dancing, and music as stuff of the devil. Scotland, England, and Ireland were countries where, during the first half of the twentieth century, and arguably in self-defense, the arts were downgraded in favour of artillery, calm in favour of armies, and fear promoted in place of love. I asked myself, *Do I give my power to these beliefs? How do I get rid of them?*

The dreams clearly instructed me to find my own answers. I recognized that, when I was not present to myself, I experienced doubt and self-sabotage. Just the previous weekend, whizzing through the trees on my skis, I'd become distracted, worrying about a conflict in a class I had facilitated that week. Boom. I found myself with my face and goggles planted in the snow. When I repeated the ski run, focused on my skis and fully in the moment, I was exhilarated. Now I reassured myself: *Thinking for myself has fuelled my growth since I was sixteen. As a teacher, I like to motivate my students to think for themselves.*

Who is the dreamer and what is the dream saying about the dreamer? In a meditative reverie, with dullness in my belly, confusion pressed on my brain like a heavy blanket. What was this? *I am your fear, your human vulnerability. I crave your recognition and acceptance. Don't banish these feelings into the recesses of your unconscious for there I will ferment, eat your vitality, and criticize you mercilessly.* All the work I had done on myself taught me that relationships were my mirrors. To take responsibility, I had to stop accusing Clive and process my own emotions to protect my children from the stinging wasps. The wasps burrowed into my right hand, my writing hand, my creative hand. I did not have confidence in my uniqueness. I heard my mother's voice. *Why bother?* Another inner adversary, an old faceless woman dressed in black, taunted me. *Ha-ha! Told you so! Who do you think you are?* I acknowledged that deep breathing and the cathartic effect of journaling helped release their negativity. These practices helped me let go of worn-out hurts, integrate my positive strengths of curiosity, awareness, and intuition.

The swami suggested I fill an imaginary box with all these criticisms, bundle them up, and send them back to Mother and Father with a thank-you note, stating, *these are no longer required.* She suggested another note that celebrated the gifts I had received from my parents: my love of wild places, my green thumb, healthy eating, education, and especially my life.

I recognized that spiritual work was not about sitting on a cloud surrounded by angels singing oms but the work of recognising my feelings, uncovering my unconscious irrational beliefs, and accepting and befriending my demons. I needed to acknowledge and accept my dark emotions like grief, irritation, and fear, and soothe them with self-compassion.

I left the workshop, skipped down the fern-clad path to the pebble beach, and disturbed a brown snake basking in the sun. Silently, it slithered into the undergrowth. My dreams about the wasps, the instructions from Swami Radha, and the snakes fitted together like pieces of a jigsaw. To continue to shed outdated WASP values, I must recognise my feelings, digest my own experiences, listen to my inner voice, embrace my sexuality, and turn up the dimmer switch on my personal goals of creative writing and facilitation. Like a snake, I must protect and nourish my tender new growth.

I followed the goddess and found my shadow. I delved into my shadow and found my bliss. Like intertwined bedmates, lovers, they danced together arm in arm in the ever-expanding vortex of my life.

CHAPTER 22
Mountain Mama

"What is passion? It is surely the becoming of a person."
~ John Boorman

Chris and Shona grew up, made their own choices, worked hard to reach their dreams, and became accomplished international athletes. I endeavoured to let go of my over-protective instinct and compulsion to give instructions.

In the winter of 2006, Clive and I travelled to Turin, Italy, to watch Shona race in the Winter Olympics. Signs everywhere said, "*Passion Lives Here.*" The women's downhill ski race was preceded by three training runs. Wide-eyed and chewing my nails, I watched the second training run. Three athletes crashed. One racer stood up and skied down the mountain. Another lay spread-eagled on the snow as if she had split herself in two. She was lifted off the course by helicopter. I crossed my arms tight over my chest when our nineteen-year-old Shona's orange and red downhill suit flashed through the gates. Turn after turn, she carved her skis and powered through the finish line. The tension seeped out of me only to return when her senior teammate crashed and hurtled into the nets. Sadly, this ended her Olympic experience and her ski career.

The next day in Turin, while Shona battled with the mountain on her third training run, we went sightseeing. In one elegant Piazza in brilliant technicolour, the NBC television replayed the accidents. The announcer did nothing to quell my fear as she questioned, "After four crashes in the training run yesterday, people here are asking, 'Is the women's downhill too dangerous?'"

In the ornate church of the pregnant mothers, as our Italian landlord described it, I lit a candle to invoke the light of the benevolent Madonna, for my Shona and her team up on the vertical ice. That night, by some strange quirk, my knee ached and I sneezed constantly. I didn't think mothers had pre-race nerves. Surely performance anxiety was reserved for athletes?

Race day on the mountain, surrounded by jagged ridges, we shuffled along with the international crowd over the snow to the spectator stand. After friendly chit-chat with other Canadian parents, I clutched my start list and climbed up the steps through the scaffold to our seats. I gave an Italian boy my cowbell and asked him, "Can you cheer for my daughter, number four?" His father gave us chocolate. There in her flaming suit, Shona stood in the start gate. My pulse raced. She looked tentative but instantly careened through the gates using her strong muscles, hard-earned skills, and her father's "go faster" genes. I proudly waved Canada's maple leaf as she hurtled down the mountain at a speed that would be illegal if she were in a car. "Sooo smooth," my friend said. In two minutes, at the bottom and intact, she smiled at the cameras. With a deep breath, I sat back to admire these world-class athletes.

Two days later at the super-combined race - a shortened downhill and two slalom runs, it snowed heavily delaying the start. In the crowded spectator tent we sipped espresso and listened to the hum of Swedish, French, Germen, Croatian, and American voices. When the sun came out, clouds like steaming cauldrons evaporated and the forerunners flew down the course. The first racer fell. After thirty minutes the officials cancelled the race.

We piled on the bus that navigated the many ferocious switchbacks further up the mountain to Sestriere. Swept along by flag-wavers, cowbells, and singing, we revelled in this astonishing international celebration and headed to the slalom stands. What joy! The floodlit slalom course with shorter turns did not look intimidating. Thrilled, I watched my daughter vigorously attack the course, competing with the world's best skiers. The announcer implored the spectators, "Make more noise." Unfortunately, Shona straddled a gate, ending her Olympic race. Head down, she placed both hands on her gold helmet, skied to the finish, and still managed a huge smile for the camera.

That night under the ochre full moon, we drove through the dusky mountains, mesmerized by a floodlit fort and church floating above the valley. A warm glow spread from my heart accompanied by immeasurable gratitude for my bold Olympian.

After four more years of sweat, tears, courage, perseverance, and dedication, Shona qualified for the 2010 Olympics held in Canada. Clive and I sat in the top row of the Vancouver stadium. The Olympic rings shone down on the international crowd that hummed with anticipation for the Opening Ceremonies. We were disappointed that Shona was training at Whistler and would not attend. Our cell phone rang. "The weather is terrible. The coaches cancelled our training. We caught the last bus." Shona giggled. I hugged Clive as her words toppled out, "The police closed off the Sea to Sky Highway. We are accompanied by helicopters and police cars. I can't wait. We'll be in time for the athlete's parade."

Clive and I kissed as I wiped a tear. It was exactly twenty years since we'd moved to Canada. I could never have predicted that Shona would represent Canada in a fast and dangerous sport. With pride, I watched my adopted country as the First Nations people enthusiastically drummed in the athletes from eighty-two nations. As the host nation, the Canadian team walked in last. A roar went up from the crowd. If I close my eyes, I can still hear it today. When K.D. Lang sang "Hallelujah" by Leonard Cohen, the crowd raised flashlights, and waves of euphoria rippled across the Vancouver stadium and around the world.

Days later, in brilliant Whistler sunshine, Chris, Clive, and I stood excited in the stands, watching the women's downhill race. The crowd, with cameras in hand, waved Swedish, German, and American flags but was dominated with red and white hockey jerseys blazoned with maple leaves and moose. Our dedicated Olympians, who believed with their glowing hearts and worked hard to make their dreams come true, inspired our entire country. One athlete's brother said, "We just want Canadians to cheer for. We are not worried whether they medal or not."

Cheering for Shona

Their preparation had been fraught with poor weather. The women racers had not completed one full training run. Once again, I watched the race with increasing anxiety as several top racers crashed. Swedish Anja Pearson, the 2006 Olympic gold medallist, lost her balance on the final jump and slid through the finish. Chris, a sponsored professional big mountain skier, was afraid for his sister. "The course is so icy and hard to fall on," he told me. "I fall in fluffy powder." The racer before Shona fell and was helicoptered off the course, causing a long delay. Meanwhile, unable to stand still, I paced and tried to focus on calming myself with my breath.

The spectators roared as Shona jumped out the start gate. She looked solid as she ripped up the course and powered through the finish line. Afterward, she told us. "With all the delays, I had to dig deep. The course was rougher than a logging road. It was all I could do to hang on."

Shona racing the Lake Louise World Cup

It was fun to watch several spectators asking for a photo with her. A few days later at the super-combined race—downhill and slalom— her highlight came when she placed twelfth and top Canadian.

A few months later, she announced she had no desire to continue. For me, it was a relief. She had learned to think big. She bought a

1986 Volkswagen van and proceeded to drive with her boyfriend to Alaska, then south to the tip of South America and back to Canada.

After high school, Chris followed his passion for free skiing to the mountains. That winter, he came in one day and announced, "I broke my skis."

"How?" I asked, nervous for his safety. He mumbled something that I did not follow.

At the end of the season, in one of his movies, I watched him fall through a cliff band. I felt relieved that only his ski was broken. As if they were birds, he and his friends loved to fly through the air, testing themselves against gravity and the mountains. When my kamikaze kid participated in a Warren Miller movie, a dream come true, there was no going back.

To support himself, Chris coached with a Free Riders program. One mother told me he'd rekindled the joy of skiing for her daughters and many other teenagers.

"He could only follow skiing lifestyle 'cause he was freakishly good at it," she said. "As a mother, it is scary to see his extreme lines. But to have a son who is a role model for many young people is something you must be proud of."

Of course, I nagged him to go to college, but he continued to forge a life for himself skiing. In his early twenties, he gave me a Mother's Day card that said, "Thank you for making me into a great kid even if I am not going to go to university."

A powder fanatic, he skied in many movies. After watching these talented, daring young men and women ski beautiful lines down vertical couloirs, I walked out of the cinema with adrenalin pumping in my body. The year after the Olympics, once again, Clive and I made our way to Whistler. In the hall, a buzz from fifteen hundred exuberant people filled the air. Elated, we watched the premiere of the movie *All I Can*, created by Sherpa's Cinema, a group of hard-working young people originally from Calgary.

Chris was one of the skiers in this well-crafted film that focused on climate change.

Working and skiing with Salomon FreeSki TV became Chris's passport to visit many of the countries Clive and I had visited: Morocco, Norway, New Zealand, Kashmir, Greenland, and Europe. My favourite movie was *Eclipse*, filmed in Svalbard, Norway, with the ambitious goal of photographing a skier in front of the solar eclipse.

Christopher

One thing I know for sure is that both Shona and Chris, with their love of the mountains, the bravado to follow their dreams, and Chris's motto—*"Best Day of Your Life"*—came by their genes honestly.

CHAPTER 23

Kashmiri Socks - Gratitude and Grace

"I think we dream so we don't have to be apart so long. If we're in each other's dreams, we can play together all night."
~ Bill Watterson

Downsizing, I emptied a drawer on the bed and sorted through my clothes. I fondled a pair of child-sized woollen socks and carefully examined their geometrical patterns of rainbow colours. Red darning wool filled the worn holes in the heels and sole. Lakshmi, a Kashmiri mother of six, who had few material possessions, had given them to my mother. They were lovingly passed down from grandchild to grandchild, and in time, to my children. I could not throw these ragged socks into the garbage bag. I folded them together. It saddened me that my children never knew their maternal grandmother.

That night, I fell onto my pillow and dreamt my wispy mother, her curly hair bouncing and her blue eyes radiant, sat beside me on the grass, admiring the Rocky Mountains with their dark cliffs and dazzling spring snow. It was like fifty years ago, when we had sat together in the Kashmiri mountains.

"Mum, I have missed you. Do you remember as a kid I whizzed down a steep hill on the fast sled. You thought I'd be terrified, but I laughed and rushed up to do it again. Now I love to ski."

She smiled.

"Back then when we walked in the park, Dorothy and I recited, 'Not last night but the night before, Three Little Monkeys came to the door; one had a fiddle, one had a drum, and one had a fiddle stuck to its bum.' How we all giggled," I said, grinning as I put my arm around her. "I guess I was the wild one in the family."

With pursed lips and wide eyes, she nodded her head in agreement.

"I know how challenging it is to begin anew. You were brave to leave Belfast. Now I see that you and me were alike. However, you found comfort in your strong faith, and I found it in the beauty of the earth. I blow my prayers to the wind and am held by the rocks, water, and light." I squeezed her shoulders.

"We sure clashed. I know I broke your heart, but I felt like a sinner judged for my sexuality and not accepting your beliefs. I was desperate to travel. I have spent a lifetime searching for an alternative to patriarchal certainties, and a misguided belief that God condemned me for my very existence. I expected to find the answer hidden in spiritual texts, or the words of yoga gurus. In the stillness, I felt a faint fluttering in my heart, a tugging of my memory, a remembrance that I am light. I have treasured my Indian star ruby ring that sparkles in the light. I found that my pain and joy, like dark and light, are intertwined in a continuous spiral of growth."

Her curls danced as she nodded her head.

"Yes, I have witnessed all of life's seasons; sadly, Ruth's, Dorothy's, and your deaths fractured my heart. My grief pushed me into therapy where I began the work of unravelling my inner world. Slowly I owned my prejudices, blind spots, and emotions. Now I'm grateful that you gave me no choice but to look within. I know life is bittersweet and I have an unknown use-by date. You all taught me not to take my health nor my life for granted. Yes, I eat my greens. I aim to live each day with no regrets and cherish the moments that are the currency of my life."

Mother hugged me.

"Clive always loved and supported me. We never went to back to live in Scotland but visit frequently. We continue to have wonderful adventures biking and hiking all over this gorgeous planet. Although I aim to dance on the edge of uncertainty, I now accept and soothe my discomfort and fears. I know that my creativity blossoms in the void."

Her brow creased, and she shook her head.

"What did you say? I can hardly hear you. You want to know about your grandchildren and my kids? Your legacy lives on in a clan of nine Scottish great-grandchildren who are flourishing, and recently my granddaughter and grandson," I said. "You know mum, the fathers I know are passionately involved with their raising their children. They change diapers, cook and play with their kids. From my experience of different cultures I worked hard to understand my children's needs, to listen, to believe in them, and acknowledge our feelings. I have learned that all control is an illusion, relationships are forged in the furnace of forgiveness, and love is letting others live life in their own way."

"Yes, yes, but how did they turn out?" I thought I heard her say.

"When we moved to Calgary to embrace the long winters, I needed to escape the city to the mountains. Ski racing looked fun, so I signed them up. If I said to Chris at bedtime, 'It's school tomorrow,' he was up and down till eleven. If I said, 'It's skiing tomorrow,' he fell asleep instantly. Both Shona and Chris became professional skiers. Yup, they get paid to play! I am their very proud mama!"

Smiling, she nodded her head.

"You know, Mum, I heard a story at a Buddhist retreat that the chances of being born human are as remote as if one turtle swimming in the Pacific Ocean puts his head through the only life ring in the entire ocean. I can only imagine how tough it was for you, with one-month-old Dorothy, to find yourself pregnant. In those days, 1948, there was no possibility of abortion and that was against your strong principles. It was only three years after the end of the brutal Second World War of which imprinted post-traumatic stress on the population. I am grateful for the life you gave me. And you generously gave me the name Grace—a gift neither deserved nor earned. I have found the courage to live my most alive life on this trembling mother earth with its starlight skies where heaven is found in the palm of my hand. I can't thank you enough for this gift."

Mother hugged me.

"Did heaven in the afterlife live up to your expectations?" I asked.

Mother smiled, her eyes softening.

"I remember a quote by the Vietnamese monk Thich Nhat Hahn that said, if and when he died, he would come back as a flower petal or a butterfly. Last summer, here in the Rockies on the first anniversary of my brother-in-law's death from falling off a Swiss mountain, I sweated up a steep ridge. As I sat on the rocky summit, a few butterflies caught my attention. One landed on my bare leg and crawled toward my hip. Another danced on my waist, flapping its brown and orange wings. I had never experienced butterflies land on my body. Although I am in no rush, I will find out about this great mystery in time. I do know that I am shaped between the visible and invisible. My diaphanous spirit stretches beyond the bookends of birth and death into the unseen world."

She beamed, and her eyes danced.

"Last summer, we hiked with Chris, Shona, and their partners. All my insecurities fell away as I puffed up the track through the wildflowers towards the pristine glaciers dancing among the clouds. Mountains have always attracted me like a magnet. With no thought in my head but awe, I wanted the day to last forever."

Clive, me, Andrew, Shona, Chris, and Jesse at Jumbo Pass, British Columbia.

I woke up with a start, holding the socks in my hand. Now I know these socks told her story—the story of how she'd spent her life looking out for others: first as a midwife, then as a mother, grandmother, and a friend. And although I have many great male friends, the socks spoke to me of something I did not understand as a snooty twenty-year-old eager to see the world. Something so precious that I only recognized when I became a grandmother myself: how women, with their boundless reserves of strength and compassion, nurture, befriend, and weave our world into being.

EPILOGUE

"We do not receive wisdom; we must discover it for ourselves. After a journey through the wilderness that no one can make for us."
~ M. Proust

In my sixties, I revisited the summer of my silent shame—the summer I became a chameleon. I returned to the Island of Harris, where I had holidayed that summer forty years ago with my friend frantically pretending all was normal. I stood by the rocky pier where we had pitched my two-person tent. There I found my distraught nineteen-year-old self, brimming with profound humiliation, confusion, and guilt. In my mind's eye, I held her, rocked her, and listened. Between her sobs, she told me how unsupported she had been and what a desolate place that was. Along with the weight of her mother's disapproval, she carried the condemnation of many thousand years of patriarchy. To them, pregnancy out of wedlock was the worst sin of all.

Bathed in brilliant sunshine, I sat with my teenage self on the silvery gneiss, watched a swirl of gannets, listened to the gulls, inhaled thyme, and allowed the waves to lull her to peace. Her angst and disgrace dropped away, washed clean by the outgoing tide. The incoming tide brought waves of self-compassion, worthiness, and wholeness. I honoured my journey as a woman now confident of her voice, sexuality, sensuality, and self-knowledge, with the wisdom to be a mother to her nineteen-year-old chameleon and the knowledge that rainbows form after the rain.

Back in Canmore, after my yoga class, I jumped on my bike and turned down the track into the cathedral of trees covered in spring greenness. Above the turquoise river, the grey spires of Mount Rundle towered into the blue skies. Here the wind sang through the trees to the accompaniment of bird song. The air filled with the sweet scent of the willow and buffalo berries. I savoured the sun on my bare shoulders and warm breezes on my cheeks.

This is my heaven, a hallowed place that soothes my soul and brings me persistent joy, inviting me to return not just on Sunday but daily. It is my whole-hearted heaven where life is a treasured gift.

APPENDIX
Meet Me on the Edge – Writing Tips

"You must surprise yourself to get to know who you are. If you didn't offer new situations to your existence all the time you'd always know your responses and won't get to know parts of yourself. It is your choice; of how to respond or react that creates suffering. Turn to flow to feel comfort, ease, and happiness."
Clarissa Pinkola Estes

In the process of writing my own life story, I came to understand how strongly internal issues and personal growth are connected. This broadened my perspective of the world and myself. Journaling and writing provides an opportunity to pull apart the threads of our experiences, examine and rethread them into a meaningful tapestry. Thus get to know and gain greater confidence in ourselves.

For readers interested in exploring their life journey or creating works of fiction, here are a few techniques I use with my students. Working in community with writers is invaluable. Do regular freefall writing from a place of curiosity, courage, creativity, confidence and liberal quantities of self-compassion. Then take these rough writings and shape them into stories. In this process, you will gain confidence in your authenticity, and create writing you can share this with others if you choose.

The Story Only You Can Tell - Spin Straw Into Gold
Revisit your life's journey, by reflecting on your past, celebrating the present, and gleaning your unique wisdom. It can be helpful to read the exercises first, do the meditation and then write. This helps you move away from the inner critic and access a deeper part of yourself. Be playful and take as much time as you need.

Writing Meditation
Find a cozy spot to relax. Minimize your distractions by turning off your mobile devices and begin to breathe, slowly and deeply. Feel your feet on the floor and keep your back upright on the chair. Feel yourself supported and held.

As you settle notice how your breath connects you to your physical body and any sensations you may be feeling. Notice the images in your mind, and your thoughts floating by. Search your body for areas of tension, breathe into them. Let go and relax. With each breath feel yourself becoming more and more relaxed.

Use the part of your mind that creates pictures. Imagine that you have roots growing out of your feet that spread deep down into mother earth. As you breathe-in, imagine energy spreading up from the earth into your body. Imagine a bright light above you and see it come in through the top of your head and move through your entire body. For a few minutes, sit with these energies mingling within you.

Now imagine you are out in nature, in a very beautiful meadow where everything is just right for you. You feel a warm breeze on your skin; smell the grass and the wild flowers, feel your feet walk on the earth, listen to the birdsong and the melody of the river. You feel very relaxed and comfortable here.

In the corner of the meadow you see a very attractive small cabin and you walk towards it. You open the creaky wooden door. Inside there is a warm fire, flowers on the table and a writing desk with everything just the way you like it.

You enter and are naturally drawn to the desk. You sit down at the table and there is a pen and journal. You pick up the pen and words flow out on to the page. Open your eyes and write in your journal...

1. **Overview your life**
   Stepping Stones - divide your life by pivotal events
   Make a map or a collage or write – be creative use post it stickers and coloured pens.
   From childhood to present day, and think about stepping stones or 5-10 pivotal events when you took leaps of faith or that just happened to you. Choose events with the most passion for you.
   I was born……
   I moved……
   Work experiences……
   Holidays……
   Relationships……
   I gave birth……
   Re-read your list to get a sense of continuity and movement in your life.
   To identify the story running through your life, create a second list of your desires as you lived your life. This is the beginning of a cycle which propels you forward to a realisation or insight. Don't judge your desires in any way, all are valid expressions of life force. There are no mistakes. Freedom to fail is a vital part of the creative process.
   Begin each item "I wanted…"

How did your desires influence your life path?
Do you see any themes or ah-ha moments?

2. **Combine both lists** by recognizing which desires may be followed by a stepping stone event. (Cut and paste)
Can you see points in your life where your desires changed and you began a new chapter?
What were your challenges, feelings, and insights at those moments of your history?
Are there clusters that go together?
Are there themes and patterns that appear?
Do you have a dominant theme?
Where and how did you face metaphorical dragons?
Are there moments of insight that led you in a new direction?
Is there something deep inside that guides and supports – your intuitive wisdom?
Read your desires and pivotal events to get a sense of continuity and movement in your life, as if it tells a story.

3. **Make a list of your insights;**
   This I know……
   At the beginning of each pivotal point you have a new desire and a struggle to achieve it. In the end you have some new learnings, and insights. *For example: Give yourself oxygen first. Never be afraid of new challenges. They will develop courage and self knowledge.*

4. **Explore each insight**
   "Perfectionism is the voice of the oppressor."
   ~ Anne Lamott
   Do freefall writing on each insight. Write about the conflicts, emotions, grief, anger, fear, anxiety and tensions you experienced to arrive at each insight. Add sensory details sight, taste,

sound, smell, touch and sixth sense. Do not judge yourself in anyway.

5. **Can you apply some of your insights** to something in your life now? As you consolidate your experience it will light up your future path.

6. **Tips to craft your insights into stories.**
Once you have explored your insights in your journal you can now craft these into stories. Each is a story in the larger cycle of your life. A story has its own beginning, middle and conclusion, the beginning and ending connect, like a snake with its tail in its mouth.

Beginning – What you wanted
Something happened to the main character and caused him/her/them to have a problem and a need. The desire is the fuel for the story and gets the reader interested to see if the character gets what she/he/they wanted. They may or may not be resolved at the end of the story.

Include: Who, What, When, Where and Why.

The Setting is where the story takes place, past, present or future? How does the setting affect your character's problem? Write in Scenes.

Middle – Muddle – What you got
The middle of the story is the struggle between the character's desire and the opposition from adversaries, what or who that stands in his/her/their way of getting what he/she/they wants. What is the character fighting within? This friction results in certain insights leading to your final realization.

Interim pivotal events – each time the desire line in a story bends or intensifies it is marked by a pivotal event. Short story may have one pivotal event but a book length memoir may have many.

This may end with a precipitating event – usually a turn of fate and usually a surprise.

The story is enriched by including the characters thoughts, feelings and actions. Sensory details sight, taste, sound, smell, touch and sixth sense. Strong emotion pulls the reader in. The writing goal is to show and not tell.

Conclusion – What you realized, your insight.
The story reaches a climax which may be a crisis or a crossroads. For example the character comes to a new moral decision, a new awareness, leaves one passage and enters the next. These are points when something dies – the character's selfishness, prejudice, or love. Find the important turning points in your life and you will be able to find the ending.

Realization – this is the point to of the story what you want the reader to know. It ties in with the beginning – why you are writing the story.

7. **Self-compassion is the secret sauce that makes everything better.**

    Treat yourself as the most precious being in the universe and ask yourself frequently;
    What is the most loving thing I could do for myself right now? What is the most loving way I could treat myself? Listen to the response of your heart and follow its guidance.

"The ability to find the spiritual shape in one's life thought writing is a gift of the genre to its practitioner even if they never share it with anyone. You may begin to see yourself as the hero of your own story even as it is happening. For me this is enormously positive."
-Tristine Rainer, Your Life as Story

ACKNOWLEDGEMENTS

Writing this memoir was not easy. I speak for no one but myself. I write to make sense of my past. I have learned from a well-inhabited life that I explored out to the edges.

My profound gratitude goes to Clive, my soul mate. Your support, boundless enthusiasm, and love made all our adventures possible.

Thank you to Christopher for teaching me persistence, patience, and love.

Thank you to Shona, who supported and believed in this book. Thank you for the priceless gift of my first grandchild.

I extend my gratitude to the myriad of wise, compassionate men and women across the globe who have supported my growth.

Thank you to the numerous Alberta writing groups and classes who supported me to take a leap into crafting my stories.

Thank you to my editor, Kimmy Beach; your insightful feedback strengthened my narrative.

Thank you for the invaluable feedback and encouragement from my Canmore writers: Bonnie, Cori, Johanne, Katrina, Linda, Sharon, Vicki, and especially Barbara Parker, my long-time writing buddy.

Only first names have been included to protect the privacy of those concerned. Some names and details have been changed to preserve the integrity of the story.

ABOUT THE AUTHOR

Scottish born Wilma Grace Rubens, educated at Edinburgh University, followed her wanderlust to India, Oman, England, New Zealand, and Australia before settling in Canmore, Alberta, Canada. Her writing is grounded in her extensive travels and decades as a facilitator of Conflict Resolution, Parent Education, Meditation and Life Writing workshops. In Calgary 2000, she received the C-cala Life of Learning Award for her work as co-writer and facilitator for The Literacy and Parenting Program.

Along with her book of poetry, Entangled Enchantments published in 2009, her writings have appeared in a number of Australian and Canadian Magazines, as well as the Anthology, The Story That Brought Me Here: To Alberta From Everywhere. (Brindle & Glass, 2011). Her story Mountain Mama received an Honorable Mention in the 2010 CBC awards.

She and her husband, who are now grandparents, have two grown children who live in Kimberley and Revelstoke, British Columbia. They are found in all four seasons playing in the mountains, their paradise on earth.

Printed in the USA
CPSIA information can be obtained
at www.ICGtesting.com
JSHW020609270824
68844JS00004B/55